THE REMARKABLE LIFE, DEATH, AND AFTERLIFE OF AN ORDINARY ROMAN

When we think of Romans, Julius Caesar or Constantine might spring to mind. But what was life like for everyday folk – those who gazed up at the palace rather than looking out from within its walls? In this book, Jeremy Hartnett offers a detailed view of an average Roman, an individual named Flavius Agricola. Though Flavius was only a generation or two removed from slavery, his successful life emerges from his careful commemoration in death: a poetic epitaph and life-sized marble portrait showing him reclining at table. This ensemble not only enables Hartnett to reconstruct Flavius' biography, as well as his wife's, but also permits a nuanced exploration of many aspects of Roman life, such as dining, sex, worship of foreign deities, gender, bodily display, cultural literacy, religious experience, blended families, and visiting the dead at their tombs. Teasing provocative questions from this ensemble, Hartnett also recounts the monument's scandalous discovery and extraordinary afterlife over the centuries.

Jeremy Hartnett is Professor of Classics at Wabash College, where he holds the Charles D. and Elizabeth S. LaFollette Distinguished Professorship in the Humanities. His book *The Roman Street: Urban Life and Society in Pompeii, Herculaneum, and Rome* was awarded the James Henry Breasted Award by the American Historical Association.

The Remarkable Life, Death, and Afterlife of an Ordinary Roman

A Social History

JEREMY HARTNETT
Wabash College

Shaftesbury Road, Cambridge CB2 8EA, United Kingdom

One Liberty Plaza, 20th Floor, New York, NY 10006, USA

477 Williamstown Road, Port Melbourne, VIC 3207, Australia

314–321, 3rd Floor, Plot 3, Splendor Forum, Jasola District Centre, New Delhi – 110025, India

103 Penang Road, #05–06/07, Visioncrest Commercial, Singapore 238467

Cambridge University Press is part of Cambridge University Press & Assessment, a department of the University of Cambridge.

We share the University's mission to contribute to society through the pursuit of education, learning and research at the highest international levels of excellence.

www.cambridge.org
Information on this title: www.cambridge.org/9781009536066

DOI: 10.1017/9781009536080

© Jeremy Hartnett 2024

This publication is in copyright. Subject to statutory exception and to the provisions of relevant collective licensing agreements, no reproduction of any part may take place without the written permission of Cambridge University Press & Assessment.

When citing this work, please include a reference to the DOI 10.1017/9781009536080

First published 2024

Printed in Great Britain by CPI Group (UK) Ltd, Croydon CR0 4YY

A catalogue record for this publication is available from the British Library

A Cataloging-in-Publication data record for this book is available from the Library of Congress

ISBN 978-1-009-53606-6 Hardback
ISBN 978-1-009-53609-7 Paperback

Cambridge University Press & Assessment has no responsibility for the persistence or accuracy of URLs for external or third-party internet websites referred to in this publication and does not guarantee that any content on such websites is, or will remain, accurate or appropriate.

Contents

List of Illustrations   *page* vii

Acknowledgments   ix

    Introduction   1

PART I THE LIFE AND DEATH OF FLAVIUS AGRICOLA   7

1   The Monument, The Epitaph, and Their Setting   12
      The Sculpture   12
      The Epitaph   15
      The Tomb   18

2   The Person, A Life, and Its Presentation   25
      What's in a Name? Flavius' Biography   26
      Flavius' Self-Presentation I: The Poetic Epitaph   30
      Flavius' Self-Presentation II: Dining   33
      Flavius' Self-Presentation III: Body   37
      Flavius' Self-Presentation IV: Cup   39
      Flavius' Self-Presentation V: Dining as a Divinity?   41

3   Flavia Primitiva: Wife, Mother, *Casta Cultrix*   44
      Marriage and Motherhood   45
      The Pharian Goddess   49
      Casta Cultrix   52
      Morality and Mortality?   55

4   Flavia Primitiva, Experience, and Community in the Iseum Campense   61
      Flavia and the Iseum Campense: An Environment Apart   61
      Flavia and the Iseum Campense: Ritual, Individual, and Community   68

5	To Eat Is to Be? Flavius' Worldview in Perspective	78
	Dining, Death, and Philosophy	79
	Flavius and Flavia – An Odd Couple?	85
	Flavius' Life Overall	90
6	Meeting Flavius at the Tomb	92
	Dining with the Dead	92
	Drinking with Flavius	95
	Dead or Alive?	97

PART II THE MANY AFTERLIVES OF FLAVIUS AGRICOLA   107

7	Flavius Agricola in Early Modern Rome	112
	Mounting Suspicion and the Inscription's Destruction	112
	Cardinal Barberini, The Palazzo Barberini, and the Continued Appeal of Antiquity	116
	Flavius Agricola Helps Tell the Barberini Tale	121
	Visitors and Viewers	127
8	Flavius in the Modern World	129
	The Politics of Art in Late Nineteenth-Century Italy	129
	Making the Rounds of the Art Market	133
	"At the Edge of a Hollywood Pool…"	138
	From New York to Indianapolis	143

Epilogue   149

Notes   155

References   176

Index   188

Illustrations

I.1	Section and plan of St. Peter's Basilica and underlying structures.	*page* 2
I.2	Sestertius of Titus with image of Colosseum, ca. 80 CE.	4
1.1	Sculpture of Flavius Agricola, ca. 160 CE.	12
1.2	Head, torso, and cup of Flavius Agricola, ca. 160 CE.	13
1.3	Funerary monument of a man and his predeceased wife, second century CE.	14
1.4	Seventeenth-century drawing of Flavius Agricola's funerary monument commissioned by Cassiano Dal Pozzo.	17
1.5	Funerary monument of a reclining girl, ca. 130 CE.	18
1.6	Reconstruction of Flavius Agricola's funerary monument.	19
1.7	Plan of the Vatican plain showing Circus of Gaius and Nero, necropolis, Constantinian St. Peter's, and Early Modern St. Peter's.	20
1.8	Plan of the Vatican necropolis.	21
1.9	Plan of Tomb S with location of Flavius Agricola's funerary monument.	22
2.1	Drawing of tomb façades, Vatican necropolis.	29
2.2	Funerary altar of Orpheus, second century CE.	36
2.3	Drawing of funerary monument of deceased couple with Hercules iconography.	41
2.4	Etching of funerary monument of Satorneinos in the guise of Dionysus.	42
3.1	Altar from Pompeii showing sacrifice.	50
4.1	Plan of the Campus Martius, Rome in the Antonine period.	62
4.2	Section of the *Forma Urbis Romae* depicting the Iseum Campense.	64

4.3	Reconstructed plan of the Iseum Campense with decorative scheme.	64
4.4	Statue of Nile river from the Iseum Campense, early second century CE.	66
4.5	Statue of Tiber river from the Iseum Campense, early second century CE.	67
4.6	"Ariccia Relief" showing Isiac rituals, early second century CE.	70
4.7	Fresco from Herculaneum showing Isiac rituals, first century CE.	72
4.8	Fresco from Herculaneum showing Isiac rituals, first century CE.	73
4.9	Sculpture of baboon in Egyptian style from the Iseum Campense, second century CE.	74
5.1	Replicas of silver drinking cups from Boscoreale, first century CE.	80
5.2	Drawing of funerary monument of Rubrius Urbanus.	84
6.1	Biclinium outside tomb at Isola Sacra.	94
6.2	Reconstruction of Flavius Agricola's funerary monument.	99
6.3	Mosaic of a reclining skeleton from tomb on Via Appia, mid second century CE.	102
7.1	Seventeenth-century drawing of Flavius Agricola's funerary monument commissioned by Cassiano Dal Pozzo.	115
7.2	Drawing of Palazzo Barberini by Giovanni Battista Piranesi, mid eighteenth century CE.	118
7.3	Plan of the Palazzo Barberini, late seventeenth century.	122
7.4	Sculpture of Latona and her children by Domenico Pieratti, 1635.	125
7.5	*La Giostra dei Caroselli* by Filippo Lauri and Filippo Gagliardi, 1656.	126
8.1	Photograph of Flavius Agricola's sculpture circulated to potential buyers, before 1936.	133
8.2	Object card of Flavius Agricola's sculpture from the Brummer Gallery, 1936–1949.	136
8.3	Parke-Bernet auction catalog entry for Flavius Agricola's sculpture, 1949.	137
8.4	Map of Midtown Manhattan with locations of Flavius Agricola's sculpture.	139
8.5	French and Company advertisement in the *New York Times*, 1957.	140
8.6	Sculpture of Flavius Agricola installed at the Indianapolis Museum of Art.	145
E.1	Sestertius of Titus with image of Colosseum, ca. 80 CE.	149

Acknowledgments

This is a book inspired by, and largely meant for, students. And so it is only right to start by thanking my students at Wabash College and at the Intercollegiate Center for Classical Studies in Rome, aka "The Centro," who inspired me in various ways over the years.

Twice the funerary monument of Flavius Agricola served as the centerpiece of Wabash's capstone senior seminar in Classics. The students in those courses – Michael Carper, Colson Crowell, Alex Gilham, Will Kline, Eddie Pingel, John Streiff, and Zachary Thompson – gamely threw themselves into the inquiry. Their questions and insights set much of the foundation for what follows. It is a delight, but not a surprise, to see them deploy similar skills across many different paths. Thanks also to students at the Centro in 2017–2018 for informal chats about Flavius' monument and to the Wabash students in Roman History in Spring 2022 for test-driving some chapters. Over the course of this project, several research assistants have been instrumental in advancing the work and readying it for presentation. My thanks to Nick Carson, Brayden Lentz, Andrew Dever, and especially Elijah Greene. Audiences in Rome, Fayetteville, Crawfordsville, Portland, Boulder, Greencastle, and Bloomington all raised superb questions that I hope to have addressed.

The research for this project has benefitted immensely from funds associated with two named chairs at Wabash College, the Anne and Andrew T. Ford Chair in the Liberal Arts, and the Charles D. and Elizabeth S. LaFollette Distinguished Professorship in the Humanities. Meanwhile, the staff at Wabash's Lilly Library have been a model of efficiency, professionalism, and patience. Thanks also to my colleagues at Wabash and at the Intercollegiate Center for Classical Studies in Rome for their friendship, smarts, humor, knowledge, and indulgence through this project's many phases: RJ Barnes, Jessica Blum-Sorensen, Mitch Brown,

Joe Day, Leslie Day, Matthew Gorey, Melissa Huber, David Kubiak, Sonia Sabnis, Matt Sears, and Bronwen Wickkiser. Additional colleagues and friends offered assistance: Danilo Allegra, Rebecca Benefiel, John Bodel, Regina Gee, Lauren Hackworth Petersen, Hedy Hartman, Matthew Roller, Molly Swetnam-Burland, and Josh Ward.

Funding from the Great Lakes Colleges Association enabled fruitful and fun collaboration with Paul Tegmeyer (John Cabot University) on Early Modern Rome. I appreciate the assistance of the staffs of the Getty Research Institute, Département des Sculptures du Musée du Louvre, and especially Robin Cooper, Marty Krause, Lacey Minton, and their colleagues at the Indianapolis Museum of Art at Newfields. *Mille grazie* to Beatrice Rehl, her colleagues at Cambridge University Press, and the two anonymous reviewers for improving this project markedly and shepherding it into print.

Strangely enough, only by teaching in Rome did I come to recognize Flavius' presence near my institution stateside. That is a testament not only to the inspiration offered by the Centro's intellectual environment but also to the tank-replenishing experience of working in the generous and competent hands of the Centro staff: Franco Sgariglia, Pina Vallefuoco, Luisa Boncompagni, Letizia Buono, Maria Baldassarre, Agata Catania, Angela Calvario, Mariya Kobik, and Rita Caramia.

Jill Lamberton's partnership means more to me than I can express adequately. As this project was initially materializing and as it was concluding, it was a special joy to walk Rome's streets, ride its *mezzi pubblici*, discover its secrets, and revel in its absurdities with her and our extended families. Thanks especially to our two children for their inquisitiveness, humor, wonder, perspective, and occasional willingness to hold the other end of a tape measure. I dedicate this book to them.

Introduction

In 1626, workers took aim at four spots marked on the floor of the largest church in Christendom, Saint Peter's Basilica in Rome. The structure's immense dome hovered more than four hundred feet above them, for they stood at the intersection of the church's nave and transept. They began to dig. These shafts, when eventually filled with masonry, would support a towering bronze tent (called a baldacchino) over the high altar. As shovels and picks hacked deep, the excavation took laborers back through layers of history. After breaking through the floor of the Renaissance church, they burrowed through the fill separating it from its fourth-century predecessor. They then cracked through that building's pavement and struck an ancient cemetery (Fig. I.1). If authorities expected to find anyone's remains, they were those of Peter himself or one of his papal successors, for they believed the key apostle and later popes were buried here.

Instead, at the bottom of the southeastern shaft, the tomb and funerary monument of a man named Flavius Agricola came to light. In his marble sculpture, he was portrayed reclining at table, and the inscription below this depiction embraced the polar opposite of Christian morality and beliefs. It encouraged readers to enjoy corporeal pleasures, especially wine and lovemaking, since "after death earth and fire consume all else." Red-faced papal authorities destroyed the inscription, though not before antiquarians clandestinely recorded its contents. The sculpture, after passing through the hands and before the eyes of families and institutions with global reach, has been exhibited in the Indianapolis Museum of Art since 1972.

Flavius' funerary ensemble, even as it offered an embarrassment for Vatican authorities, reveals the fascinating biography, family, worldview, and choices of a man whose lineage was only a couple generations – if that – removed from slavery. This book delves, as deeply as the evidence will allow, into the details of Flavius' life, his commemoration in death, and his sculpture's many

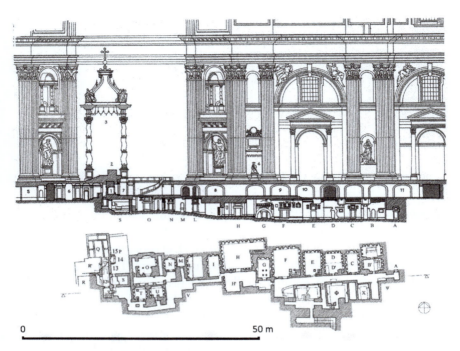

FIGURE I.1 Successive layers of history are visible in this cross section of St. Peter's Basilica in Rome. The Renaissance church stands atop a crypt, where its predecessor, "Old St. Peter's," was itself built atop a Roman cemetery (also in plan below). The high altars of both churches were positioned above what was believed to be the tomb of St. Peter (P). Flavius Agricola's funerary monument was discovered a mere four meters away in Tomb S when Baroque-era workers were digging foundations for the southeastern column of the towering baldacchino. (Courtesy of the Fabbrica di San Pietro in Vaticano.)

subsequent travels. The picture afforded by Flavius' portrait, epitaph, tomb, and cemetery not only permits us to explore the lived experience of this particular Roman but also sheds light on how captivating realms of Roman life – sex, religion, philosophy, dining, notions of the body, low-brow fluency in high culture, and more – were experienced by many excluded from Rome's halls of power.

This Roman Life

If asked to imagine "a Roman," most people would likely flash to a big-ticket name like Julius Caesar, Livia, or Constantine. After all, they are famous for a reason – their lives were extraordinary, their impact and legacy

Introduction

immense. Even among Roman powerbrokers, they were atypical. And when we place them within the broader contexts of the senatorial class, the population of Rome, or of the whole of the Roman Empire, the peculiarities of their lives stand out in still-higher relief. And yet, in documentaries, books, and even plenty of Roman history classrooms, Caesars, Livias, and Constantines dominate our attention.

This book focuses on "a Roman" of a markedly different type. Flavius Agricola existed far below Rome's innermost circles. In the grand scheme, Flavius' life was not nearly as impactful as these others. But his experience is certainly more representative of the way more Romans lived: not peering out from the palace but gazing up at it. That perspective alone offers one reason to dedicate the following pages to this individual, his life, his family, and, ultimately, the travels of his monument between Rome and Indianapolis. Why else?

I want to offer several additional and intertwined responses to this question. Recent decades have pushed back against "great man" history, which focuses on prominent individuals (predominantly men) and brings the accompanying assumption that these individuals were the foremost agents in shaping the course of history. Instead, scholars of ancient Rome and other periods have trained their attention on broader swaths of the population. Coordinately, focus has expanded from military matters and politics to any number of different realms: family, leisure, medicine, commerce, freedom and enslavement, gender, and others. Scholars usually lump together these topics under the banner of "social history." Flavius definitely took his place amid this broader mass of Romans, and his funeral ensemble explicitly draws our attention to spots beyond the battlefield and senate house.

One particular challenge of looking beyond the halls of power is keeping track of individual experiences. Let me illustrate this through a familiar lens. Just about everyone recognizes the Flavian Amphitheater, even if they call it by its medieval moniker of the Colosseum, and many understand that the vast majority of the texts that come down to us were written by and about the senators and other elites who sat in the amphitheater's first few rows, since seating was organized by legal rank. (It was not the case that middle-class folks could save their bucks and buy arena-side seats.) Those are the faces we are usually able to see, whose details we can make out. When we want to look beyond the front rows, our vision become hazier, since the further one ascends the less we have written by, or surviving from, individuals. As a result, one approach has been to study these ranks of society in the aggregate by, for instance, statistical analysis of their funerary

FIGURE I.2 This coin, issued by the emperor Titus, exemplifies the challenge of writing the history of individual Romans. We see one face, that of the emperor, while the masses are undifferentiated from one another. (Courtesy of the British Museum.)

inscriptions, plotting the sizes and locations of houses of different scales, or, to take an example from my own scholarship, examination of the streetside benches on which they perched when they needed a rest from a city's bustle. While these approaches can trace general contours of an issue, they also end up feeling like coins showing Colosseum crowds from on-high (Fig. I.2). We see lots of heads, but the only face we encounter is that of the emperor on the other side.

Zooming in on Flavius, then, allows one story to unfold. Flavius and his life are not meant to be stand-ins for all Romans and all stories, but only what they are – a case study as closely examined as the evidence will allow and reasonable reconstruction may permit. In fact, that they are *not* stand-ins is part of the point. There can be a tendency, when questions are asked about Roman daily life, to respond with something akin to, "*This* is what Romans did" or "*This* is what Romans believed." The truth, of course, is more complicated, as all individuals had their own experience and worldview, depending on their legal status (free, freed, and enslaved), their gender, race, and place of origin, to name a few of many distinguishing features. This is Flavius' story, his family's story, and no one else's. The following pages aim to explore a few of his experiences and beliefs, and, to the degree possible, to situate them within a broader context.

Part of the point of examining Flavius' life is to walk all the way around it. So many treatments of the Roman experience splinter everyday life into categories: work, religion, sex, entertainment, politics, and the like. This is understandable, for grouping sources by topic makes logical sense. And yet we know intuitively that reality does not cleave cleanly in this way but that life's inevitable messiness tends to weave many realms together in richly

Introduction

textured and complicated patterns. In the pages that follow, I will treat topics serially for the sake of organization, but not with any expectation that, if we find the right key, everything will click into place unproblematically. Rather, sniffing out the tensions and contending with them is part of the point.

And then there is Flavius' story. Most treatments of Rome's lower classes take the shape of a funnel: they start with some broad topic at the top and then trickle down to the best illustrations of the issue at hand. By contrast, this book is more pyramidal, starting with the specific point of Flavius' life and then expanding outward as we encounter and wrestle with the various features of that life and its legacy. The result, I hope, is a narrative that illustrates one way "to do social history," with the reader as a partner in the intellectual inquiry.

Outline

The pages that follow are divided into two parts – one discussing Flavius' ancient existence and one tracing the sculpture's travels from Rome to Indianapolis.

The opening chapter of Part I introduces the various pieces of Flavius' funerary ensemble, positions them within the Vatican necropolis, and contends that they combined to form a cohesive, carefully conceived whole. Who was Flavius Agricola and what did he want people who saw his funerary ensemble to know about him? Chapter 2 guides readers through his self-presentation, discussing the ways his epitaph borrowed phrases from famous poems, the surprising potency of at-home dining, and the thin line separating mortals from the divine in the Roman world. Of the fifteen lines in Flavius' epitaph, seven offer a subbiography of the deceased's wife of thirty years, Flavia Primitiva. The next two chapters consider her portrayal. As we shall see, Flavia is described both through stock terms for Roman women and also as an adherent of the cult of Isis. Chapter 3 weighs this tension before Chapter 4 imagines Flavia's experience within Rome's principal sanctuary of Isis. Such worship brought certain outlooks that contrast with what Flavius espouses in his monument. These different worldviews and the challenges of reconciling them occupy Chapter 5, while Chapter 6 shifts focus from Flavius' life to the experiences of those visiting his tomb after his death, particularly as they raised a glass alongside Flavius' sculpture.

Papal panic after the discovery of Flavius' monument and the obliteration of his epitaph were only the first of many different responses, manipulations, and reframings that Flavius' monument underwent between its discovery in 1626 and its current exhibition at the Indianapolis Museum of Art. Part II offers what has been called an "object biography" of Flavius' sculpture as it has moved through contexts as diverse as Baroque palazzi in Rome, the Parisian workshop of an infamous art dealer, Manhattan galleries and auction houses, and the pages of the *New York Times*. Through these different settings, the artwork passed before the eyes of cardinals, royalty, leading artists of early twentieth-century France, mustache-twisting American industrialists, and bargain-hunters on the lookout for the perfect finishing touch for their Hamptons estate. These travels and audiences do not just offer colorful stories but document the malleability of the past in the hands of the present. Flavius has had many garments of meaning draped across his chiseled abs, from totem of paganism and emblem of ancient majesty to focal point of national identity and symbol of classy classicism. Chapter 7 and Chapter 8 follow those threads and invite us to entertain the complex ways that our current perception of artworks is shaped by, and entangled in, those past understandings.

PART I

The Life and Death of Flavius Agricola

The Life and Death of Flavius Agricola

The circumstances in which we encounter an artwork are bound to shape the ways we understand it. And the Vatican could hardly offer a more illustrative example of such a phenomenon. Every year, nearly seven million people visit the Vatican Museums: a set of galleries, chambers, courtyards, and hallways stretching dozens of kilometers in length and housing everything from prehistoric pottery to artworks of the last decade.[1] Students of ancient history will want to linger over favorites such as the portrait of Augustus from Primaporta and the sarcophagus of Lucius Cornelius Scipio Barbatus. Yet the overwhelming number of visitors renders uninterrupted pondering impossible. To lend some perspective, about one in every one-thousand people on Earth passes through the Sistine Chapel in twelve months, making it one of the most visited rooms on the planet. And it can sure feel every bit that number, as museum authorities herd the hordes along a set of prescribed routes to maintain security and keep the traffic flowing. The result is a cattle-call experience that threatens to overwhelm the glories on display.

A respite is available only a couple of hundred yards away at the so-called *scavi Vaticani*. Here pilgrims and archaeology buffs tour an imperial-era necropolis (city of the dead) buried deep below St. Peter's Basilica.[2] From the beginning, the experience feels exclusive and even fun. Visitors must secure prior reservations. After passing through an airport-style security checkpoint, they present their paperwork to Swiss guards dressed in stripey Renaissance-style pantaloons. A salute sends aspirants for admission along the basilica's southern side toward the *ufficio scavi*, the excavations office housing the no-nonsense personnel who oversee the site. A guide, contracted by Vatican authorities, leads groups of about a dozen through a small door in the basilica's side, down a ramp, and to an "airlock"-style set of sliding glass doors that offer both security and climate control.

What follows is an expert explanation of superbly preserved tombs from second- and third-century Rome. Their state of conservation results from a flurry of activity on the part of the emperor Constantine. Over less than a decade in the early fourth century CE, he expropriated the land and began construction on a monumental church stretching over the cemetery.[3] Constantine located the structure immediately above the spot that early Christians thought housed the bones of St. Peter. Much debate circles about the authenticity of the bones on display.[4] Both the degree of certainty and the reasoning vary guide-by-guide. Those questions aside, groups standing near the apostle's purported resting place can peer up to take in a remarkable view: from the level of the Constantinian basilica, through the floor of the Renaissance church, and ultimately up to the cupola hovering more than 150 meters above them. Overall, this intimate, behind-the-scenes, subterranean, and curated visit could hardly contrast more starkly with what one encounters elsewhere in the Holy See.

And yet things would have been so much different 1,700 or 1,800 years ago, before Constantine initiated the first St. Peter's. It is hard, when one feels the weight of successive layers of history piled high atop one another – dome above floor, floor above crypt, crypt above cemetery – to remember that this necropolis was once open to the sky and bathed in sunlight. Flavius' tomb and its neighbors formed a prominent part of the suburban landscape, their façades rising alongside a busy road. People walking or riding along the Via Cornelia as they headed toward or away from Rome's bustling and smoky center would have heard birdsong amid the clip-clop of hooves and the clattering of iron-rimmed wagon wheels on basalt pavers. Perhaps they encountered tangles of workers slapping mortar on bricks for tombs sprouting up nearby or maybe they spotted the occasional squatter using the necropolis as a makeshift dwelling. And travelers might have caught a whiff of foodstuffs being prepared and made out stories and song rising up from clusters of people gathered to pay their respects to their departed family and friends.

In short, it can be a challenge, when examining cultural artifacts like Flavius Agricola's funerary ensemble, to consider them within their original contexts. It involves thinking away the environments in which we encounter them today, such as an overstuffed gallery, a dusty storeroom, or a museum space in the American Midwest. It entails setting aside our own experiences of where they once stood, like archaeological sites peeping out in a living city or – in the case of Flavius Agricola's tomb – open-air spaces now buried deep beneath buildings of totally different purpose. And it requires research,

Part I The Life and Death of Flavius Agricola

recontextualization, and occasionally even some imagination to place the ancient protagonists – both marble and flesh – back where and as they once were. Part I of this book aims to recapture ancient experiences – of Flavius, of his family, and of visitors to his tomb. We start with the facts: the physical form of the sculpture, the content and layout of its epitaph, and the architectural and topographical contexts of the monument.

CHAPTER 1

The Monument, The Epitaph, and Their Setting

Since nearly all our evidence for reconstructing Flavius' life comes from his funerary ensemble, it makes good sense to dive into what was found, how it originally looked, what visitors could see and read, and where it rested within the necropolis and city more broadly. This chapter seeks to reunite the now widely scattered data points.

The Sculpture

Flavius' funerary monument enjoys remarkable preservation (Fig. 1.1).[5] Carved from white marble streaked with gray veins, the life-sized sculpture displays Flavius reclining on his side atop a high-sided dining couch, routinely called a *lectus*. A cushion sags slightly under his weight, which

FIGURE 1.1 The sculpture of Flavius Agricola depicts him crowning his head, holding a vessel, and reclining seminude atop a dining couch (*lectus*). A circular cutting near his foot likely held an urn containing his ashes. (Courtesy of the Indianapolis Museum of Art at Newfields.)

The Monument, The Epitaph, and Their Setting

is borne on his left hip and left elbow. The mattress slopes upward near Flavius' bare right foot, while his left foot is tucked beneath his elevated right knee. A cloth garment encircles Flavius' body, draping his left shoulder, emerging from behind his right flank, and bunching above his pelvis. His left hand cradles a sizable cup outfitted with one handle, while Flavius' right arm lifts his hand above his ear. The thumb and first two fingers close together on a round coil of material; it begins at the figure's right temple, circles behind his head, and reemerges above his left temple (Fig. 1.2). Several small holes dot the space on Flavius' forehead between these endpoints, and the back of his head is unfinished; it is instead a diagonal plane pocked with chisel marks. This suggests that a metal object was inserted in the holes to hide the crown of Flavius' head and to complete the roll ringing it. Wrinkles crease Flavius' forehead and trail down his hollow cheeks. Incised irises and drilled pupils mark his eyes; slight bags hang on either side of a pronounced nose; and his beard splits into two points below his chin. Together with his closed mouth, the eyes give little hint of Flavius' emotional state, but suggest a man of mature age, perhaps in his late fifties or into his sixties. By contrast, Flavius' body is portrayed in the bloom of youth, with taut skin over ample musculature and no hint of flab.

In the "mattress" a circular cutting, approximately five centimeters deep, is nearly centered on Flavius' right foot. Like the back of his head, it presents an unfinished surface, which suggests that something was set into the depression. (Records make no mention of any discovery.) The

FIGURE 1.2 Holes in the sculpture's forehead probably held a metal wreath. Also visible is a darker vein in the marble, which frames the figure's face. (Courtesy of the Indianapolis Museum of Art at Newfields.)

FIGURE 1.3 A funerary monument in Rome shows the honorand with his arm around a bust of his predeceased wife. A small opening behind his head held her cremated remains. (Photos: author. Courtesy of Ministero della Cultura, Museo Nazionale Romano.)

best candidate is Flavius' cinerary urn, a stone vessel containing his ashes.[6] A funerary monument in Rome that likewise depicts a reclining figure offers a point of comparison (Fig. 1.3). Carved into the couch itself near the deceased's shoulder is a depression, which once contained the woman's ashes; we know as much because its lid (now sadly lost) was inscribed with the contents *ossa Iuliae C. L. Atticae*, "the bones of Julia Attica, freedwoman of Caius."[7] She also appears as a bust around which the main figure wraps his arm – a depiction of a sculpture within a sculpture. How should we envision Flavius' urn? If it was cylindrical and stuck to the proportions of well-known examples, it would have risen to about thirty centimeters in height, putting its top approximately level with the top of Flavius' knee.[8]

A few awkward bits mar the sculpture. The transition from Flavius' chest through his abdomen and toward his pelvis is not fully successful, as the artist struggled to render the pectorals vertically and the abdominals on a nearly horizontal plane. Moreover, Flavius' left elbow and shoulder appear to dip into the woodwork of the couch because the right extreme lacks sufficient space. In an otherwise well-sculpted piece, one explanation of these oddities lies on Flavius' head, where a darker vein in the stone appears. The sculptor, I suspect, encountered this irregularity and then tried to minimize it by making the vein frame Flavius' temples and face in a perfectly symmetrical pattern. If the figure's head were positioned slightly to the viewer's left, the vein would have crossed Flavius' face at an angle and distracted from the artist's intended impression.

Even if this one issue disrupts the composition, the sculpture suggests careful conception and execution overall. For example, the line of Flavius' right shin is picked up by his right forearm to draw the viewer's eye toward his face, which is the most prominent feature of the sculpture to break the "frame" of the couch. Flavius' forearm also forms one side of a triangular arrangement that dominates the right side of the composition: a line from his elbow to the cup traces along the bottom of his chest muscles, while the cup and his head are linked by the folded garment running over his left shoulder. And, while attention now concentrates on the right side, we must remember that, with an object inserted into the cutting at the left, it would occupy some of the negative space and form a visual counterpoint to the cup in Flavius' hand.

The Epitaph

The monument's internal cohesion continues with the Latin inscription found carved into the sculpture's base.[9] It consists of fifteen lines of poetry:

>   Tibur mihi patria, Agricola sum vocitatus
>   Flavius, idem ego sum discumbens, ut me videtis,
>   sic et aput superos annis, quibus fata dedere,
>   animulum colui nec defuit umqua Lyaeus.
> 5   Praecessitque prior Primitiva gratissima coniuncx
>   Flavia et ipsa, cultrix deae Phariae casta,
>   sedulaque et forma decore repleta,
>   cum qua ter denos dulcissimos egerim annos.
>   Solaciumque sui generis Aurelium Primitivum
> 10 tradidit, qui pietate sua coleret fastigia nostra,
>   hospitiumque mihi secura servavit in aevum.
>   Amici, qui legitis, moneo, miscete Lyaeum
>   et potate procul redimiti tempora flore
>   et venereos coitus formosis ne denegate puellis;
> 15 cetera post obitum terra consumit et ignis.

>   Tivoli was my fatherland; I am called Flavius
>   Agricola. I am the very one reclining as you see me,
>   just as I did all the years of my life which the fates granted me.
>   I took care of my little soul, and the wine was never lacking.
> 5   Primitiva, my most pleasant wife, passed away before me.
>   She herself was a Flavian, a chaste and attentive worshipper of Isis,
>   attentive to my needs, and of beautiful appearance.
>   I spent thirty wonderful years with her;
>   as a comfort, she left me her son, Aurelius Primitivus,

10 to tend our house/tomb dutifully;
   and so, herself released from care, she has kept a welcome for me forever.
   Friends who read this, I admonish you: mix the wine,
   drink deep, wreath your head with flowers,
   and do not refuse to make love with pretty girls.
15 After death, earth and fire devour all the rest.

You are not seeing the inscription itself because Vatican authorities, scandalized by its salacious content, destroyed the stone. The version we have is courtesy of seventeenth-century antiquarians (enthusiasts for ancient material) who transcribed the epitaph surreptitiously.[10] Poor lighting and threat of punishment hampered their efforts, and may have introduced some errors in particular words or spellings. For instance, instead of the participle *redimiti* in line 13, the imperative *redimite* makes more sense, since it would run parallel to other imperatives: *miscete* and *ne denegate*.

Setting these details aside, the epitaph's overall structure is clear. It divides cleanly into three sections. The first, encompassing lines 1–4, introduces the deceased – or, rather, has Flavius introduce himself in the first person. It draws attention to his origin, bodily posture, and lifestyle. Lines 5–11 constitute the second section, which concentrates on Flavius' family, most notably offering a minibiography of his wife. Flavius' voice returns in the final portion to implore a lifestyle rich in pleasures. Such ring composition bridges the parts and helps the epitaph cohere. In particular, these sections draw attention to the interaction between viewers and deceased, as in the first section onlookers' very act of seeing Flavius (*ut me videtis*, "as you see me") is paired with a double-underscored *ego*: *idem ego sum discumbens* (I am the very one reclining). Meanwhile, at the end, viewers become lectors (*qui legitis*, "you who are reading"), and the text doubly admonishes by deploying the first person and then issuing second-person imperatives.

In fact, these parallels not only band together Flavius and his viewer-readers but also emphasize the interplay between epitaph and sculpture. The text initially references the figure's most obvious feature – Flavius' reclining at table – before ultimately offering a nearly perfect caption for its actions. We see Flavius following his own advice by crowning his head with flowers. The large cup implies both wine mixing and drinking, which could have been even more apparent if the cutting near the figure's feet held the Roman equivalent of a punch bowl. (Cinerary urns in this shape have been found through the Roman world.)[11] The instructions for sexual matters are not represented, perhaps for propriety's sake.[12]

The Monument, The Epitaph, and Their Setting

FIGURE 1.4 A seventeenth-century drawing, commissioned by the antiquarian Cassiano Dal Pozzo, shows Flavius Agricola's funerary monument, including its base. The area between the base's "feet" housed Flavius' epitaph before it was removed by papal authorities. (Courtesy of the Royal Collection Trust / © His Majesty King Charles III.)

Such coordination prompts the question: How was this poetic epitaph presented on the monument? The inscription's loss obviously prevents direct inspection, yet several resources help us picture its appearance. First, a seventeenth-century depiction of the piece survives (Fig. 1.4); it was commissioned by Cassiano Dal Pozzo, an Italian scholar who served as the secretary of the very cardinal whose gardens hosted the sculpture soon after its discovery.[13] Notably, the drawing includes something that is now missing – a lower section consisting of a broad panel framed by two "legs" carved in relief, as though the couch's "wood" were spindle-turned. (That lowest section of the monument was, as we shall see in Part II, lopped off at a later date.) Epitaphs were routinely displayed here in this type of funerary commemoration – which scholars term *"kline* monuments."[14] Second, an eighteenth-century document confirms the pattern for Flavius, noting that the inscription was sculpted "in beautiful letters" below the sculpture.[15] Third, verse inscriptions were not typically displayed in antiquity as Greek and Latin poems are printed in books today, with each metrical line on its own. The text instead ran from one end of the stone to the other without line breaks. Therefore, we should not imagine Flavius' sculpture occupying a tall base that accommodated all fifteen lines as I have reproduced them; rather, the broad and squat space in the drawing would have sufficed.

FIGURE 1.5 A young girl's *kline* monument, now at the Getty Villa in Malibu, displays her epitaph between the spindle-turned legs of the couch. It thus offers a parallel to the location and size of Flavius' inscription. (Digital image courtesy of Getty's Open Content Program.)

The drawing and the lettering on similar monuments cement our understanding of the epitaph's layout. Dal Pozzo's representation suggests the space between the legs measured 1.56 m in width and 0.16 m in height.[16] How many letters of what size would this zone accommodate? A *kline* monument of a life-sized young girl at the Getty Villa in Malibu, of comparable date to Flavius' sculpture, provides a reference point (Fig. 1.5).[17] It has two "feet" sculpted in relief that frame a one-line inscription of about seventy-seven characters. Horizontally, each letter averages 1.52 cm in width, which was typical for *kline* monuments in Rome.[18] If the 552 characters of Flavius' inscription were inscribed with letters of the same size, they could squeeze horizontally into five lines or fit comfortably on six. The Getty text is 2.5 cm high; tellingly, characters of the same height on Flavius' monument would allow for six lines of text with spaces between lines. Detective work thus underscores that the slab between the couch's legs was perfectly suited for Flavius' epitaph.

The Tomb

The sculpture's outward gaze, the epitaph's first- and second-person voices, and the bonds between art and text all indicate a carefully choreographed engagement with an audience (Fig. 1.6). This prompts us to consider the physical circumstances in which viewer-readers encountered the funerary ensemble. When Flavius' monument was erected, it stood amid a growing necropolis beyond the western edge of Rome's *pomerium* – the sacred boundary ringing the city and separating it from enemies, war, the dead,

The Monument, The Epitaph, and Their Setting

FIGURE 1.6 A reconstruction of the sculpture, cinerary urn, and epitaph of Flavius' funerary monument grants some sense of the composition's original appearance. (Drawing: Elijah Greene.)

and other threatening outside forces. The tombs lay about one kilometer west of the newly constructed Mausoleum of Hadrian, not far from the Via Cornelia, a road that ran from a bridge over the Tiber, through the Vatican plain, and out of Rome's built-up area to Etruria beyond (Fig. 1.7).

This open area offered the fanciest Romans space for private gardens and larger building schemes. Among these was the Circus of Gaius and Nero, a venue for chariot racing amid the gardens (*horti*) of Agrippina. Running largely east–west, the circus had starting gates near the mouth of the present-day Piazza di San Pietro; its curved end lay southwest of the Renaissance St. Peter's.[19] The Via Cornelia ran along its northern edge. Unsurprisingly, given the reputations of both Gaius (aka Caligula) and Nero, the circus fell into disuse not long after their reigns. With the structure's abandonment, humble burials sprung up along the road, many in the simple so-called cappucin-style of roof tiles tented over the deceased's body.[20] Flavius commissioned a nicer brick structure, termed Tomb S by excavators, that was one of several house-like structures constructed in a row north of, and parallel to, the Via Cornelia in the mid second century CE (Fig. 1.8).[21] These had their rear walls embedded in the Vatican hill and thus presented their face to the road.

It is important to remember that, when Flavius' tomb was constructed, the necropolis was not as we see it today but was still taking shape. Like teeth that grow in one by one, tombs rose along the roadside: A, O, and

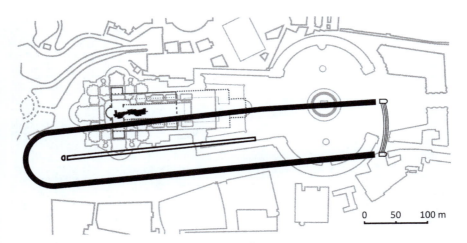

FIGURE 1.7 The "Vatican necropolis" stood near the Via Cornelia, which ran along the north side of the Circus of Gaius and Nero (both in black). The chariot racing venue had fallen into disuse by the time Flavius' tomb and monument were created. The construction of the original St. Peter's Basilica (in charcoal) buried and thus preserved the necropolis. In turn, its Renaissance/Baroque successor (in gray) was built over "Old St. Peter's." (Drawing: Elijah Greene.)

G were first; Tombs B to F narrowed the gaps between them; and L, I, and H followed Tomb O to the west, thus completing the arrangement before Flavius constructed Tomb S. Development continued apace in subsequent decades. Not long after Tomb S's creation, it appeared to get "pushed back," as R/R', T, and U projected their façades southward. Did another row of tombs later obstruct these western ones from the road – as happened in the east with the construction of V, Z, φ, X, and Ψ? Likely so, but the area has not been subject to excavation.[22] Additional finds and testimony confirm that the line of tombs extended eastward to the Tiber and, given the Via Cornelia's prominence, similar structures undoubtedly stretched some distance westward into Rome's suburbs as well.

To understand the tombs' exceptional survival, we have to look backward and forward in time. Sources hold that, well before Flavius' and others' tombs were constructed, St. Peter was killed at the command of Nero on the central spine of the Circus of Gaius and Nero during the *Neronia*, a set of games honoring the emperor. By 160 CE, when Tomb S was being constructed, early Christians were gathering to pray at a small, columned monument at the immediately adjacent Field P, where they believed Peter was interred. The spot's connection with the apostle drew Constantine, and

The Monument, The Epitaph, and Their Setting

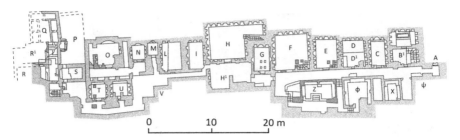

FIGURE 1.8 Flavius' tomb (S) was located among larger structures along the north side of the Via Cornelia. The construction of "Old St. Peter's" by Constantine buried all these tombs. The church's high altar was located above the supposed spot of the apostle's burial, labeled P on the plan. (Courtesy of the Fabbrica di San Pietro in Vaticano.)

in the early fourth century the emperor ordered the building project of what we now call Old St. Peter's. He expropriated the necropolis' land and had tombs filled with rubble and buried, thus essentially sealing them for more than a millennium. Together with purpose-built retaining walls, the tombs helped to support the massive church above. "Old St. Peter's" stood as the touchstone of Christendom until the early sixteenth century, when it was razed and its successor was erected. The Renaissance structure's floor level rested about three meters above that of Constantine's structure and seven to eleven meters above the necropolis' second-century sloping ground. Only in the twentieth century would the tombs be explored systematically and, decades later, the *scavi Vaticani* would be visitable by archaeologists, tourists, and pilgrims.[23]

Back to Flavius' tomb. Its bricks were set closely together with minimal mortar – a sign of expense. Though Tomb S had a smaller "footprint" than its neighbors, a glance from the Via Cornelia did not reveal as much, since it presented a façade of similar width. Like nearby tombs, a doorway trimmed with travertine opened on its façade, and an inscription likely hung above its door. Unfortunately, that portion of the façade is among several lost due to Constantinian reworking and Baroque-era interventions.[24]

Much of Tomb S's interior is no longer visible. After seventeenth-century workers dug the hole for the baldacchino's foundation (inadvertently discovering Flavius' monument in the process), they filled the cavity (and thus much of the tomb's core) in order to form the stable pylon holding up the lofty bronze tent (Fig. 1.9).[25] Excavators in the 1940s reached the tomb from a different angle, however, and removed Constantinian fill around the support to unveil the remainder of the tomb's interior space. In the small

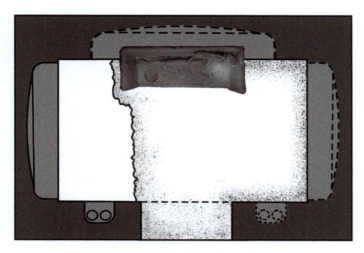

FIGURE 1.9 Tomb S featured small archways (*arcosolia*) on its west, north, and east walls as well as small niches for cinerary urns. The irregular outline of the hole made (and later filled) by seventeenth-century workers makes clear that Flavius Agricola's funerary monument nestled under the arch in the north wall of Tomb S. In this spot, the monument enjoyed great visibility. (Drawing: Elijah Greene.)

area (3.40 m × 1.86 m) a mosaic carpeted the tomb's floor, and small marble slabs traced its perimeter. Holes in the marble allowed mourners to pour libations for the deceased, whose cinerary urns were placed below the floor.[26] A narrow cornice about one meter above the floor divided the walls into two zones. Below the cornice, gold and purple panels of fresco decorated the walls. In the southern wall flanking the door, cremation burials were set within small niches painted with flowers; and *arcosolia* – arched niches accommodating a sarcophagus or a similarly sized monument – opened on both side walls and also the rear one. Near the *arcosolium* on the west wall appears the common motif of a hippocamp – an animal with a horse's torso and sea-serpent's lower body.[27] Above the cornice, it appears that additional niches intended to host cremated remains ringed the tomb.

No surviving documents identify the location of Flavius' monument within Tomb S, but several clues allow us to pinpoint its display. First, since the sculpture's rear face is unfinished and still shows dimpled marks from the sculptor's tools, we can surmise that it was pushed up against a wall. Which wall? It would not have fit in the western *arcosolium* or the symmetrical one on the east; anyway, the former was occupied by a terracotta sarcophagus with its body.[28] What is left is the back wall, which makes good sense as the location. After all, as we have seen, the monument self-consciously makes an impact; in addition to the features mentioned above, the piece's large scale and fancy material emphatically impressed. Placing the monument anywhere but the most visible spot would be odd, especially since the funerary monument and its architectural shell were apparently built as part of a single project.[29]

I had wondered if this placement could be confirmed. It struck me that the pylon's footprint is not regular. While the edge of the support's base is almost perfectly straight along the west side, a bulge of about 30 cm protrudes near the tomb's northern wall. Why would there be such an irregularity? The Baroque-era workers must have had some reason to deviate from a straight line and to expand their hole in the northern part of the tomb. The answer: the larger opening served to extract Flavius' monument from the rear wall. Some calculations confirm this. Side to side, the sculpture measures 1.78 m, while the tomb spans 3.40 m east–west. The monument, if centered on the tomb's rear wall, would have left 81 cm between its sides and the tomb's lateral walls. The drawing of the pylon's footprint shows the Baroque hole stopping about 70 cm from the tomb's western wall, thus proving that the monument was centered on the rear wall.[30] That accounts for the horizontal positioning, but what about the z-axis? According to the Dal Pozzo drawing, the monument's original total height was about 90 cm, thus allowing it to nestle under the rear wall's *arcosolium*, just below the cornice that ringed the room.

• • •

Let us take stock, starting first with the collection of information about Flavius Agricola. We have his life-size portrait, the lengthy text he commissioned to accompany that rendering in marble, the structure in which his monument once stood, and much of the broader necropolis where he was entombed. This data set is remarkably rich for someone of Flavius' social station. Too often social historians are limited to only one or two of these categories when considering Romans beyond the fanciest folk.

If the dossier of evidence is rich, it is also the product of four centuries of scholarship. Gutsy antiquarians risked papal reprisals to transcribe his epitaph before it was carved out of the monument. A twentieth-century scholar's keen archival sleuthing reconnected the monument's sculpture and epitaph, both reasonably well-known but separated in the scholarship for centuries. Archaeologists dug their way through millennia of material to revisit the Vatican necropolis and bring more of this fascinating site into view. Further detective work now establishes and adds more details, such as the layout of the inscription and the positioning of the monument within the tomb. In this slow churn of advancing knowledge, every generation is beholden to, and yet also builds on, what has come before.

And so let us consider these newest facts regarding the monument within its setting. At the rear wall's center, Flavius' sculpture and epitaph were dominant visually and spatially, confronting visitors the moment the door was opened and southern light flooded in. Other people entombed here were, from the ensemble's very design, celebrated more modestly in less prominent positions, their ashes placed in urns circling the wall or their bodies encased in simple sarcophagi. Flavius', by contrast, were the only remains that we know of to receive sculptural adornment or, so far as we know, a sizable inscription. This hierarchical organization points us in two related directions. First, it underscores the obvious point that Flavius' commemoration was not merely about capturing his life but in fashioning and presenting it in favorable terms with respect to others, both within the tomb and the necropolis more broadly. Second, while we concentrate on this rich funerary assemblage of brick, marble, metal, and plaster, we of course must not forget that it does not merely offer an object of study itself but was intended as the final resting place for a particular individual of sinew, bone, and flesh. Thankfully, from the inscription and commemoration, through signs both more and less intentional, a hazy biography of Flavius emerges. Chapter 2 aims to breathe as much life as possible back into this individual, and to examine what Flavius wanted others to know or remember about him.

CHAPTER 2

The Person, A Life, and Its Presentation

From Pompeii's lesser-known cousin of Herculaneum comes the story of a remarkable individual that lends some perspective to the evidence we have for Flavius' life. L. Venidius Ennychus was an enslaved person, later gained his freedom, and emerged as a Junian Latin (a legal status akin to a protocitizen). He was awarded Roman citizenship after marrying, producing a child who lived to one year of age, and trekking to Rome with his wife and toddler to present themselves before an official in the Forum of Augustus. Somewhere along the way, Venidius appears to have purchased a sizable house near Herculaneum's civic center and engaged in substantial commercial transactions. After earning citizenship, he stood for the highest recognition he could attain as a freedman, namely membership among Herculaneum's Augustales, a sort of pseudomagistracy that granted freedmen and out-of-towners visibility and status while leveraging their money for the public good.

This biography comes into view thanks to a very rare source – a dossier of wooden tablets from Venidius' house. Documenting his business and legal affairs, this cache was carbonized in the heat of Mount Vesuvius' eruption in 79 CE. Many folks kept similar stashes; indeed, tablets from other spots along Venidius' street pour forth rich episodes. Aside from a few select spots on the Bay of Naples, however, similar tablets from elsewhere in the Roman world have simply decomposed, burnt, or otherwise been lost to time.[1] If they had survived, the type of rich, bottom-up archival work that is possible for researching nonelite lives in other times and places, such as Renaissance Florence, would be possible for ancient Rome.

By contrast with Venidius and with famous Romans – whom we can study by examining literary and historical texts, inscriptions, coins, structures, artwork, and other evidence – Flavius left us less to work with. No archive, no house and artifacts, no other epigraphical evidence like

Venidius' tablets. Yet Flavius' sculpture, his inscription, his tomb, and its neighbors can enable us to piece together a fair amount of his life. Even if they offer less of a résumé than what we encounter for Venidius, these elements offer the opportunity to understand how Flavius *wished* to be seen, which can be nearly as revealing.

What's in a Name? Flavius' Biography

To start, the sculpture offers some clues of when Flavius lived. In particular, the detailed carving of his eyes, his facial features, and his curly beard have convinced scholars that the monument dates from the middle part of the second century CE, probably around 160 CE and the dynasty of the Antonine emperors.[2] Our hero's name also suggests some possibilities. As was becoming typical in the second century CE, his inscription offers only two names rather than the three names (*tria nomina*) that had been standard for Roman citizens. In Flavius Agricola, we read the second and third of those names – the *nomen* and *cognomen* – but not the first, the *praenomen*. Since only a few different *praenomina* were in use, their utility had never been very profound, especially since the same *praenomen* was often given to all males in a family.[3]

Flavius' *nomen* is suggestive, however, since he shares it with a family that ruled first-century CE Rome – the three emperors of the Flavian dynasty. Flavius was unlikely to be related to them by blood. Probably, given the location in Rome, someone in his family had been enslaved in the imperial household. We suspect this because, while enslaved people generally had only one name, freedmen kept that name as a *cognomen*, to which were appended the *praenomen* and *nomen* of their former master. Not surprisingly, Italy was peppered with individuals bearing *Iulius* as their *nomen*; these were freedmen of the Julian dynasty and the freedmen's descendants. That explains the likely continuation of the Flavius *nomen*.[4] Now, Flavius Agricola himself was probably not a freedman of the Flavian emperors, since his monument was created more than a half-century after they ruled (69–96 CE). Instead, someone in our figure's background, possibly his father, was likely a slave of an emperor in the Flavian dynasty who was freed and took on the *nomen* Flavius, which he passed on to future generations. Alternatively, he himself may have been manumitted by a former slave of the Flavian household – the freedman of a freedman.[5]

By evoking Tibur (modern-day Tivoli) as his hometown with his epitaph's opening words (*Tibur mihi patria est*), Flavius conjured a host of resonances. Tibur had long offered a popular location for elite Romans to construct luxurious retreats as an escape from a chaotic and cramped life in Rome. Members of the prominent Metellus family, for instance, passed a villa in Tibur through several generations during the Republic, and the trend only blossomed as Julius Caesar, the poets Catullus and Horace, and their early imperial successors Martial and Juvenal all had property nearby.[6] Tibur's attractions included a beautiful location in the Apennine foothills, abundant water from the Anio river (and a stunning waterfall of the same), and proximity to Rome, which allowed villa dwellers to scamper back to the city if business called.[7] When the emperor Hadrian (117–138 CE) constructed a villa outstripping all its predecessors, Tibur became an important alternative center of power. It is hard to know whether such connections aided Flavius as he migrated to Rome or even why he moved in the first place. The Flavian dynasty had little connection to Tibur but owned a lavish villa near Tibur's one rival for the title of Rome's premier suburban getaway, Tusculum in the Alban Hills southeast of Rome.[8] Did Flavius mention Tibur to distance himself from the Flavians' well-known power centers, Rome and the Alban Hills, and thus to underscore his free birth? All we can say with certainty is that somewhere along the way he married Flavia Primitiva and a young man named Aurelius Primitivus entered his life. The marriage lasted three decades until Flavia's death.

A lack of details clouds other aspects of Flavius' life course. His splashy funerary monument, together with the tomb apparently purpose-built to house it, speak to his financial means. An inscription embedded above the entrance of Tomb A of the Vatican necropolis hints at the cost of a structure like Flavius'. It declares itself a codicil to the will of Gaius Popidius Heracla, who asks his heirs to "build me a tomb ... at the cost of 6000 sesterces."[9] Though we do not know how "deep" Tomb A went into the hillside, its breadth of about 4.5 m was consistent with Flavius'. A comparable sum or even a bit more likely went toward Flavius' sculpture and its base, to judge from sculptures from North Africa and Italy whose cost is known. Across the 147 examples, the median cost is 5,000 sesterces.[10] The size, personalization, and material involved in Flavius' sculpture would have pushed the cost of his representation higher. To put these figures in context, merely subsisting in the Roman world required 200 sesterces annually, and a Roman legionary's salary was 1,200 sesterces.[11] Translating those figures into today's currency is challenging. It is more profitable to consider what other public act someone might bankroll with 10,000 to 15,000 sesterces in the second century. Refurbish a public bath in a small city, repave about 600 feet of a public street, or establish an endowment whose interest funds an annual banquet for several dozen diners reclining on triclinia.[12]

Commissioning a portrait in marble had additional resonances beyond forking over funds for a luxury material. Henner von Hesberg has documented the growing use of marble in funerary contexts over the first two centuries CE. It was sometimes deployed on façades to give tombs a temple-like aspect or, by using large blocks, to lend an appearance of solidity and therefore permanence. And, as with Flavius' tomb, marble was increasingly deployed *within* tombs, von Hesberg contends, because its durability granted a sentiment of long-standing memory and eternity. One section of Statius' *Silvae*, a first-century CE collection of poems, consoles a man who has lost his wife. Addressing the deceased, it seeks consolation and pinpoints the material of her statue within the tomb: "Duration of time will no longer weaken you; and the labors of years will do you no harm: such care is taken for your body, so great is the wealth that the venerable marble breathes out."[13] In this view, a marble sculpture freezes time, as though the deceased had always appeared this way and would continue as such forever. It is easy to understand the appeal such shades of meaning would have for folks like Flavius, whose past – marked not by distinction but by servitude – benefitted from a recasting.[14]

Flavius appears eager to be laid to rest amid striking tombs of well-to-do Roman families. Crowned by temple-like pediments, Tombs E through H, for instance, outwardly impressed through fanciful decoration around their doorways and windows, as inset brickwork of various colors formed eye-catching architectural displays, scrollwork, and figural representations (Fig. 2.1). Visitors to the necropolis could read about the owners from inscriptions within eyeshot of the door. In addition to Tomb A's Gaius Popidius Heracla, readers would learn about Titus Aelius Tyrannus, an imperial freedman who worked as a secretary in Northern Gaul (Provincia Belgica); Titus Matuccius Pallas, who was the patron and former owner of Entimus and Zmaragdus, two linen merchants who built Tomb O for him; and Tullia Secunda, the daughter of Lucius Tullius Zethus (builder of Tomb C) and wife of Marcus Caetennius Antigonus (likely builder of Tomb F).[15]

Just as impressive as these epigraphic boasts were the views offered to anyone who peered through the tombs' iron gates, for the household's wealth and size were discernible from the decorative program and numerous openings for cinerary urns. Tombs F and H, for instance, both boasted elaborate schemes of plasterwork niches and relief work, while the latter was designed to hold 170 individuals.[16] This number offers more of an index

The Person, A Life, and Its Presentation

FIGURE 2.1 Tombs near Flavius' sought to distinguish themselves through elaborate brickwork decoration and gabled façades. Shown here are the elevations of Tombs H through E (left to right). (Courtesy of "L'Erma" di Bretschneider, *Die heidnische Nekropole unter St. Peter in Rom* (1995).)

of someone's ambition than a strict reflection of *familia* size, however, since a tomb's commissioner did not have a firm idea of how many people's remains the structure would eventually hold. So, a greater capacity was a claim of what a big deal you expected your family to be in the coming years. Gaius Valerius Herma – who, according to the inscription above its door, built Tomb H for himself, his wife, their children, their freedmen and freedwomen, and their descendants – shot too low, for his structure designed for 170 ultimately housed 250 individuals' remains.[17]

Flavius did not inject himself into a field of upstarts but established himself amid rich and flourishing households. And he appears to have largely measured up. His tomb was much shallower – probably because of space dedicated to St. Peter's tomb to the north – but its frontage was not out of scale. The ten tombs built before Tomb S average 4.8 m in breadth, while Flavius' tomb measures 4.4 m. The upper sections of the tomb that would have born ornament were lost through later reworkings of the space, but the quality of the brickwork along Flavius' façade are consistent with its fancy neighbors.[18] And it likewise boasted niches and *arcosolia* for household members, though more on the order of dozens than hundreds. Over the years, these were filled with the bodies of his family and subsequent generations.[19] Moreover, in a potential mark of differentiation, Flavius' funerary ensemble is one of only two tombs from the Vatican necropolis to include a portrait, and it is the lone life-sized freestanding sculpture.[20] Such were Flavius' resources and ambitions.

How Flavius earned the financial capacity to afford this funereal ensemble in this spot is unclear. Is the *Agricola* of his name a playful allusion to a source of wealth, as at least one scholar has suggested, making the first line read something like "Tivoli is my hometown, I am a farmer, and my name is Flavius"?[21] Unfortunately, there is nothing to confirm or deny this conjecture. The lack of details may be disappointing, but we should not lose sight of what, even to Western readers, can feel like a remarkable degree of social mobility. Over the course of one or two generations, Flavius' family likely passed from being someone's property to shaping this form of legacy.

Many people have a vision of the ancient world as one split between the "haves" and the "have nots," "elites" and "non-elites." A first and obvious point is that many more gradations than this simple division existed, even if scholars have struggled to tease them out, whether through examination of texts or archaeology.[22] Second, the situation was hardly a caste system set in stone from one generation to the next. The absurdities and complexities of social mobility come into focus through the character of the outrageously wealthy freedman Trimalchio in Petronius' *Satyricon*, an over-the-top satirical novel of the early empire. The one-time slave had schemed his way to freedom and then struck it big in trade before he acquired such a vast fortune that he did not know the extent of his own holdings.[23] In the novel, he seems to miss the mark time and again in his social presentation (at his dinner table, in his house decoration, at his tomb), which traffics in the stereotype of the "rich freedman." Advancing such caricatures also speaks to the anxieties of those pushing such a narrative, which reinforced the boundaries between new money and "true" status.[24] The difference between being rich and having respectable status proved a tough knot for Romans to untangle, but what went unquestioned was the idea that someone could make his way rapidly from slavery to owning substantial amounts. To put it differently, Trimalchio is a fiction, but the processes and dynamics this character points up were real, even if much slower. And Flavius was a distinct example of such currents.

Flavius' Self-Presentation I: The Poetic Epitaph

The "self-presentation" of this and the following subtitles might seem odd, since we most often think of family members/survivors as the designers/commissioners of a funerary marker for the deceased. In the Roman world, however, considering one's final resting place while still alive was common.[25] From Pompeii arrives the striking story of a woman named Naevoleia Tyche, who outlived her husband and, after his death, forsook the tomb he had designed for the two of them and instead commissioned her own more elaborate monument. We know as much not only because we have two tombs for Naevoleia, but because she, on her solo monument, specified that she was *viva*, living, when she built the structure.[26] While Flavius makes no such direct claim, the monument's heavily personalized and carefully orchestrated character suggests the deceased's direct hand, and the first-person voice only adds to this sensibility. Moreover, the other possible commissioner would be Aurelius Primitivus; the only supporting evidence for his candidacy, however, is the minibiography of his mother and the light praise he draws for his pious cultivation of the tomb.

Flavius' hand was unlikely to have been the only one in the monument's creation, for, as our eye soaks in Flavius' funerary ensemble, his epitaph's verse form should demand our attention. Poetic inscriptions were hardly unknown in the Roman world. Indeed, nineteenth-century German scholar Franz Bücheler collected more than two thousand (Flavius' is n. 856).[27] Excavation at Pompeii, meanwhile, has revealed lines of poetry – from heavy hitters like Vergil and Ovid to other lesser-known authors – scratched into the city's plaster walls, which suggests that everyday folk a four-day wagon ride from the *caput mundi* had both knowledge of literary works and felt the urge to rewrite them.[28] All that said, only 1 or 2 percent of Latin inscriptions are metrical, which makes Flavius' very decision to commemorate himself in poetry important, not least for practical reasons, as it most likely involved commissioning a poet to write the epitaph and coordinating between that artist and the sculptor who put chisel to marble.[29]

Is it a successful or good poem? Certain features may have raised eyebrows. Latin poetry followed a certain rhythm or "meter" (or at least was supposed to). Of the fifteen lines in Flavius' epitaph, five defy easy scansion into clean hexameter (a pattern consisting of six "feet" per line), and the remaining lines all contain a hiccup or two.[30] Another is the poet's frequent recourse to alliteration, not only in the "pr" of his wife's introduction (*praecessitque prior Primitiva*) but also *denos dulcissimos*, *solacium sui*, *moneo miscete*, and *potate procul*. Ancient rhetoricians warned against excessive use of this device, faulting none other than Ennius, the father of Latin verse, and singling out a line of his *Annals*: *O Tite, tute, Tati, tibi tanta, tyranne, tulisti* (O Titus Tatius, you tyrant, what greatness you have brought for yourself).[31] Similarly, Flavius' epitaph frequently employs conjunctions, particularly *et* and *-que*. This tendency could favorably be characterized as polysyndeton, the repeated use of conjunctions between clauses, often to elicit a heightened sense of excitement or action.[32] In Flavius' inscription, however, a critic might point to the repeated appearance of identical words in the same metrical foot in neighboring lines – *-que* in lines 9 and 11, *qui* in 10 and 12, *et* in 13 and 14 – and raise more questions: Would a greater degree of variation have been welcome? Were these words inserted simply to make the lines scan into hexameters (to the degree that they do in the first place)?

On the other hand, readers who were conversant with "classics" of Latin poetry would have recognized that Flavius was drawing on notable phrases from well-known poems in his epitaph. The very first words echo a snippet of famous verse. Augustan-era poet Ovid wrote *Sulmo mihi patria est* (Sulmo is my fatherland) near the beginning of one notably biographical poem, and he uses a similar formulation – *Pisa mihi patria est* – in a still more circulated work, the *Metamorphoses*, when the nymph Arethusa speaks this line to introduce her wanderings.[33] Flavius' *Tibur mihi patria est* references both origin stories while also setting the stage for his epitaph's first section, which closely tracks a poem by Horace in honor of a famous native son of Flavius' hometown of Tibur, L. Munatius Plancus.[34] Horace, after praising Tibur's landscape, urges Plancus to be wise, to put an end to his labors, and to enjoy soothing wine, whether in a military camp or in "your Tibur." Acting in this way would make his experience parallel a Greek hero, who crowns his *tempora*, "temples," and takes up the *Lyaeus*, "wine" – two of the very acts and phrasings that Flavius' epitaph describes and his sculpture embodies.[35] Referencing Horace's poem, with its Tibur-specific celebration of acts in which Flavius takes part, set Flavius within a tradition of figures mythological and local.

Flavius' poetic resonances extended to more recent imperial circles. When he claims that he cultivated his little soul (*animulum colui*) in line 4, Flavius echoes a poem that Hadrian penned shortly before he passed away, according to the *Historia Augusta*, a series of biographies of emperors.[36] The poem addresses Hadrian's *animula*, which he describes as *vagula, blandula | hospes comesque corporis*. The phrase's full range of meanings cannot be captured easily; indeed, a website has cataloged forty-three different versions in English alone.[37] Essentially, Hadrian addresses his little soul as the tender guest and companion of his body. To what colorless, ruthless, and bare spots will this little wanderer depart now, the poem asks, abandoning the little soul's accustomed jokes. The free-spirited sentiment and the emphasis on the joys of this life, in addition to the particular invocation of an *animulus/a* links Flavius to this famed imperial predecessor.

We have barely gotten past the epitaph's first section and have already landed on several examples of Flavius' evocation of famous poets.

Additional examples appear throughout the epitaph, which leads to why Flavius and his poet would echo these other works.[38] The phenomenon comes into focus when we consider another funerary inscription that is very self-consciously in verse. Found in Rome, it too draws on Ovid's formulation: Its speaker declares *Roma mihi patria est* (Rome is my fatherland) before describing himself as someone "skilled in reciting the legacy of poets in strains sweet as the Muses and swans, skilled in delivering poetry pulsating with Homeric verse." Scholars have noted at least four Ovidian works represented in the inscription.[39] In other words, this inscription makes explicit what is usually implied – that hinting at, or redeploying the words of, well-known poets was part and parcel of showing that you were "skilled" at poetry. We might think of this as an ancient parallel of a musical artist today "sampling" the bassline and drums of an older track. It is not just about, say, reusing Marvin Gaye's groove but about paying homage to, and showcasing your knowledge of, predecessors. Recent scholarship has highlighted how poetic "sampling" like Flavius' offered Romans an opportunity to display their "literary literacy" – their fluency with poetic tropes as well as with the *oeuvre* of elite circles of poets.[40] Even if it was something of an insider's game – you needed to know the sampled body of work in order to "be in on" the game – it marked Flavius as someone both in the know and with tastes beyond the prosaic.

Flavius' Self-Presentation II: Dining

Outside of Flavius' poetic cultured-ness, the monument's design concentrates overwhelmingly on dining and drinking. Why would that be? For one thing, elite Romans often concentrated their funerary outfit on offices held, public honors awarded, benefits showered on their fellow urbanites, and the like. As an example, an inscription on the sarcophagus of M. Annius Proculus described him as "town councilor of the colony of Ostia, priest of the divine Vespasian, patron of the Ostian ship-builders." All this despite his death at the age of twenty-five.[41] Put simply, folk like Flavius did not enjoy these higher-ups' public visibility nor their perks of office.

And Flavius does not even hint at such realms of representation, which is important. Scholars long presumed that Roman elites were the tastemakers, with everyone below them on the social scale scratching for whatever shreds of elite status-markers they could afford.[42] Instead, we are recognizing that, particularly over the first two centuries of the empire, regular Romans sought out alternative means of presenting themselves in the funerary realm. One strategy involved tying your commemoration to pride in your labor, as we see in, for example, a cobbler who includes forms for shoes above his portrait in one monument, a metalsmith who showcases the range of tools at his disposal and assimilates himself to mythical figures who relied on sharp blades and numerous other individuals who were simply commemorated by their name and occupation.[43] Flavius, by contrast, pins his memorial to the pleasures of life, most notably feasting, conversing, reclining comfortably, and downing the never-lacking fruit of the vine.

In choosing this form of depiction, Flavius stepped along a well-trod path in funerary commemoration. Greek and Etruscan predecessors from the fifth century BCE onwards likewise depicted the deceased at table in a scene labeled by scholars as the *Totenmahl* motif, or "meal of the dead."[44] Roman uses of this tableau, however, did not develop organically from their predecessors. Rather, after a break from the practice in the Republic, the motif emerged only late in the Augustan era and continued for less than two centuries before appearing to die out. Paul Zanker contends that such a break from the past reflected the different purpose of the Roman motif, spotlighting how the use of *kline* monuments offered "a neat cipher for private, domestic well-being, since ... it recalled one of the central rituals of private life."[45] Part of the appeal lay in the jocularity of the occasion. Despite the popular notion of Roman overindulgence at table, enjoying a banquet was not a matter of gluttony and drunkenness. Or not those things alone, at least. Rather, feasting in groups pervaded every corner of Roman life: Banquets were thrown by elite members of society to forge or solidify relationships either among themselves or with their dependents; religious holidays saw banquets at which images of the gods might be plopped down to enjoy the repast next to devotees; the dedications of civic buildings were marked by public feasts; and members of guilds and funerary clubs celebrated their ties through communal meals. Even if their meals were less frequent and more modest, the ranks of ordinary Romans, freedmen, and enslaved people hosted and partook in group feasting as well.[46] These occasions drew together communities, articulated hierarchies, and greased the interlocking gears of power, information, and access in Roman society. So, Flavius' depiction of dining hardly represented more than a simple statement about a favorite pastime but articulated a claim about the social rituals that he marshalled, in which he participated, and from which he derived meaning.

Even if many people up and down the Roman social ladder took part in banqueting on occasion, it was a regular occurrence for very few folks. Rather, most urban dwellers had little space of their own to host such affairs,

The Person, A Life, and Its Presentation

let alone the time, money, expertise, assistance, or facilities. Without artificial refrigeration, Romans worried about spoilage; moreover, shopping for ingredients was time-consuming, while smoke and fire were annoying and dangerous, particularly in small spaces. Instead, many urbanites took to streetside cookshops for a quick bite to eat, a splash of wine, and the opportunity for stimulation and socializing. The remains of Pompeii, for instance, have yielded over 160 such eating and drinking establishments, even though about 30 percent of the city remains unexcavated.[47] Estimating Pompeii's population is a challenging endeavor, and we do not know for sure how many cookshops remain buried, but a conservative estimate of their proliferation suggests one for about every seventy-five inhabitants – a density on par with street-food vendors in the developing world.[48] Additionally, many poorer folks received *sportulae* – handouts that could include food – from their patrons, and many inhabitants of Rome received heavily subsidized or even free grain from the government.[49] In other words, Flavius showcases a luxury that was rarely attainable by the vast majority of Rome, who usually ate and drank in much different circumstances.

Though Flavius is depicted alone, his portrait encodes numerous claims about his standing. We can start with the elegant high-backed couch with its turned legs, on which a cushy mattress and a soft cushion have been set.[50] A crown of flowers joins the parade of luxuries. But we should not overlook Flavius' bodily position, which also signals a host of associations, as other depictions of the dining dead make clear. For example, the relatively humble funerary altar of Marcus Orpheus, now in the Capitoline Museums in Rome, shows the deceased at table in a scene shared with three other figures (Fig. 2.2). Stretched out on a high-boarded couch, Orpheus reclines in the same posture as Flavius, his left hand holding a cup and his right knee elevated. A three-legged table holds victuals in front of him. And, notably, a woman is shown sitting near his feet on the couch and holding his right hand; she is presumably his wife or concubine. Meanwhile, two smaller figures stand in tunics at the scene's far edges. Both standing figures hold objects – a vessel for wine and something indiscernible because of damage – which marks them as enslaved servers, probably handsome young boys who were especially prized in this role.[51]

Dining as Flavius or Orpheus did, then, was not just enjoying a repast but was a mark of elite distinction. A diner like these two, Orpheus' altar makes clear, possessed wealth sufficient to afford fancy furniture, coverlets, abundant wine, and slave boys who waited on the banqueter. Moreover, internal signs within the altar also emphasized the differences and the banqueters'

FIGURE 2.2 A funerary altar from Rome shows the deceased reclining atop a *lectus* and surrounded by household members whose dress, posture, and activities serve to cast his relaxation in higher relief. (Musei Capitolini, Centrale Montemartini; courtesy of Archivio Fotografico dei Musei Capitolini / © Sovrintendenza Capitolina ai Beni Culturali, Roma.)

privilege: The prone Orpheus occupies the most comfortable position among a three-tier hierarchy. Likewise, his clothing underscores his superiority, as his mantle (or even toga, it is hard to tell) outclasses the tunic-clad slaves. And, in addition to the high-prestige couch and table, Orpheus is the lone person enjoying food and drink, while the slaves serve it. As Matthew Roller summarizes the relief: "The privileged, reclining, free adult male ... is the focal point of a number of pleasures ... He also enjoys the companionship of the woman, and the prospect of the sexual pleasure that she and the slave boys provide."[52] Overall, what we witness explicitly in Orpheus' relief is implied in Flavius' funerary monument – leisured conviviality of the type enjoyed by Rome's elite men.

Pinning his funerary commemoration to the world of leisure was not only a matter of reaching upwards for Flavius but also entailed pushing downwards. It is true that ordinary Romans were by no means unified in concentrating their funerary commemoration on their work and that this trend was lightening by Flavius' era, but such connections were a mainstream phenomenon.[53] By contrast, Flavius appears to swim against

The Person, A Life, and Its Presentation

this current by emphasizing anything but the *labor* entailed in such presentations. His is a world of *otium*, leisure, which ancient texts and the very etymology of the word contrast with *negotium* – occupations, business, or duties that were the negation of leisure. In Cicero's *De Oratore*, for example, one personage describes debating state affairs with graybeard politicians by day before the group adjourned in the evening to the dining couches. Such was the contrast in atmosphere, the figure says, that "among these men the day seemed to have run its course in the senate-house, but the dinner party seemed to have unfolded in Tusculum." The analogy runs that the forum is to a rural villa retreat as gloomy business is to festive relaxation.[54] Closer to Flavius' own time, Martial shows the distinction's continued vibrancy: "Neither the forum nor summons papers are known to us: our job is to recline on dolled-up couches." Even what Romans wore, it seems, emphasized the difference, as the "speaker" here is actually a set of fancy dining clothes.[55] And so, given this stark contrast between the worlds of work/business and pleasure, *labor/negotium* and *otium*, Flavius' depiction of dining and drinking appears not only to be a claim of fancy luxuries but to entail a pushback against representational strategies of a broad swath of ordinary Romans.

In sum, then, Flavius' representation and others like his complicate the "trickle-down" model of taste-making in ancient Rome. His commemoration is not tied to senatorial or equestrian models of funerary self-presentation. Indeed, no one of that rank is commemorated with dining motifs, and in Flavius' epitaph we read no list of offices held, battles won, cash splashed for the public good, or the rest. In other words, his funerary ensemble copies elite practices in life, not their self-presentation in death. At the same time that he looks up, he also looks down to respond to modes of commemoration that certainly did not threaten him but that presented an opportunity for him to claim a step above. Whether this situation offers an example of a self-defined and self-conscious upper-middle class, a so-called *plebs media*, as some scholars would have it, is questionable.[56] It nevertheless rebuffs models both above and below in avoiding a depiction of past achievements in some field and instead emphasizing present leisure.

Flavius' Self-Presentation III: Body

That addresses the overall content but could leave us asking about specific features of Flavius' representation. One of the largest gaps between modern and ancient reactions to his sculpture might be in the apparent difference between Flavius' face and torso: the one undeniably aged, the other looking as though every waking hour was spent in a gym. What we read as a disjuncture was not all that strange for Romans, however. As Christopher Hallett has pointed out, ancient cultures were rife with initially odd combinations that resolved in one being, such as Pegasus, the Minotaur, the Sphinx, or Nike.[57] Against this backdrop, combining a youthful body with an older head was not so extreme. But, when we dig deeper, a more seamless confluence of two practices is evident.

Flavius' presentation broadcast two messages. His wizened face likely reflected reality, in that he probably was in his fifties or sixties at death, considering his long marriage to Flavia Primitiva. Yet even displaying his full age might surprise us, since many obituaries today include a photograph of the deceased in the full bloom of youth, not with a face scored by wrinkles and creased by crow's feet. The difference may lay partly in today's elevation of youth, but it equally arises from the status afforded to those rare few who had achieved an older age in Roman society. To them deference was due on account of their having experienced life's perils and accumulated its lessons with resolve and determination. The Greek historian Polybius' famous narration of an elite Republican funeral, for instance, fixates on the lifelike, warts-and-all masks that actors wore to impersonate the progenitors of the deceased in the funeral cortege and once they took their places atop the rostra, where the character of those men and the deceased was praised.[58] A face like Flavius' signaled steeliness and resolve, *severitas* and *gravitas*. In fact, we might even note that Flavius' face feels somehow exaggerated in its agedness, as though it is playing up the cracks and crevices. Such prominence could reflect the sculpture's setting in a minimally lit tomb, but it also parallels similar representations of elderly male portrait subjects, whose faces reflect a sort of hyperrealism that scholars have termed "verism." This artificially amped-up version of reality, in other words, emphasizes a Roman ideal of the experienced, serious, and world-wise man.[59]

Flavius' torso likewise presents an ideal, but one drawn from a different background, namely Greek precedents. In Greece, male athletes, rulers, and mythological figures were rendered with few or no items of clothing, which eventually offered, in the words of one scholar, a sort of visual shorthand for "action" as well as "physical strength, manliness and courage."[60] As Rome's dominion expanded through Hellenistic Greece, a taste for such iconography of idealized human form seeped into Roman sensibilities, so that Romans slowly shrugged off anxious attitudes toward nudity or its near equivalents until even Roman generals and emperors were depicted in the buff or in minimal clothing. (Interestingly, *nudus* in

Latin can denote someone stark naked or wearing minimal clothing that hides the sex organs; lack of clothing was often associated with servile or poor persons who could not legally wear certain garments.) By the time of the empire, a portrait depicting its subject in (near) nudity characterizes that person as "self-consciously stepping back into the world of heroes," evoking associations with virtue and courage.[61] It was especially popular in representing and designating the deceased, like Flavius, who had moved on to the world beyond.[62] I will return to this theme in a moment.

Whereas we might see a disconnect between a young body and old head, Roman sensibilities were quite differently attuned. For one thing, in Roman sculpture, they served different purposes: Individuality was rarely if ever distinguished through the representation of the body and its dress; that was the head's job, as we have seen in Flavius' portrait.[63] Next, confusion is very much a cultural expectation created by circumstances. Though Greek and Roman art were distinctly naturalistic, in that they typically sought to capture forms like wildlife or humans in various media, at times they presented distinctly unnatural images. Many of those, like a bust in a museum, do not strike us oddly, since we are accustomed to them: They are convention, and so we do not think that there existed a person with a head, shoulders, and nothing else. Hallett's example of this "suspension of disbelief" is really nice – even when we see modern actors in strange costumes performing Shakespeare's *Antony and Cleopatra* in Elizabethan English, we do not have any trouble imagining them as ancient folks, since it is expected.[64] And so, when ancient folk looked at Flavius' sculpted representation, they did not see a disconnect but an example of code-switching as two idealized messages were articulated via different signifiers for different signifieds.

Flavius' Self-Presentation IV: Cup

Though our eyes may fly straight to Flavius' head and body, the vessel in his hand may have drawn a Roman's gaze. After all, the form of serving ware – be it a red Solo cup or a piece of fine Riedel stemware – bears meaning for the type and register of event underway. Despite restorations, the basic form of Flavius' cup is clear: a slight lip tops an almost semispherical body, while a long, flat handle outlined with simple decoration terminates in a half-moon.[65] Similar shapes in the artifactual record take bronze, silver, and even glass form. Which material was meant to be depicted here is not immediately clear, since the marble couldn't be carved beyond a certain thinness. The simple trimming and lunate endpoint find parallels in the

190 bronze examples of this shape found at Pompeii, while silver vessels typically receive more ornate decoration along the handle.[66]

We might be tempted to puzzle out the vessel's meanings by scouring ancient literature for mentions of its name. The issue, however, is that scholars have attached several terms to this shape – *casseruola*, *patera*, or *trulla* – but ancient artifacts, absent packaging, are rarely labeled. So, while we do not know what Romans called these vessels, it is tempting to abide by scholarly convention and search ancient texts for these terms. For Flavius' cup, each term inflects our approach to the vessel because of the assumptions embedded in the word: *trulla*, a ladle, presumes immersion; *patera*, beyond a drinking cup, is connected to offerings of wine; and *casseruola* derives from Italian bakeware.[67] Truth be told, we often do not know if we are pairing a textual descriptor with the correct artifact, or if Romans were flexible about terminology – if someone asked you for a "cup," how many vessel shapes and materials might come to mind? There is ample opportunity for circularity.

Better, then, to approach the vessel from a material culture perspective. No Pompeian bronze example of the form at the Naples Museum shows any sign of discoloration from direct flame, so it was not used for cooking.[68] Meanwhile, one or two examples of this shape appear in hordes of silver vessels – such as from Boscoreale, the Casa del Menandro in Pompeii, and Hildesheim in Germany – yet always amid drinkware with more elaborate decoration, which suggests that they were routinely part of an assemblage of silver, but not at the top end of it.[69] Indeed, a painted representation of a twenty-plus piece silver assemblage from a Pompeian tomb omits them altogether.[70] And what about the form itself? It contrasts to similar vessels with shallower receptacles and round handles, which took less care to contain the liquid and also facilitated pouring with a twist of the wrist. The flat handle of Flavius' vessel helped maintain a level position, and its deeper bowl mitigated spillage. Many drinking vessels had smaller handles or none whatsoever, which raises the question of why a handle was desired at all. It potentially insulated Flavius and other users from the frigid or hot water that was mixed with wine. Yet Flavius' left hand cradles the vessel's bowl, which would minimize this effect or perhaps communicate a moment when the wine has yet to be poured or has already been drained. Overall, this quick survey highlights potential pitfalls of nomenclature, outlines paths forward, and shows that, to paraphrase Freud, a cup is never just a cup. Rather, Flavius' vessel stands apart from the fanciest drinkware, yet, because of its depth, signals a hearty thirst for the festivities already underway or about to commence.

The Person, A Life, and Its Presentation

Flavius' Self-Presentation V: Dining as a Divinity?

If we take Flavius' activity, dress, adornment, and cup together, they may add up to a still grander set of associations, for Romans on occasion drew explicit connections between the deceased and divinities by portraying the dead as a god. Interestingly, at least two other *kline* monuments from Rome were explicit in forging such associations. One displays the deceased, like Flavius, with a bare chest and holding a cup in his left hand (Fig. 2.3).[71] He appears bald, wears a garland around his neck, and drapes his right arm around the shoulder of a woman who shares the couch. Most notably, a lion skin lies behind the man's shoulder, and the hero's quiver round out the connection with Hercules. This was a not-uncommon association for men of his age – about three dozen examples survive.[72]

As if a hero's full iconographical ensemble were not enough, the dead-divine connection could be made explicit, such as on another *kline* monument from Rome, which we now only know from an engraving (Fig. 2.4). Like Flavius, the deceased, named Satorneinos, is shown reclining, holding a cup in his left hand, appearing bare-chested, and wearing a crown atop his head. Unlike Flavius, he appears youthful through his face, and holds a garland in his right hand. Additionally, a Greek inscription runs between the legs of his couch that records the wish of the deceased's parents that he be portrayed "in the guise of Dionysus." And we read about similar statues of individuals made to look like Bacchus in the literary record.[73] In this

FIGURE 2.3 A *kline* monument from Rome depicts a deceased couple. The man's ample iconography (lion skin, drinking cup, and quiver) associates him with Hercules. (Courtesy of the Royal Collection Trust / © His Majesty King Charles III.)

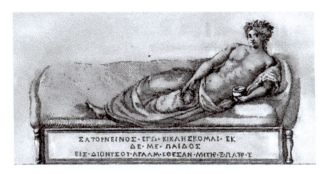

FIGURE 2.4 This etching of a now-lost funerary monument from Rome was dedicated to a young man named Satorneinos, whose parents specified that he be portrayed "in the guise of Dionysus." His wreath, cup, and seminudity align with their wishes. (N. Foggini, *Del Museo Capitolino* (1782).)

light, if we reimagine a metal wreath affixed to Flavius' head, then his sculpture likewise also cultivates connections with Lyaeus, the god twice invoked in his epitaph as a stand-in for wine.

Flavius may have played the situation a bit more subtly than Satorneinos' parents, but if the boy's monument cast the lad in the guise of Dionysus, then Flavius' similar accoutrements could invite a parallel conclusion or at the very least an understanding of Flavius as a member of the *thiasos*, the god's giddy retinue. Anxieties about drunkenness that often tagged along with the god might have been lessened by Flavius' sober face. And we should ask: Are we to think that these figures are represented as gods, or, like a friend who dons a LeBron James jersey, someone *dressed in that role*? Did that costume bestow on the individual a divinity's attributes or simply provoke a positive association? Though these answers are not immediately forthcoming, we are nevertheless witnessing a fascinating overlapping of the celestial and terrestrial realms that casts yet another shade of meaning on Flavius' presentation in his tomb. He clearly alighted on alternative means of highlighting his standing and forging ties to social realms above and beyond.[74]

• • •

If Flavius' audience picked up a connection to divinity even in part, then it chimed with much else that they soaked in from his monument. From the poetic epitaph and its literary callouts to the sculpture and its material, scale, content, and depiction of Flavius, the whole ensemble cast Flavius in special terms. As the preceding pages have shown, none of these efforts are unusual on their own, and they individually align with and underscore broader Roman obsessions with status and impulses to claim one's spot, to articulate hierarchies, and to mark out social differences. And yet the unity of spirit across several realms suggests a comprehensive effort on Flavius' part to make clear that he was anything but a run-of-the-mill Roman. Was this an example of compensation for his background, or even overcompensation? Unfortunately, at this point we bump up against the limits of our evidence, for all we have is Flavius' own self-portrait, which concentrates most intensely on his lifestyle while leaving much more of his life virtually undiscussed. We would love to know, for example, how he gained the funds required for this impressive assemblage, with whom he interacted at banquets and elsewhere, what obstacles he had to overcome, and where else he spent his time – the very sorts of things that Venidius' dossier of tablets at Herculaneum discusses or at least hints at because of their procedural character. This is one challenge of "doing social history" of Romans beyond the uppermost social strata – we are at the mercy of the immediate evidence.

That said, we are granted a firmer scholarly foothold when Flavius moves away from himself and instead turns the epigraphical focus on his family, especially his wife Flavia Primitiva. Over the course of a few lines of the inscription, we learn about her characteristics and life course, at least as Flavius portrays them, and in the process some of both of their experiences come into greater focus.

CHAPTER 3

Flavia Primitiva: Wife, Mother, *Casta Cultrix*

Of the fifteen lines of Flavius' epitaph, nearly half are not about him at all but concentrate on two other figures: his wife of many years Flavia Primitiva and Aurelius Primitivus, who piously cares for Flavius and Flavia's household. Lines 5–11 of the inscription read:

> Praecessitque prior Primitiva gratissima coniuncx
> Flavia et ipsa, cultrix deae Phariae casta,
> sedulaque et forma decore repleta,
> cum qua ter denos dulcissimos egerim annos.
> Solaciumque sui generis Aurelium Primitivum tradidit,
> qui pietate sua coleret fastigia nostra,
> hospitiumque mihi secura servavit in aevum.

> Primitiva, my most pleasant wife, passed away before me.
> She herself was a Flavian, a chaste worshipper of Isis,
> attentive to my needs, and of beautiful appearance.
> I spent thirty wonderful years with her;
> as a comfort, she left me her son, Aurelius Primitivus,
> to tend our house/tomb dutifully; and so, herself released
> from care, she has kept a welcome for me forever.

That such commemoration occurred is not entirely surprising, as Roman epitaphs occasionally dwell on people beyond the deceased themselves. In most cases, however, it is the dedicator whose biography receives attention, not another party. For instance, the tombstone of a freedman named M. Aurelius Zosimos – dating from the early empire and found on the Via Appia – lavishes praise on the deceased's patron and former master, M. Aurelius Cotta Maximus. It thanks Maximus for financial support and for advancing the political career of the deceased's son. Maximus certainly also erected the inscription.[1]

The extensive attention paid to Flavia is one sign of Flavius' affection for the spouse that predeceased him. Moreover, as we shall see, Flavia's portrayal manages to balance both generic descriptors attached to Roman matrons – beauty, industry, and sweetness – and features particular to Flavia, especially her devotion to the "Pharian goddess," longhand for the Egyptian goddess Isis. The length and specificity of Flavia's portrayal suggest that we should take this biography seriously on its own. Yet even as we examine Flavia's depiction in the inscription, we should simultaneously recognize that Flavius created such a portrait, which formed part of his own broader "packaging." In this way, Flavius' words in these seven lines begin to flesh out his own *curriculum vitae* and also broaden our scope: to a family, to the experiences and beliefs of its members individually and collectively, and to a richer picture of Roman social relationships.

Marriage and Motherhood

Somewhere between Tibur and Rome, Flavius Agricola and Flavia Primitiva wed and lived together for thirty years before her death. The *Flavia* of her name perhaps indicates that she likewise descended from a freedman of the imperial household or was herself a freedwoman of the emperor. Line 6 of the inscription may emphasize such a descent, as *Flavia* completes her name and *et ipsa*, "and she herself," draws attention and adds emphasis. The *cognomen* Primitiva is most common among freeborn women. Meaning "first," it often refers to birth order, which could also hint that whoever named her was counting freeborn children. Unfortunately, as with Flavius, Flavia's status and background is uncertain.

Calling Flavia his "most pleasant wife" (*gratissima coniuncx*) and celebrating a marriage may have been mild novelties in Flavius' family. If we are correct that one of his ancestors was enslaved, then that person had been denied legal rights in servitude, including legally recognized marriages. Enslaved people could, and often did, form informal marriage-like partnerships among themselves, but their continuation was subject to a master's whims, therefore making the partnerships themselves tools of manipulation. Being liberated gave freedmen legal standing to conduct business, enter into contracts, write wills, become citizens in the case of most men, and also marry. Not surprisingly, individuals who, when enslaved, had endured what has been called "social death" trumpeted their freshly minted marriages as freedmen, portraying themselves side-by-side, joining hands, and decked out in toga and stola, the sartorial markers of citizenship for men and marriage for women.[2] And so, in Flavius' featuring of Flavia on his epitaph as his wife, we may be seeing an epigraphic reflection of that same sensibility, even if it had grown paler after a generation or two.

Many descriptors attached to Flavia are routine formulae for Roman matrons, as her grace, beauty, and dutifulness all come in for praise. In fact, one woman's epitaph, the so-called *Laudatio Murdiae*, records a eulogy delivered by her son. It laments:

> Since the funerary speech for all good women is wont to be simple and similar, because their natural qualities preserved under their own charge do not require variations of phraseology, and it may be enough for all of them to have done the same good deeds worthy of a good reputation, and, because it is hard for a woman to find new praises since their lives are upset by fewer variations, it is necessary for us to commemorate their common values so that nothing may be lost from just precepts and besmirch the remainder. On that account my dearest of all mothers deserved the greater praise from everyone because in modesty, honesty, chastity, obedience, wool-working, diligence and trustworthiness she was the equal and the model of other upstanding women.[3]

Ironically, this very lament about formulaic expressions of women's virtues may itself have been formulaic.[4] On the whole, Roman woman enjoyed more power and freedom than their Greek counterparts. The fifth-century BCE historian Thucydides famously has the Athenian statesman Pericles append a brief note about women to a speech praising Athens and its soldiers who had fallen in the Peloponnesian War against Sparta:

> If it is necessary for me to say something about excellence to you women who will now be widows, let me say it in this brief advice. Your glory will be great in not falling short of your innate character; and the greatest glory will belong to her who is least talked of among men, whether for good or for bad.[5]

As we can already see with Flavia, Romans did not shy away from praising women, and numerous other differences separated Roman women from Greek, such as their ability to inherit property and occasionally be honored as public priestesses (though we do not know exactly what that role entailed). Some behaviors that come in for stock praise ("trustworthiness," for one) underscore a degree of independence, yet others – such as "obedience," "modesty," and "chastity" – put a heavy finger on the other side of that balance. They sound like the "love, honor, and obey" from bridal vows of old. As one scholar has put it, "The reward of the 'good' woman in Rome was likely to be praise in stereotypical phrases; in Athens she won oblivion."[6] In the end, the repetitive nature of women's epitaphs underscores the narrow range of endeavors and categories of activity to which Roman society constricted women.

That does not mean that Flavius' sentiments were not genuine. Or perhaps they served in part to reassure readers, who next encountered what seems to have been a slightly unusual circumstance. Although nothing is stated explicitly, it appears that Flavia had a son by someone other than Flavius. The most obvious piece of evidence to suggest this is the son's name, Aurelius Primitivus, which obviously does not reflect that of Flavius Agricola but instead shares a *cognomen* with his mother. Second, the text roundaboutly describes Aurelius as the *solacium sui generis*, the comfort of Flavia's own *genus*, a word that encompasses a host of meanings. It can denote something as broad as "race" or "nationality" or as intimate as "offspring" or "family"; somewhere between it has the qualitative sense of "kind" or "character/nature."[7] Whatever our understanding, the phrase emphasizes Flavia and Aurelius' connection. (It may simply be a way to say "son" with more panache.) Last, the verb used to describe Flavia's act of leaving behind Aurelius, *tradidit*, implies a handing over or a bestowing, which would be an odd choice if Flavius were Aurelius' father.[8] All in all, the balance of evidence points toward an earlier relationship that yielded Aurelius.

Aurelius Primitivus does come in for his share of praise. First, he is a comfort. Second, the epitaph both mentions and demonstrates Aurelius' piety with its description of Aurelius' cultivation of *fastigia nostra*, literally "our gables." *Fastigia* could equally apply to a house or a tomb, or it could have a metaphorical sense: "our eminence/social position."[9] Third, both Aurelius and Flavius are subjects of the verb *colere*, "to cultivate," thus drawing a parallel between the two men and linking them to Flavia, who is described as a *cultrix*, a "cultress." (And this set of words, as agricultural as religious, could pun on Flavius' *cognomen* Agricola, "farmer.") Yet we should not lose sight of how the portrayal of Aurelius also reflects positively on his mother. When Aurelius is described as a comfort (*solacium*) for Flavius, the statement speaks both to the depth of Flavius' sense of loss (he really needs consolation) as well as to the warmth between the men (as Aurelius is able to provide the comfort).[10] Similarly, Aurelius' piety implies his mother's positive shaping of his character. Overall, the two lines dedicated to Aurelius lend texture to some otherwise fairly stock praise. In the words of English 101 instructors everywhere, they show and do not merely tell.

If Flavia brought Aurelius to her marriage with Flavius, then their relationship reflected broader demographic patterns in the Roman world.

As is clear from a famous tombstone discovered in Rome, Roman men typically were older than their wives. In this case, the girl was wed at age seven (!) to a fellow freedman, whom she describes as "truly like a father to me."[11] Scholarly opinion differs on just how extreme this example was, as some camps posit an average age at first marriage of around eighteen for females and twenty-eight for males, while others would push for younger ages for both sexes, with males still significantly older than females.[12] Such a situation commonly meant, for first-time marriages, a substantial difference in the worldliness and experience levels of the couple, which could easily perpetuate the power imbalance between husband and wife.[13]

The pattern also meant that it was common for women to outlive their husbands, thus leaving widows as a significantly larger portion of the population than they are today, in the United States at least.[14] Or perhaps Flavia was divorced, though that seems unlikely, since children of a divorced couple largely remained under the legal authority of their father.[15] In either case, why did Flavia apparently wed again? There may have been legal and financial motivation, as legislation passed under Augustus incentivized widows to remarry within two years (by limiting their right of inheritance if they did not).[16] It could have been a matter of practicality, as Flavia was drawn to the economic protection that Flavius afforded her and her son, particularly if she were herself a freedwoman.[17] And it would be foolish to rule out emotional attachment, both because we see love identified as a motivating factor in marriage – a tombstone from Rome describes a couple as "bound by mutual love"[18] – and because Flavius, though not quite so lovey-dovey, does deploy warm language ("sweetest years") to recount their marriage.

Regardless of how and why Flavia and Flavius' marriage took shape, its example points to the variety of forms that families took beyond what we might initially imagine. In Rome, for example, it was hardly out of the question to manumit one's female slave in order to marry her. That was the case, for instance, for Acte and Euphrosynus, whom we know from their daughter's funerary altar, which was found on the Via Flaminia in Rome. The inscription on the front shows that Euphrosynus had freed Acte, they had married, and to them was born a daughter, who died at eight years old. Some scholars see love as the motivating factor for such slave-to-wife manumissions, while others envision a more complicated relationship. The rear face of the Acte and Euphrosynus altar, for instance, shows just such a circumstance. An added text curses Acte for committing adultery and abandoning Euphrosynus.[19] Forming a family, in this world of high and sudden mortality, often involved adoption, as when families could not produce living children, when someone was left parentless, and especially

Flavia Primitiva: Wife, Mother, *Casta Cultrix*

when inheritance and preserving a family's wealth were at stake. It was even possible to adopt someone in your will, so they became your son or daughter upon your death. And, on the flip side, exposing unwanted children was a matter of life for families with too many mouths to feed. So, a circumstance like the one we seem to encounter, with a "blended family," was not particularly odd – aside, perhaps, from its long duration.[20]

The Pharian Goddess

Back to Flavia and her descriptors. By contrast with stock praise of wifely traits, a more particular identification names Flavia as a *casta deae Phariaes cultrix*, a chaste/pure devotee of the Pharian goddess, namely Isis. The goddess' worship was long-standing, tracing back to third millennium BCE Egypt. In the Hellenistic period it spread widely through the Greek-speaking world, which was soon enveloped within Rome's sphere of power. This deity, like other foreign cults, met with suspicion not long after her arrival in Italy in the late second century BCE, because adherents met privately and were initiated into mysteries through clandestine rituals.[21] By Flavia's lifetime in the second century CE, however, worship of an Egyptian goddess in Rome was not unusual, as the cosmopolitan city boasted several shrines to Isis; the largest enjoyed financial backing from the emperor.[22] The locational adjective "of the Pharos" (the lighthouse that marked Alexandria's port in Egypt) even anticipates a reader's familiarity with Isis' epithets, perhaps even specifying Flavia's veneration of a particularly Alexandrian manifestation of the goddess.[23] For the remainder of this chapter, I want to trace two related questions. Based on Flavius' portrayal of Flavia as *casta deae Phariaes cultrix*, what can we tell about her relationship to the cult of Isis? And what features of the cult may have appealed to her?

It seems best to begin, however, by establishing a baseline of traditional Roman civic religion.[24] The front face of an altar from Pompeii's forum offers a useful starting point (Fig. 3.1).[25] It depicts preparations for a key mainstream religious practice, namely offering a sacrifice. We first note the ritual's setting – not enclosed within a temple but at an altar in front of its columned façade. The undertaking, in other words, was a public affair conducted for the common welfare before a crowd of onlookers. Yet the clothing of the participants makes clear that not all were equal, for only one figure wears a toga – the priest with his head covered. The bundled rods (*fasces*) poking out at the upper left belong to his attendants, which mark him as a public official, thus underscoring the deep connection between religion and matters of state in the Roman world. Everyone else's role is

FIGURE 3.1 An altar from Pompeii's forum exemplifies the public, communal, and hierarchical nature of traditional Roman civic religion. (Photo: Wikimedia Commons.)

subordinate, especially the half-naked figures who lead the bull and will undertake the gory business of dispatching it. The animal is one of several offerings made to secure the gods' goodwill. We see at left a tray of foodstuffs and instruments for a libation. Meanwhile, the pipe player in the background drowns out extraneous sounds so the priest's formulaic prayer will unproblematically reach divine ears.[26] Romans had no set of sacred texts. Instead, Romans spoke of *cultus deorum*, "the worship of the gods," which meant continually appeasing the gods through gifts and offerings of valuable items such as we see depicted. In the crassest terms, this was ritualized bribery. Civic religion did not ask much of most participants, nor did it offer much aside from a spectacle, perhaps a chunk of meat, and reassurance that matters would be okay. Polytheism was of course the order of the day, and Romans' pragmatic approach to cult extended to enlarging their Pantheon as they expanded their domain. When they conquered another territory, they might ritually invite its deities to abandon that place/people and to be welcomed into Rome.[27]

How did the worship of Isis compare to civic religion and why might it have attracted Flavia? For one thing, the cult of Isis did not involve everyone by default as civic worship did. Rather, like other so-called mystery cults, it was constituted by members who chose to take part in a voluntary association and who were initiated into the group's membership after a period of preparation. Such a difference introduces two important elements, namely the decision on the part of a worshipper and the cult's promise of a before-and-after change on an individual level. If civic religion largely served to cement the social status quo and to keep matters pointed in the same direction, elective cults like that of Isis offered transformation in their adherents' lives as well as incorporation into a self-selecting group. We see these features illustrated most directly, even hyperbolically, in Apuleius' *Metamorphoses*, a novel penned in the second century CE. The protagonist/narrator, Lucius, after being transformed into a donkey early on, spends the majority of the novel in a literally asinine state. Late in the work, however, he prays to Isis, returns to human form, and undergoes initiation into the cult. Flavia and others hoped for something less drastic in degree yet nevertheless similar in nature.

Isis may have appealed to Flavia because the goddess' worshippers thought she wielded all-encompassing features and power. When Lucius, while still in donkey form, has a vision of Isis, he addresses her as queen of heaven and then raises the possibility that she is known by other names: Ceres, Venus, Diana, and Proserpina. Near the end of his speech, the donkey implores Isis, "By whatever name, with whatever ceremony, in whatever aspect it is right to invoke you, support me now amid the extreme depths of my distress, strengthen my fallen fortune, grant me peace and rest after cruel tribulations."[28] In reply, the goddess takes Lucius' vision of universality still further: "I am mother of nature, commander of all the elements, the original offspring of the ages, loftiest of the deities, queen of the shades, foremost of the heavenly beings, single form of gods and goddesses."[29] She confirms Lucius' litany of alternative identities and tacks on still more goddesses and regions – the Phyrigians call her Pessinuntia, she brags, the people of Attica Minerva, the Cyprians Venus, the Cretans Diana, the Sicilians Proserpina, the Eleusinians Ceres, still others Juno or Bellona or Hecate or Rhamnusia. She concludes with, "The Ethiopians and Egyptians . . . venerate me with the rites that are truly mine, and call me by my real name, queen Isis."[30]

How should we understand this seemingly encyclopedic phenomenon? It is not monotheism, the belief in one goddess to the exclusion of others, for other deities do exist in both Lucius' and Isis' formulations. Rather, it has been described by the modern term *henotheism* – from the Greek εἷς ὁ θεός, "the one god" – a belief system that acknowledges other deities but considers one supreme.[31] Isis is not just preeminent in the catalog but also ranges widely in geography, spanning the eastern Mediterranean before tracing herself back to Egypt. Rome's pantheon, just like its cosmopolitan population, drew from the whole Mediterranean, but one goddess reigned supreme, Isiac worshippers believed. Those other deities' attributes and spheres of influence were subsumed within Isis, whom they regarded as the omnipotent and universal original. For worshippers like Flavia, Isis offered a distinctly "one stop shop" and comprehensive catalog of divinity. This was a different type of enterprise from normal polytheism.

Casta Cultrix

What was the degree of Flavia's investment in venerating Isis? Inspection of Flavia's characterization as a *casta cultrix* lends contours to her participation. Let us start with *cultrix*. The term describes a female "reverencer" or "worshipper" as well as a woman who cares for any sort of thing or who dwells in a place, religious or not.[32] Unfortunately, Flavia represents our only *cultrix* of Isis in inscriptions and literary texts, and very few *cultrices* of any deity appear in pre-Christian inscriptions at all.[33] For that reason, we are not able to speak specifically about a *cultrix*, but we may identify actions undertaken by others like Flavia in their devotion to Isis. We know, for example, of women priestesses, and no fewer than five female *sacerdotes* appear in inscriptions. One of these was also a *pastophorus*, likely a shrine-bearer in processions. We also read of an *ornatrix* who probably decorated the goddess' shrine and ornamented her statue. And one woman in Rome is listed as a *melanep(h)ore*, a title that implies she wore black to grieve the goddess.[34] In other words, while inscriptions outline some specific roles for women in the cult of Isis, Flavia is not identified by any of them, but is granted a more generic descriptor, like "adherent" or "devotee."[35]

These various roles do underscore another possible appeal of Isis to Flavia, namely the greater opportunity for participation afforded to women as well as the positions of responsibility they could hold. In civic cult, it is true that a few important positions were open to women – the Vestals most famously – yet they were limited to the senatorial class or local elites. In addition to specific tasks enumerated above, we read of female

Flavia Primitiva: Wife, Mother, *Casta Cultrix*

Isiac worshippers described as *Bubiastica* (a devotee of the goddess Bubastis, an aspect of Isis) or *Memfiana* (after a major site of Isis worship in Egypt).[36] In this way, women could occupy prominent positions within the cult that, on occasions when worship took on a public face, as at annual processions, translated into public recognition.

On to Flavia's characterization as *casta*, "chaste." If Flavia had a child, technical virginity was not in play. Rather, *castitas* in the Roman mindset reflected a moral standing in the world; it applied not only to people but even to structures and abstract ideas. In Horace, for instance, we read of a *domus* (a house, including both its architecture and occupants) that is *casta*, not because of a lack of intercourse – indeed, mothers are praised for their newborns in the very same lines – but because it is not polluted by any *stuprum*, a word that defies easy translation but which encompasses illicit sex such as adultery and rape.[37] *Pudica* would be a more appropriate adjective to emphasize sexual purity.[38] What counted as sex that was out-of-bounds? It depended on who one was. The prevailing ideology held that respectable women were to remain virginal until marriage and thereafter to sleep with their husband alone. Meanwhile, a man was held to no such standard but could have relations with others outside the marriage, male and female, provided he took the active role, avoided other men's wives and daughters, and did not gain a reputation for being oversexed.

Where *cultrix* broadcasts a vibrant if imprecise devotion to Isis, its combination with *casta* moves beyond standard formulations of wifely virtue to get more specific about Flavia's religious practices. First, despite the general acceptance of Isiac worship, certain aspects proved hard to shake in the popular imagination. For female devotees, suspicions circled about their sexual activity. Juvenal's wildly misogynistic Satire 6, for instance, pictures an adulteress getting dolled up more than usual and seeking out the sanctuary of *Isiacae ... lenae*, "Isis the procuress," for a liaison. Ovid similarly paints the shrine of Isis as space of transgression and transformation: If a young man is looking for a partner, the poet encourages him to seek out Isis, for she turns girls into mistresses. And Martial mocks a rival who does not want to have sex, listing the Iseum among the spots he consciously avoids. In general, dogging the temple of Isis and its devotees was a reputation as a hook-up spot rife with morally malleable women.[39] In this light, *casta* reflects a defensive correction.

Yet Flavia's identification as a *casta cultrix* also embraces specific practices of Isis devotees. Isiac worshippers practiced sexual abstinence both as a portion of their initiation as well as for ten days annually thereafter. In preparation for his initiation, Apuleius' narrator, Lucius, rents a room in the temple precinct and then reports:

> I had known from careful study that the obligations of her cult were hard, that the abstinence required by the rules of chastity was quite demanding, and how with caution and circumspection you had to protect a life subject to innumerable vicissitudes.[40]

According to Plutarch, the result of initiates' "strict regimen and abstinence from many kinds of food and from the lusts of the flesh" was a curbing of their unbridled ways and an encouraging of patient service in the shrines.[41] Other evidence for abstinence among Isis worshippers derives from male love poets who bemoan their beloved's abandonment of a shared bed. Propertius, for example, seems to feign irritation at Isis at the beginning of one poem:

> The dismal rites have returned again for poor me: Cynthia is currently occupied for ten nights. If only these sacraments – which the daughter of Inachus sent to Italy's matrons – would perish! The goddess (whoever she was) who has separated impassioned lovers so often has always been harsh to her worshippers.[42]

Such nocturnal separation deserves recompense, claims Propertius' narrator elsewhere: Once his beloved has performed her vigil for Isis, she should pay back the ten nights vowed to him.[43] A woman wishing to manipulate her pursuer, we read in another set of poems, should arouse his desire and then stave off intercourse on the pretext of a headache or Isis worship.[44] Sex, then, was very much a theme in participation in, and reaction to, women's Isis worship.

Funerary commemorations celebrate such close bonds between chastity and piety among Isis worshippers. A verse epitaph from Rome, for instance, identifies (the appropriately named) Alexandria as a "shrine-bearer of the goddess of the Nile" and describes her as *pudica* in the next line.[45] In a similar vein, on a funerary altar from Ostia, a mother and an especially devout father mourn the passing of their twenty-four-year-old daughter, calling her "most chaste and most devout" (*pudicissima[e et] religiosissim-[ae]*), thus cementing the link between veneration and a lack of venereal matters.[46] And, to prove that the emphasis is on abstinence in service to the goddess and not just a splash-over from formulaic female descriptors, a statue base honoring a male priest of Isis at Ostia lists important positions he held and celebrates his *sanctimonia castitas*, "holy abstinence."[47] All told, Flavius' portrayal of Flavia as *casta* held several levels of resonance: a generic value of Roman matrons, a defense against slanderous portrayals, and a reflection of Flavia's degree of devotion to Isis and her precise adherence to cult practices.

Morality and Mortality?

The requirement of chastity helps to introduce additional appeals of Isis' cult for someone like Flavia: a life conducted according to moral expectations as well as potential answers to what awaits after death. In Apuleius' *Metamorphoses*, when the goddess appears to Lucius (still in donkey form) and addresses him, she spells out an important nexus of expectations: "If by attentive obedience, dutiful service, and determined chastity you are worthy of my divinity, know that I alone am able to extend your life beyond the limits determined by fate."[48] Let me make two points, one looking backward and one forward. First, Isis' words here again emphasize chastity and add another adjective, *sedulis* (attentive), that also modifies Flavia in her husband's epitaph. It is a common descriptor applied to Roman women, and that is how I have rendered it in my translation. But it might equally apply to Flavia's worship of the Pharian goddess: She is both chaste and attentive as a *cultrix*, thus checking two of the three boxes in Isis' admonition to Lucius.[49] Second, in posing an if-then statement, Isis here traffics in the mainstream of much of Greco-Roman religion, for reciprocated behavior in the form of vows (if I win this battle or recover from this disease, deity X, I vow to give you Y) or along the lines of *do ut des* (I give so that you might give) was commonplace. Yet what she requires (a certain form of behavior) and what she offers (an extension of life) were hardly typical.

Many people today look to religion not only to answer big questions – What is the point of it all? – but also to consider how we should live: What should we do or not do? In the ancient Mediterranean, by contrast, morality and ethics were hardly the concern of traditional civic religion. Myths overflowed with "bad" behavior, as, in Roman eyes, the gods were as jealous, greedy, plotting, and lustful as you and I. Yet matters occasionally differed for certain sects, including Isiac worshippers. In addition to periodic sexual purity, other restrictions apparently governed worshippers, as Lucius reports that a priest ordered him "to control my desire for food for the next ten days, to avoid eating any meat, and not to drink wine."[50]

Such abstinence and fasting might be dismissed as stringent requirements for purity if not for a further framework that saw moral/ethical deeds rewarded and missteps punished. The case of Lucius again offers a useful starting point, for, immediately after he transformed back into human form, his experience as an ass is described by the high priest: "Not your birth, nor your standing, nor even your fine education brought any help to you; but on youth's impulsive and slippery path you skidded into servile pleasures and brought upon yourself the adverse rewards of ill-starred curiosity."[51] Despite Lucius' high status, he got what he deserved, according to the official, because of his pursuit of bodily delights and his lack of restraint. We read elsewhere of other Isiac worshippers who likewise interpret their misfortunes as punishments for transgressions. Ovid reports: "I've seen one kneeling before Isis's altar who confessed to outraging the divinity of linen-robed Isis. Another, robbed of sight for a similar reason, was shouting through the street that he'd deserved it."[52]

If punishment awaited offenses, what correspondingly positive behavior or value system was expected of the cult's adherents? A fascinating source are hymns in honor of Isis, called aretalogies, that have been found inscribed in her sanctuaries around the Mediterranean. The hypothesis is that these would be sung in praise of the goddess and thus imprint on devotees her stories, mythic lineage, and values.[53] One aretalogy claims, "She instituted justice, that each of us might know how to live on equal terms," before describing her giving of laws so that cities "enjoy tranquility, having discovered not violence legalized, but law without violence."[54] In a similar vein, another aretalogy has Isis offer a first-person litany of her accomplishments: bringing down tyrants, ending murders, ordaining that truth should be considered good, inventing marriage contracts, establishing penalties for practitioners of injustice, honoring those who defend themselves while in the right, and so on.[55] Worshippers like Flavia who recited, chanted, or otherwise soaked in these words were reassured that Isis wielded power, as other gods did, but with a distinctly ethical and egalitarian orientation.

Such an Isiac framework of principles shared overlap with "popular morality" in Roman society. This general set of behavioral expectations – as extracted from fables, sayings, and repeated *exempla* – likewise placed an emphasis on concepts like justice.[56] What differentiates the Isiac material was less content or coverage and more consequences. Isis worship instructed its adherents how to live and told them that their comportment would be assessed. This belief anchored ethical behavior and incentivized it, ensuring that someone like Flavia not only undertook an action because it was right but also because Isis would dole out benefits or unleash punishment. Such reassurance should not be discounted in a world where inequality reigned and individuals rich and poor, connected and dependent, had wildly different access to resolving problems justly.

On to the reward promised by Isis. Flavius' portrayal of Flavia hints that concerns about "the beyond" governed her Isiac worship. The epitaph says she "preceded" him (making no mention of death), and is now *secura*, "free from care," which suggests a peaceful existence. The remainder of the line, in saying that Flavia has preserved a welcome for Flavius forever (*hospitium ... mihi servavit in aevum*), underscores the placid sensibility and extends it perpetually. In this way, the inscription may reflect an Isiac sensibility about "the beyond" on Flavia's part as filtered through Flavius.

If this description feels vague, it may be less Flavius' fault and more a reflection of divergent views across Isiac worshippers. When Isis addressed Lucius, we might remember, her words were also unclear, pledging that, if he should live in service, obedience, and chastity, then she will extend his life beyond the limits of fate. Should we take the goddess' words at face value and contend that all she promises Lucius is to extend his life? Other parts of Lucius' fictional experience suggest images of death and rebirth, but on a symbolic level, as when he receives preinitiation instruction from the high priest:

> Both the gates of the underworld and the safeguarding of life are in [Isis'] hands, [the priest] said, and the very act of initiation is akin to a voluntary death and salvation through her grace. In fact, those whose lifespan was drawing to its close and who already stood on the final threshold of light, if the cult's unspoken mysteries could be entrusted to them safely, the power of the Goddess could select these ones to be in a manner reborn through her providence and to set forth once more on the course of renewed life.[57]

While acknowledging Isis' power over issues of mortality, the high priest outlines an initiate's prolonged life after a symbolic and voluntary death, all thanks to Isis. And Lucius, emerging from the initiation, describes the experience in similar terms, stating, "I reached the very gates of death and, treading Proserpine's threshold, passed through all the elements and returned."[58]

Meanwhile, some funerary inscriptions spell out a clearer hope that the deceased will enjoy an existence beyond this one.[59] One Greek epitaph found in Rome commemorates a child's death yet hopes for his eternal afterlife. It begins: "O Markos Hortorios Eleutheros, sweetest child, at the age of 10 years, 3 months, and 3 days, you left for the immortal house to live (there) forever. May now Osiris give you the refreshing water."[60] Osiris was Isis' brother-cum-husband and lord of the afterlife, whom worshippers credited with the life-giving annual flood of the Nile in Egypt. The deceased, as one scholar puts it, "was notionally bathed" in the refreshing waters "in order to receive eternal life" thanks to Osiris.[61] Other inscriptions spring from the same font – "May Isis grant you the grace of Osiris' pure water," runs one, while another hopes the deceased will be "of good cheer in the company of Osiris."[62] These references suggest an expectation that the dead will find their eternal refuge with the afterlife's tutelary deity.

Expecting clarity about Flavia's sentiments about the Isiac "beyond" is foolhardy, since a statement about her sensibilities would be more fitting for her own epitaph than the indirect homage offered by Flavius. Nevertheless, if there is some meaning to be extracted and guesses to be hazarded, then the stillness and eternity evoked for Flavia suggest a vision of an existence beyond this realm, where she awaits her beloved. And such a calm and nourishing vision would hold understandable appeal.

• • •

As this final discussion makes clear, the view of Flavia Primitiva that we are granted comes through the lens offered by her husband, Flavius Agricola, and therefore likely reflects his interests. It is not surprising, then, that Flavia comes in for some stock praise – according to him, she is beautiful, pleasant, and attentive. Leaving those features out or substituting other ones could have raised eyebrows or generally reflected poorly on him. And yet, as much as Flavia's portrait is penned in by common descriptors that reflect gendered expectations of her (and other women's) behavior, we do not want that to stand in the way of recognizing the totality of Flavia's life course, the ways in which it was unique, and her potential agency in giving it shape.

For one thing, Flavius' brief portrait suggests that Flavia's life was hardly a smooth continuum, but one cleaved into chapters. Widowhood and remarriage – if our reading of the epitaph is correct – lent a second phase to her life. And it was apparently a relatively prosperous and content one, given her warm commemoration by Flavius on *his* funerary monument and within a tomb she likely did not inhabit. But concentrating on these final segments and reducing Flavia's life to widowhood and wifedom would bypass her experiences in infancy, girlhood, marriage, as a mother, and so forth. We intuitively know about these temporal and transformational dimensions as we bury grandparents, endure puberty and junior high, get dumped by crushes, and try our hand at something-like-independence at college, in the military, or elsewhere. And so, even as we have a vision of Flavia's later years, we must not lose sight of the roads she took to get there, and the many different Flavias there were before the one we encounter.[63]

Flavia Primitiva: Wife, Mother, *Casta Cultrix*

Which brings us to another point about Flavia as she was presented on Flavius' epitaph: being named as a worshipper of Isis, and apparently a serious one at that. We do not know at what point in her life course she dabbled with and then committed to the goddess' worship, but the previous pages intimate the sense of change, order, and protection it offered. Her devotion was not a rote parroting of anything Flavius believed: what she was to the *Dea Pharia*, he was to *Lyaeus*. (We will see in Chapter 5 how that difference may have played out.) All of which points to two things: First, that Flavius, in recording this aspect of his wife, was honoring something of deep importance or even definitional to her; and second, that it was Flavia's choice to venerate the goddess.

Across the many appeals of Isis worship that we have traced through this chapter, the theme of personal transformation has run strong. Amid a civic religious landscape that largely enshrined the status quo and in the face of a society that (like nearly all of them) tried to reinscribe the hierarchy, the appeal of change shines forth. When Lucius emerges from the temple after his initiation, he is dressed in new and resplendent clothing, is revealed to the gathered crowd, and then undertakes several celebratory meals with them. The world looks different to him; he looks different to it.[64] Part of Lucius' fervency is explained by the safeguarding he confesses to feel under the goddess' watch, particularly amid life's challenges. He addresses Isis: "You, holy and perpetual protector of humankind, who are always benevolent in nurturing mortals with the sweet affection of a mother to the afflictions of the wretches."[65] We must not overlook that existence, both in Roman times as now, can be grueling and hard. Feeling part of something surer – with rules and promises and protection and like-minded folk who agree to live by the same precepts and who share special knowledge – must have held great appeal. And not just for former donkeys, but also widows, those poorly served by society, and many others.

Flavia's voluntary participation in the cult of Isis entailed an outlook, behavioral expectations, and (at least ideally) a way of life and death that ran parallel to, or perhaps even beyond, the mainstream. While many of the chapters of Flavia's life may have *happened to her* or been the product of sociocultural expectations, all signs point to these practices and beliefs springing from her initiative. Whether it was the chance for ritual participation or responsibility, a desire for a sense of belonging, a quest for justice and fairness, or queries about life's deep issues, Flavia sought in Isis answers or at least salves to the questions and challenges she faced.

We will never know what combination of factors drew Flavia to the worship of Isis along the course of her life and its many chapters, but considering what unfolded within the sanctuary of Isis as she worshipped, participated in ritual activities, and even spent time with her fellow adherents can deepen our understanding. That is, to this point, our consideration of Flavia's relationship to Isis has remained largely focused on personal matters. When we set Flavia in contact with other Isis worshippers inside the physical framework of their place of worship, we not only gain a view of interaction among Isis devotees, but also the role of these spaces and activities in shaping their sense of belonging and community. As we shall see, the temple and what unfolded within it also helped to engender a sense of devotion and personal change for Flavia.

CHAPTER 4

Flavia Primitiva, Experience, and Community in the Iseum Campense

In Chapter 2, we lamented having little sense of where Flavius spent his time. We can study his eternal resting place but not the spots he haunted while alive: his places of business and socializing, his dwelling, or, more particularly, his dining room(s). But if Flavius took a break from overseeing his tomb's construction, a thirty-minute walk or litter ride would have brought him to a spot of deep importance to Flavia: the Iseum Campense, Italy's most important sanctuary of Isis. Once standing in the Campus Martius – an ample plain carved out by the Tiber's curve – the sizable sanctuary (about 75 m × 225 m) now lies buried beneath several meters and nearly two millennia of urban buildup. Nevertheless, through a host of sources, it is possible to piece together the Iseum's structure and decoration, to consider the artworks that were meaningful to Flavia, and to take stock of the space's atmosphere. Such issues set the stage for this chapter's ultimate question: When Flavia visited the sanctuary and participated in its activities together with her fellow Isiac worshippers, how did it shape her devotion to Isis?

Flavia and the Iseum Campense: An Environment Apart

As Flavius made his way along the Via Cornelia from the Vatican plain, past the Mausoleum of Hadrian (Fig. 4.1(1)), and toward the Iseum, his travels presented a timeline of Roman history. Military exercises in the Republic granted the Campus Martius, the "Field of Mars," its martial moniker. Its open and level ground gave rise to emperors' extensive building projects that came to carpet the area. Working his way eastward along the Via Recta (the "Straight Street" preserved as Via dei Coronari), Flavius encountered the Greek-style Stadium of Domitian (Fig. 4.1(2)), one of the Flavian emperors whose dynasty likely gave him his name. Today the

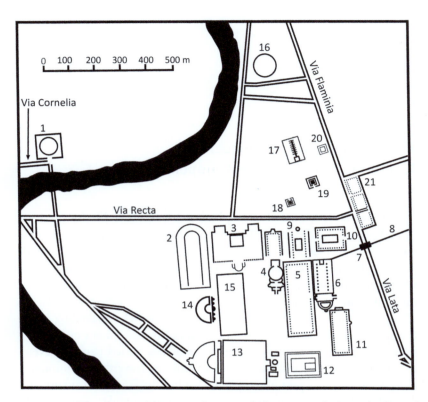

FIGURE 4.1 The Campus Martius in the time of Flavius Agricola boasted a host of structures built by emperors, including the Iseum Campense (6) constructed by Domitian. (Drawing: Elijah Greene.)
Legend:
1. Mausoleum of Hadrian; 2. Stadium of Domitian; 3. Baths of Nero; 4. Pantheon; 5. Saepta Julia; 6. Iseum Campense; 7. Arch of Claudius; 8. Aqua Virgo; 9. Temple of Matidia; 10. Hadrianeum; 11. Divorum; 12. Porticus Minucia; 13. Theater and Portico of Pompey; 14. Odeon of Domitian; 15. Stagnum of Agrippa; 16. Mausoleum of Augustus; 17. Solarium of Augustus; 18. Ustrinum of Antoninus Pius; 19. Ustrinum of Marcus Aurelius; 20. Ara Pacis; 21. Insulae

Piazza Navona maintains the stadium's outline, as the intervening centuries used the structure as foundations for palaces, churches, and the like. He passed the Baths of Nero (Fig. 4.1(3)); their reputation contrasted with that of their creator: "What is worse than Nero? What is better than his baths?" quipped one poet.[1] Only a few scraps of Nero's construction remain visible, but Hadrian's Pantheon (Fig. 4.1(4)), now a church, stands nearly whole and evokes the original grandeur of the Iseum's setting.[2]

Flavia Primitiva in the Iseum Campense

About 100 meters to the Pantheon's east – just beyond the Saepta Julia (Fig. 4.1(5)), a massive voting enclosure begun by Julius Caesar – rose the Iseum Campense (Fig. 4.1(6)). Flavia venerated the goddess and perhaps also Serapis, the goddess' male consort, in a complex erected by the emperor Domitian after a catastrophic fire razed much of central Rome in 80 CE.[3] This imperial patronage and the Iseum's location among public structures speak volumes about Isis' acceptance in Rome.[4]

When Flavia visited the Iseum, she undoubtedly felt its importance. Though the Iseum Campense was not Rome's only sanctuary of Isis – a handful of lesser shrines are attested[5] – the words of one Isis worshipper give voice to the common sentiment that it had a Mediterranean-spanning reputation. After being initiated into the cult near Corinth in Greece, the narrator of Apuleius' *Metamorphoses* reports:

> I hurriedly packed my things and boarded a ship to Rome ... I arrived safe at Ostia; from there I sped in a fast carriage, reaching that holy city on the evening before the Ides of December. Next, my foremost goal was to offer daily prayers to the supreme power of Queen Isis, who is the subject of special veneration under the name Isis Campensis (of the Field), which comes from the site of her temple. From then on, I was constant worshipper: a newcomer to this shrine, sure, but a native of the faith.[6]

The character's urgency offers an index of this space's preeminence for Isiac worshippers throughout Rome's expanse. This was the spot to seek out, even if it entailed traveling much greater distances than a stroll across Rome.

Though the sanctuary is buried today and has never been subject to large-scale excavation, a wide set of sources allow us to picture what Flavia encountered. To start, we know much about the sanctuary's layout thanks to the *Forma Urbis Romae* (FUR), more descriptively known as the "marble plan" of Rome (Fig. 4.2). Created in the early third century CE for public display, the FUR survives only in small part – about 10–15 percent, much of it unlabeled – thus making it the world's most tantalizing yet lousiest jigsaw puzzle and a trigger for abundant scholarly debate.[7] Thanks to surviving sections of the FUR and Renaissance drawings of now-missing pieces, we know that the Iseum consisted of three areas during Flavia's life (Fig. 4.3): First, a central courtyard awaited visitors, who passed through monumental archways on the east and west; second, to the north a large court (ca. 70 × 150 m) was accessible through a narrow doorway; third, to

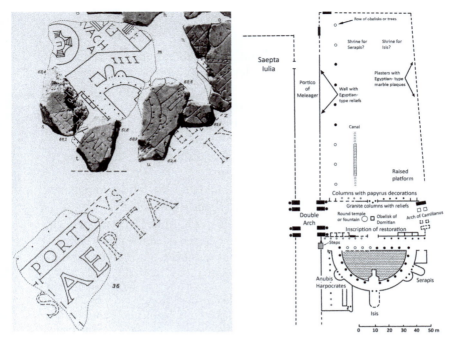

FIGURES 4.2 AND 4.3 Even though the Iseum Campense has been subject to minimal formal archaeological investigation and remains largely buried, a host of sources and extensive archival work have established much of the building's plan and decorative scheme. Sections of the *Forma Urbis* – either preserved or known from Renaissance drawings – suggest that it was divided into a central section, whose openness to the public appears to have contrasted with more limited access to the northern and southern sections. A number of artworks and architectural elements that decorated the sanctuary were imported from Egypt or carved in an Egyptian style. (Drawing: Elijah Greene; *Forma Urbis*: G. Carettoni et al., eds., *La Pianta Marmorea di Roma Antica: Forma Urbis Romae* (1960) / © Sovrintendenza Capitolina ai Beni Culturali, Roma.)

the south was a semicircular colonnaded courtyard, again reached through a small entryway, that featured a large water basin surrounded by niches. This architectural arrangement has suggested that the central area was open to anyone, but access to the northern and southern sections could be limited to cult adherents, either temporarily (such as during certain ceremonies) or permanently.

Artifacts and furnishings contributed to the atmosphere that greeted Flavia. An obelisk dominated the central courtyard; quarried in Egypt, carved with hieroglyphics in Rome, it stood in honor of the emperor Domitian, addressing him in almost pharaonic terms.[8] Additionally, three towering monolithic granite columns, decorated with low reliefs of sacred processions, limited access and visibility at the entrance to the northern section.[9] That huge area is not well-documented by the marble plan. One small fragment depicts four circles spaced thirteen meters apart and ten meters from the sanctuary's west wall. If the circles represented vertical elements, such as columns, such broad spacing would not support a roof. They might stand in for trees or obelisks, six of which were found in this part of the Iseum. Also suggesting that the northern section was open to the sky are water channels found running north–south; accessible via a pair of wide travertine steps, they likely served to imitate the Nile.[10] The most comprehensive study of the sanctuary proposes a garden-like setting that hosted temples of Isis and Serapis. It is also possible that the two deities shared one building.

Much besides temples crowded the sanctuary. One five-by-fifteen-meter trench dug in the northern section in 1883 produced a staggering mass of finds: an Egyptian obelisk, a host of sculptures (a sphinx depicting a pharaoh, two baboons, a crocodile), two candelabra bases, Egyptian reliefs in red granite, and a granite column that Italian artists adorned with reliefs.[11] Recovered from the southern section were large statues personifying the Nile and Tiber rivers (Figs. 4.4, 4.5); they likely reclined on the small peninsula jutting into the semicircular pool, while statues of other Egyptian deities occupied the niches around the water basin. Our mental images of sanctuaries typically involve a temple standing before an empty square. The evidence at the Iseum makes us wonder how Flavia could have seen through all the objects on display.

German archaeologist Katja Lembke has painstakingly compiled the discoveries made in this area over the centuries. She has cataloged more than 131 sculptures, architectural remains, and inscriptions. Of these, 29 percent were Egyptian pieces imported from Egypt – the oldest a bust of the pharaoh Amenemhat III, who reigned in the nineteenth century BCE. (It was as much of an antique for Flavia as her husband's sculpture is for us.) And about 60 percent of the objects found were in an Egyptian style. A fair portion of the materials told the same story, as 56 of the 107 sculptures and architectural remains were carved from stone that originated in Egypt. Red and gray granite was quarried in Aswan before making a 2,000-mile journey to Rome.[12] Some scholars even raise the possibility that animals native to Egypt – crocodiles, ibises, and baboons – were housed in the precinct.[13] In sum, from the surfaces that she ran her hand over to the motifs on which her eyes alighted, so much of the

FIGURES 4.4 AND 4.5 Within the Iseum Campense, sculpted personifications of the Nile (with abundant babies and sphinx) and the Tiber (with Romulus, Remus, and the she-wolf) presented similar poses, while intentional differences between the portrayals invited comparison between Egypt and Rome. (Nile photo: Wikimedia Commons; Tiber photo: Azoor Photo/Alamy Stock Photo.)

Iseum summoned and stirred in Flavia thoughts of a distant and exotic land of deep religious significance.

And yet the Iseum stood smack dab in Rome's monumental center. How might Flavia have understood this juxtaposition? Comparing the paired statues of the Nile and Tiber is helpful. The distinct parallels shared by the two personifications – they strike similar poses and are carved in the same (Greco-Roman) sculptural style – serve to draw attention to their intentional contrasts: the Nile's calm posture and the Tiber's more tense pose, the Nile's abundance of babies versus the Tiber's Romulus and Remus, and reliefs of humble folk working in different manners on each base.[14] Just as the Nile statue was to the Tiber, so too was the Iseum Campense to the broader Campus Martius. It was, in some senses, a *heterotopia* amid imperial Rome. This concept, promulgated by French philosopher Michel Foucault, draws on notions of *u-topia* (where all is good) and *dys-topia* (where all is bad) to build an image of a place where things are *hetero-*, different. A *heterotopia*, in short, is a world within a world, one that is part of, but distinctly apart from, its surrounding context.[15] Some examples today might include cemeteries and summer camps, both of which draw meaning from their contrast with

FIGURES 4.4 AND 4.5 (cont.)

everyday life and spaces. Within the heterotopic Iseum, Flavia did not leave behind her normal world, but – in a parallel to her initiation into the cult that contrasted with civic religion – she encountered a realm self-consciously and meaningfully transformed.

To conclude this section, I want to highlight how the story of the Iseum Campense showcases the challenges of piecing together ancient Rome's layout. What we call the "urban process" has steadily churned along in Rome for more than two-and-a-half millennia, as the "eternal city" has been burnt, flooded, wrecked by earthquakes, built and rebuilt time and again in support of grand powers or merely by peasants struggling to survive.[16] As a result, many Roman buildings like the Iseum reside deep underground, broken, degraded, and with much of their constituent parts robbed out, reclaimed, or scattered. For the Iseum, artworks and fragments now pepper Rome's landscape (and, indeed, Italy's and Europe's more generally) due to their being prized by emperors, popes, aristocrats, and others from the fourth century onward.[17] Lions from early Ptolemaic Egypt flank grand stairs to the Capitoline, Domitian's obelisk crowns the Piazza Navona's central fountain, and a giant marble foot wearing an Egyptian-style sandal stands on a street corner.[18] Meanwhile, the Nile and Tiber sculptures are displayed in the Vatican Museums and Louvre, respectively. Other pieces reside in Germany, Russia, Denmark, and the USA (Tennessee).

We can draw several lessons from this quick survey. First, the ways the Iseum has been prized apart by later generations make clear that what we encounter in Rome (or elsewhere) is not the result of a neutral process like the slow churn of tectonic plates. Rather, it is an urban landscape highly edited by multiple parties with their own agendas. (We will see some of these in Part II of this book.) Second, this situation makes us grateful for the Vatican necropolis' relatively good shape (aside from Flavius' tomb!). Its archaeological "formation process" – involving Constantine's requisitioning of the cemetery and its speedy burial underneath a mammoth basilica – is much simpler. Finally, this stocktaking helps us appreciate the scholarly work involved. In a central storyline of Egyptian mythology, Osiris was killed and dismembered by his power-hungry brother, who spread Osiris' body parts hither and yon. Isis, Osiris' heartbroken sister and wife, collected the pieces, revived Osiris, and soon thereafter gave birth to Horus. Lembke's scholarly gumshoeing through old excavation reports, centuries-old inventories of art collections, and so many other oddball scraps of evidence has allowed – in a modern parallel of Isis' trekking throughout Egypt to reassemble Osiris – the Iseum to be pieced back together.

Flavia and the Iseum Campense: Ritual, Individual, and Community

While we can marvel at how we can gaze upon some of the same objects that Flavia encountered and mentally place them within their architectural framework, we should not convince ourselves that this is an endpoint. It would be akin to visiting a house but not encountering its residents, knowing their stories, or witnessing their interactions. We need to fill this stage set with a script and actors. Such a practice can be a challenge under normal conditions but is especially tricky for a "mystery cult" like Isis' that, by definition, kept some activities secret. Unsurprisingly, the events involving Isis worship that receive the greatest description in literary texts are the ones celebrated in public, such as the *navigium Isidis*, a spring festival whose procession of priests receives extensive discussion in Book 11 of Apuleius' *Metamorphoses*.[19] What about the events that unfolded behind closed doors?

The novel gives some description of the narrator's initiation but stops short of revealing all. Lucius' morning presentation before the temple involves a priest bringing forth books "in characters strange to me" (likely

Flavia Primitiva in the Iseum Campense

hieroglyphics[20]) that outlined the necessities to be secured prior to initiation. After Lucius is feted with gifts and the uninitiated ordered to depart, he is conducted into the goddess' inner sanctum, at which point he gets cryptic:

> You, diligent reader, might perhaps be eager to know what was said and what was done next. I'd tell you, if it were permitted; you would know if you were allowed to hear. But ears and tongue would cause harm equally ... Therefore, I shall speak only of what can be revealed to the minds of the uninitiated without need for later atonement, things which though you have heard them, you may well not understand.[21]

The ceremony complete, the narrator emerges to the uninitiated and rejoins the story: Curtains are pulled back to reveal him dressed in twelve robes, holding a torch, and wearing a crown of palm leaves. Two feasts complete the occasion.

When scholars have tried to imagine the workings of the Iseum Campense and other sanctuaries of Isis, they have largely tried to puzzle together how the initiation unfolded amid its surroundings. We are likewise interested in that question, since Flavius gives us every reason to believe that Flavia was initiated into the cult. And yet this passage from Apuleius reflects a fundamental challenge of understanding the inner workings of Isis worship or other cults that revealed "secrets" to their initiates: If we are fortunate, we can piece together the setting for these acts, but – to adapt Apuleius'/Lucius' words slightly – though we have seen them, we may not understand. The initiation was the most important ceremony but likely also the least traceable.

What such a fixation on initiation leaves out are Flavia's previous and subsequent visits to (or stays at) the Iseum for worship, for aiding in administering the sanctuary, and for other activities. These occasions, after all, both outnumbered her experience of the sanctuary as an initiate and also served to stir and cement her devotion. Presuming that, contrary to what satirists suggest, Flavia was not looking for a date, what else might she have done within the Iseum on the regular? A useful starting point is offered by the late-Republican poet Tibullus. In addressing his girlfriend and then the goddess, he adds to our image of temple activities:

> What use is your Isis to me now, Delia? What use is the bronze that you rattled so often in your hand, or, while you worshipped with holy rite, I remember, your bathing in pure water, sleeping in a pure bed? Now, goddess, help me now (since the many pictures in your temples witness that you can heal), so my Delia fulfilling her midnight vows might sit before

your sacred doors, shrouded in linen and twice a day be bound to speak your praise, conspicuous with loosened hair among the Pharian crowd.[22]

Tibullus' image of Isis devotion includes shaking the sistrum (a bronze rattle particular to Egyptian gods), taking up housing within the sanctuary (something we also encountered with Lucius), paying nocturnal vigil at the temple while dressed in special clothing, enjoying purification, and expecting healing from the goddess. In other words, a visit involved more than prayer and extended to many other possibilities.

Visual evidence enriches the picture and emphasizes the importance of group activities in Isis worship. The Ariccia Relief – a second century CE marble slab found reused in a tomb southeast of Rome[23] – depicts a sanctuary of Egyptian deities (Fig. 4.6). Statues in the upper register spread out from the central figure of Isis; Bes, baboons, Apis bulls, and other zoomorphic evocations of deities appear within a portico. The lower register features dancers ecstatically waving their limbs and beating dowels together in the center, while, at the right, figures atop a garland-bedecked platform enthusiastically clap to provide encouragement. Further below ibises strut and peck while a crab skitters along what may be a canal. Some scholars, noting Isis' centrality, contend that the relief depicts the Iseum Campense itself.[24]

FIGURE 4.6 The Ariccia Relief depicts a group of ecstatic revelers amid an artwork-packed sanctuary dedicated to Isis. (Photo: author. Courtesy of Ministero della Cultura – Museo Nazionale Romano.)

That question aside, the relief adds to the nature of goings-on that unfolded in a place like the Iseum. It also helpfully weds our previous discussions, making clear that neither buildings/decoration nor people make a space on their own – it is their combination that matters. Here, the zealous and noisy action jumps out of the relief, as it does from a fresco found at Herculaneum that likewise appears to depict a sanctuary of an Egyptian deity (Fig. 4.7). The frontal view shows some individuals in supplicatory position alongside an altar as well eager figures dancing atop a temple-like structure; a few sistrum-shakers again encouragingly set the beat. Flavia may have danced, chanted, clapped alongside others in this way. And yet, before we channel Juvenal and other poets to characterize the Iseum solely as a place of wild frenzy, another fresco from Herculaneum, identically sized and therefore likely a partner painting, is infused with a much different atmosphere (Fig. 4.8). Nearly everyone stands still: two ranks of devotees are aligned before a temple-like structure flanked by sphinxes and palm trees. Atop the steps and around the altar, officiants assume prominent spots. Staid and hierarchical, the scene underscores that a space like the Iseum could take on multiple spirits. Indeed, some of its dynamism may have hinged on tense inhaling during solemn rituals and energetic release upon their conclusion.[25]

While capturing the Iseum's potential emotional range, the paintings, relief, and Tibullus poem all make the obvious point that Flavia did not encounter the Iseum on her own. The differences in revelers' dress, gender, and accoutrements imply a diverse crowd. It likely consisted of some individuals who had partaken in initiation, others in the formative stages of instruction, and priestly types as well. Yet communal undertakings like these would have shaped Flavia's experience of the sanctuary, her relationship to Isis, and her bonds with other members of the crowd. In the Iseum Flavia shared specialized knowledge of the goddess' powers and mysteries that she had gained through rituals; perhaps she helped in the preparation of aspiring initiates or undertook behind-the-curtain work in organizing and conducting the rites. Adherents danced together, chanted in unison to cheer on fellow adherents, struck instruments rhythmically, and listened to sacred hymns expounding on Isis' reach and righteousness. For the meals mentioned across our sources, folk needed to acquire the raw materials and then cook and serve.[26] And then there was the shared experience of undertaking voluntary abstinence while periodically taking up residence in the Iseum. The broad expanse of

FIGURES 4.7 AND 4.8 Two identically sized frescoes from Herculaneum depict scenes evoking sanctuaries in honor of Egyptian deities. Their content contrasts markedly in spirit, the one showing rampant revelry, the other portraying a much more staid tone. (Museo Archeologico Nazionale di Napoli; photos: Album / Alamy Stock Photos.)

the Iseum's northern garden-like section – equivalent to one-and-a-half soccer fields in area – could have accommodated numerous temporary residents, both inhabitants of Rome, such as Flavia, and also pilgrims who, like Lucius, had traveled a long way.

By and large, we can only speculate about what personal relationships Flavia fostered and what conversations flowed through these activities. Did she plan her periodic visits to the Iseum together with a repeat cast of associates and friends, with whom she essentially camped out? In what ways were her sentiments about Isis strengthened or rekindled when she witnessed, or even aided in, the initiation of new members? How might Flavia and her colleagues have processed the emotional swings between tightly wound ceremony and euphoric dancing and chanting? How did they make sense of certain sensory

FIGURES 4.7 AND 4.8 (CONT.)

experiences – the view of imported Egyptian stone, the feel of the water running through the canal, the movements of ritual dances, or the distinctive sounds of rattled sistra and clapped sticks?[27]

We could go on asking such questions, and a useful guide in answering them on a general level arises from scholarship in the sociology of religion. It underscores the power of ritual in triggering group experiences, reinforcing belief, and creating community. According to this school of thought, belonging is not a fact that one achieves and thereafter wields like a diploma but has to be created and routinely recreated. Believers might feel most connected, for example, when renewing their baptismal vows, breaking fast at sundown with loved ones during Ramadan, or retelling stories around a Passover Seder table. But these dynamics do not only operate in contexts involving Religion and Ritual but also in circumstances far from churches, mosques, synagogues, and Isea: helping to clean up from

FIGURE 4.9 A sculpture of a baboon from the Iseum bore three inscriptions around its base: one in Greek dedicating the sculpture, another in Latin recording its placement by officials in 159 CE, and another in Greek recording its creators as Phidias and Ammonios. Extensive wear on its right hand suggests that Isiac devotees made a habit of touching or rubbing the sculpture. (© Governate of the Vatican City State – Directorate of the Vatican Museums.)

Thanksgiving dinner, cheering on a sports team, or doing volunteer work alongside others. And so, the type of intense, repeated, and collective undertakings and conversations in which Flavia and her fellow Isiac worshippers engaged – whether grand or intimate, as someone on stage or working behind the scenes – likely helped them to restore and reinforce their connections with a community by reaffirming shared values and inculcating a sense of belonging.[28]

If pinning down specifics about this process has proven difficult, one artwork recovered from the Iseum showcases concretely the intersection of personal action and group meaning-making in the sanctuary. Standing just over one meter in height and sculpted from bluish-gray basalt in an Egyptian style, the statue represents a baboon sitting on its haunches, knees pulled up to its chest, in a form evoking the god Thoth (Fig. 4.9). The baboon's head is missing, and part of its plinth has chipped away.[29]

Flavia Primitiva in the Iseum Campense

Several inscriptions around the base lay out the artwork's biography. On the left side, in Greek, we learn that the artists "Phidias and Ammo(nios), [sons] of Phidias, made it." As names, Phidias recalls Pheidias, the renowned classical Greek sculptor of cult statues in Athens and Olympia, while Ammonios echoes the Egyptian deity Amun. The front records the baboon as a dedication – the Greek for "has set up" (ΑΝΕΘΗΚΕΝ) survives, though the name of the dedicator is lost.[30] Finally, on the right, a Latin text conducts business: "The place was assigned by Aulus Caelius [and] ... illianus Maximus, curators of sacred temples and public works. [The statue] was dedicated on the ... of September, when Quintillus and Priscus were consuls." These officials served in 159 CE.[31]

One initial lesson from this piece is the sanctuary's constant evolution. After Domitian funded its construction, no single agent was responsible for its decoration; rather, what survives reflects a constant accumulation of material on the part of many people, including devotees. Second, the sculpture embodies a personal mark of veneration, as the donor marshaled the necessary resources, decided on the (Egyptian) content, commissioned the artists, and then liaised with the curators to arrange for the piece's installation. The name on the inscription, though now lost, made the personal public, as it commemorated the gift on the base's most visible face. We can only imagine the pride filling the heart of dedicators upon seeing their artworks or other fittings within the sanctuary. Did they inspect their gifts on every visit, show their friends, or return home after a pilgrimage secure in the knowledge that their dedications remained with the goddess in the Iseum?

If the primary inscription points to the sculpture's importance for its dedicator, then another detail expands the meaning-making to sanctuary visitors. While the majority of the sculpture is marred by nicks and cuts, the basalt on the baboon's right hand shows signs of being gently worn away, to the point that the cuttings marking out the fingers have been erased. The most likely cause is repeated rubbing on the part of worshippers, who habitually pressed their hand to the baboon's, perhaps as a sign of reverence or in hope of a bit of luck. In fact, other Egyptianizing sculptures show similar "touch wear" on their hands/paws, such as a statue of Bes in the Vatican Museums.[32] Were these pieces familiar touchstones of the sanctuary for visitors from near and far, like the foot of the medieval bronze of St. Peter set up in his eponymous basilica today? When Flavia and others felt the wear, did they sense a link to previous generations whose hands had also passed along the statue? We normally consider religion a mental/spiritual/emotional endeavor, but the wear on the baboon's hand underscores the ritualized tactile engagement that Flavia and her fellow devotees had with Isis and other divine figures.

Last, a remarkable variety of "languages," both literal and artistic, present themselves in the artwork and inscriptions: Latin for administrative details, Greek for the artists' signatures and dedication, and an Egyptian style for the artwork itself. That is, we have "Egyptian" art made on Italian soil by artists assuming names resonant of Greek and Egyptian lands. Such a mélange of identities and influences derives partly from the nature of Roman imperialism, as peoples, cultures, and languages from around the Mediterranean converged, collided, and convulsed in the *caput mundi*. But it is also a reminder of the ways that the Iseum brought together diverse individuals, each of whom made the choice of membership in what was, ideally, a community of like-minded people devoted to the same goddess and seeking some of the same answers to life's challenges and questions.

• • •

Why spend so much time on Flavia's time in the Iseum when so many questions, if answerable at all, have responses couched in the subjunctive or conditional moods? For one thing, it is easy to follow Flavius' words and affirm that, yes, Flavia cultivated a serious adherence to the cult of Isis. These are labels and descriptors, however, not actions. By considering the Iseum – some of whose spaces required membership or special permission to access, and whose atmosphere consciously evoked an ancient and mysterious land at least a half-month journey from Rome – we gain greater perspective on Flavia's participation. Here she likely found meaning and perhaps a degree of responsibility/recognition amid a community of familiar faces likewise committed to the life-changing power of this foreign goddess.

Since Isis worshippers drew their sense of belonging from the belief that meaningful differences (rituals, spaces, sounds, aesthetics) distinguished them from others, they, like members of other groups, constructed mental categories not only of an Us but also a Them of outsiders.[33] And here is perhaps where examining the Iseum sheds the greatest light on Flavius and Flavia. We do not know how Flavius responded to Flavia's participation in Isiac rites and visits to the Iseum. If anything, his epitaph's characterization would seem to offer a quiet nod of affirmation. But it seems unlikely that he stepped within the Iseum's more restricted zones or even knew much of what to make of the obelisk in the Iseum's central area or the towering columns of

Flavia Primitiva in the Iseum Campense

Egyptian granite decorated with oddly styled motifs nearby. In other words, while considering Flavia's interactions with and within the Iseum might not reveal all, it opens up a rich set of possibilities for her own sense of Rome's geography and her network of personal connections, ones quite apart from her husband's and perhaps also her son's. At the Iseum she likely set aside maternal and wifely responsibilities, found a different set of folk with whom to spend time, and engaged with a set of activities, objects, and outlooks that she found meaningful. Worship of Isis was unlikely to have been a solo path, as it is presented when we view it in the inscription alone, but an avenue to a rich set of associations beyond the local, the familial, and the traditional.

Throughout our discussion of Flavius' portrait of Flavia, an apparent tension has festered: Was Flavia a standard and upstanding Roman matron or was she an ardent adherent of a foreign goddess? Was she the woman of formulaic generalities – beautiful and assiduous – or a fervent follower of the Pharian goddess? The truth, of course, is that she need not have checked only one box. There was "room" in Roman culture and society for both of these sides of Flavia's life. The degree that we may struggle in trying to square the circle of Flavia's different roles reflects the pigeonholing that we tend to do of the Roman world. "*This* is family; *that* is religion," we are tempted to say, when we must recognize that individual experiences did not sequester different parts of a life from one another.

And it is telling that Flavius honors, celebrates, and seemingly boasts about these sides of Flavia, not least because, on first reading, they outline additional tensions and prompt more questions. If Flavia indeed was a regular visitor of the Iseum and, as the epitaph suggests, stuck to periods of ritual abstinence from sex while camped out there, what were her thoughts about Flavius (if she had any at all) as she withdrew from society at large and took up her place within the sanctuary and her religious community? Was she worried about his behavior? After all, if he lived as he encouraged others to do, she may have had cause for concern. Or we can flip the question somewhat: What were Flavius' views on life's Big Questions, which Flavia's worship of Isis appears to have partially supplied answers for? The next chapter dives into the two figures' worldviews and considers how those outlooks intersected.

CHAPTER 5

To Eat Is to Be? Flavius' Worldview in Perspective

Flavia's description as a *cultrix deae Phariaes casta* helps to trace her adherence to a framework of beliefs that involved moral/ethical tenets as well as the potential promise of something beyond the mortal realm. It invites us to ask what Flavius' sculpture and inscription say about his own outlook. First, it is obvious that he claims to have one, since his portrait and epitaph both present him as something of a philosopher. His beard and carved pupils reflected recent trends in Rome popularized by the emperor Hadrian (117–138), during whose reign Flavius was coming of age. The bearded appearance of Greek intellectuals, particularly philosophers, partly inspired the philhellenic ruler's facial hair, which was a novelty for emperors.[1] Meanwhile, we cannot rule out a connection between the emergence of drilled pupils and a greater philosophical concentration on the eyes as the windows of the soul.[2] Paint had previously highlighted eyes on sculpture.

Flavius' philosophizing extended from marble to words. Pondering a life course is both described explicitly by the text – as he seems to boast that he "cultivated" his "little soul" (though *animula/animulus* is so lightly attested that it may mean something as simple as "little life"[3]) – and embodied in his final first-person directions (lines 12–15):

> Amici, qui legitis, moneo, miscete Lyaeum
> et potate procul redimiti tempora flore
> et venereos coitus formosis ne denegate puellis;
> cetera post obitum terra consumit et ignis.

> Friends who read this, I admonish you: mix the wine,
> drink deep, wreath your head with flowers,
> and do not refuse to make love with pretty girls.
> After death, earth and fire devour all the rest.

"Live it up!" he says, because that will not be possible after death. To be sure, the epitaph's final four lines hardly constitute a fulsome treatise; they are more what gets slurred after the *n*-th cup of wine. Nevertheless, Flavius does not merely showcase his enjoyment of life's pleasures but dresses up those practices in philosophical clothes. What was his philosophy and how might we understand it amid contexts both broader and narrower?

Dining, Death, and Philosophy

This presentation was not about posing Flavius as a philosopher and sticking him at table but was part of a broader portrayal of dining. For Romans a convivial setting routinely occasioned conversation about life's deep issues. The nine books of Plutarch's *Quaestiones Convivales* (or *Table Talk*), for instance, pose over 100 questions that engage the work's interlocutors in dialogue. They all start with "whether philosophy is a fitting topic for conversation at a drinking-party."[4] (The characters tellingly debate the question in a rather philosophical manner and decide in the affirmative.) Similarly, the learned discussion of philosophy, food and wine, sex, and literature in Athenaeus' early third-century work *Deipnosophistae* (literally, "the dinner philosophers") unfolds among guests at a series of fictional banquets. In other words, Flavius' philosophizing, almost as much as his cup and posture, signaled a certain type and register of occasion.

The dining-philosophizing connection, perhaps surprisingly, also folds death deeply into its nexus. Indeed, a popular motif for banqueting accoutrements involved representations of skeletons. These could be small models, almost like dolls, that were made of precious metals.[5] Sometimes their limbs were articulated so diners could toy with them amid the feast, posing or freezing them in a diner's reclining posture, for instance.[6] In Petronius' *Satyricon*, just such a skeleton is produced during the feast, which occasions a poem from the host:

> Eheu nos miseros, quam totus homuncio nil est.
> Sic erimus cuncti, postquam nos auferet Orcus.
> Ergo vivamus, dum licet esse bene.

> Woe for us poor mortals! How this little guy is absolutely nothing.
> It's exactly how we all will be, once Orcus takes us away.
> So, let us live while we can still do so well.[7]

My translation does not capture a key pun in the last line, as *esse* can both mean "to be," as I have rendered it above, and also "to eat," so that Trimalchio's final line is about gobbling up the goodies while still alive.

A pair of silver drinking cups – discovered at Boscoreale near Pompeii and now in the Louvre – offers a still more striking portrayal of skeletons, who represent both revelers and named Greek philosophers (Fig. 5.1).[8] On one cup, a banqueter-cum-skeleton adorns his head with flowers, while another wears a wreath, and a third strums a lyre. Others infuse the cup with philosophical musings: one skeleton studies a butterfly (understood to represent the soul in antiquity); and another spouts "life is a stage."[9] The second cup continues the pageant with anonymous wisdom-spouters, such as a skeleton who pours a libation over a mass of bones next to a caption reading "reverence the worthless dung."[10] A gaggle of skeletons labeled with the names of famed Greek intellectuals parades by. Playwrights such as Euripides and Sophocles appear. So do philosophers: Epicurus, Zeno the stoic, and Monimos the cynic, among others. Additional iconography helps to identify these figures, such as the pun-ful dogs between Monimos' legs. Cynic means "dog-like," as cynics rejected normal measures of success; plus, they barked at people. Together the skeletons form a near encyclopedia of ancient philosophical schools. For revelers who lifted the silver to their lips, in the words of Katherine Dunbabin, the cups proclaimed, "Life is a stage; we play our part and die; all revels come to this; the greatest of poets come to this; the wisdom of

FIGURE 5.1 Silver cups from Boscoreale play on Roman connections among death, philosophizing, and drinking by showing skeletons, labeled with the names of Greek intellectuals, partying and cracking wise. (Photo: Wikimedia Commons; originals at the Musée du Louvre.)

philosophers, their maxims, and their conflicts, offer no escape; piety and religion can do nothing to save us; therefore enjoy the moment while it is here."[11] While Flavius' philosophizing has at times been seen as consonant with an Epicurean focus on pleasure, that characterization traffics in a popular caricature. Rather, this pair of cups suggests that his celebration of life's good times was paired with a rejection of philosophical schools of thought. It was, in itself, a sort of philosophy.

What is fascinating about such a worldview was that Flavius and others did not only embrace it while alive but espoused this life path from beyond the grave. "Eat, drink, play, c'mon!" runs a standard formula with multiple variants, all imploring the living to celebrate life's gustatory and erotic joys. Some also bewail their loss in death: "What I ate and drank, I have with me. What I left behind, I have lost."[12] Others expand or reshuffle the list of pleasures, playing up a list of "baths, wine, and love/sex," *balnea vina Venus*. One epitaph writes that these things "break down our bodies, but make life worth living"; another claims they "make our destiny speed up."[13] The irony that these inscriptions traffic in, that the very things that make life worth living are also those that hasten death, remains funny today, even if they strike us as odd subjects to address from the beyond.

Not that Romans really needed many additional prompts to keep death in mind. Scholars and the popular imagination make much of so-called *memento mori* motifs – depictions in Roman art that reminded viewers that death was near, such as a mosaic from Pompeii that shows a skull hanging from a level and balancing atop a wheel of fortune.[14] We might be tempted to think that this artwork sent a message along the lines of "remember that you will one day die." But the truth is that, in comparison with what many of us experience today, Romans confronted death more frequently and at closer range. They hardly needed any reminders. About a third of babies born did not survive to their first birthday, and roughly half of them did not reach ten years old.[15] Like today, some died of neonatal causes such as labor, while we suspect others perished due to diarrhea or pneumonia, which of course could not yet be treated with antibiotics. How many of us as children endured earaches, tonsillitis, strep throat, or another infection that could not have been easily remedied in Roman times? Yes, treatments for symptoms existed, but nothing that would quickly eliminate bacteria. All of this meant that very few children would grow up without the experience of losing a sibling or a playmate.

While Romans would have a life expectancy into their mid-twenties at birth, those who made it to ten years old could realistically envisage a life stretching into their forties on average. But it was not a simple coast to the grave, for many mortal threats persisted and reminders of death were regularly before Romans' eyes. Something like the food supply, for instance, was hardly as stable as we expect today, since the city of Rome survived on grain imported from overseas and especially Egypt. Crop failure in Egypt – though less of a threat than elsewhere in the Mediterranean basin, because irrigation derived not from irregular rainfall but from the Nile's annual flooding – could have devastating consequences in Rome. So too could disruptions in the "supply chain," which entailed overwater shipping via barges that were subject to extreme weather, brigandage, and other threats.[16] Tacitus reports that two hundred ships were lost in Claudius' harbor in 62 CE due to a storm, and another hundred were burnt in an accidental fire after sailing up the Tiber for safety's sake.[17] Events such as these brought about shortages or famine in Rome. Ten such examples are recorded in the literary record from an otherwise stable century of the early empire – almost certainly a sizable undercount.[18]

Potential quick-hitting disasters likewise combined natural and human causes. Floods occasionally inundated Rome, fires threatened to ravage the city, buildings swayed and collapsed, and in the absence of a central law enforcement authority, the threat of violence lurked in the streets.[19] Outbreaks of infectious disease could sweep through Rome's close quarters, with devastating consequences. It is estimated that, in the decades following the construction of Flavius' funerary ensemble, about 10 percent of the empire's population died from what is commonly called the Antonine plague – likely smallpox. One witness in 189 CE recounts 2,000 victims dying on a daily basis in Rome.[20]

By Flavius' time in the high empire most residents of Rome were insulated from the threat of military defeats, as the frontlines had long shifted to the empire's edges. Nevertheless, monuments such as the Column of Marcus Aurelius – a nearly 140-foot-tall cylinder of stone erected in central Rome not long after Flavius' death – featured low-relief narratives of Roman military campaigns that brought home war's horrors.[21] The scenes capture the gruesomeness of battle: villages burning, captives being led off, and even Romans suffering amid this carnage. In one particularly gruesome scene (LXI), for example, members of the Marcomanni (the Germanic tribe that were Rome's principal enemies in Marcus Aurelius' conflict) are forced to behead their own tribesmen. Witnessing death by semimartial means remained a possibility, for Romans could soak in what some scholars have termed a "fossilized" version of Roman imperial expansion if they ventured to the amphitheater for gladiatorial shows.[22] Fewer fighters died in the arena than is popularly imagined, but the execution of criminals – a means of demonstrative justice – was more common than many people understand. And, venturing beyond the human realm, we must remember the spectacle involved in animal sacrifices, when a one-ton cow might be ritually slaughtered, cut open, and then butchered before a crowd.

My point is not to depict Rome as a dystopic and death-strewn mess, for, even in the face of these numerous threats, the benefits of urban life were substantial. Instead, this list of dangers underscores the precariousness and unpredictability of life for Roman city dwellers as well as how much more visible death could be. Unsurprisingly, many Romans wore amulets or other articles that they thought might ward of such threats to their health and well-being.[23] In sum, to a degree that we may not recognize, Flavius' sentiment and the *memento mori* motifs were not simply about remembering death but about enjoying life. To sharpen the point further, they did not encourage living it up because you will not be able to someday. Rather, that "someday" could easily have been tomorrow, given the potential dangers to life brought about by unpredictable fates.

This paradoxical dance between a fuller life and an earlier death receives a remorseful spin in another funerary monument that paired a relief sculpture and a verse epitaph (Fig. 5.2). Like Flavius, C. Rubrius Urbanus is depicted reclining on a *lectus* cradling a cup. But, by contrast, he did not live this way, as his inscription makes clear:

> While life was granted to him, he always lived sparingly saving for his heir, mean too with himself. Here he bade himself be artfully sculpted by skilled hand, merrily reclining after his own demise, so that at least he might rest recumbent in death, and enjoy assured repose there lying.
>
> His son sits on his right, who followed soldiering and died before the sad funeral of his own father. Yet what good does a merry image do the dead? This is the way they ought rather to have lived.[24]

Other than the regret that infuses the epitaph, little is resolved in the words accompanying the image. At issue are at least two tensions: between the life one leads and what follows in death, and between a sculptural representation and its efficacy. Urbanus seems to have thought that a representation of himself enjoying life's pleasures (a "merry image") offered something of a remedy, a salve for both tensions. And yet the final two lines twist the knife as they question the usefulness of Urbanus' sculptural choice, rebuke his chosen lifestyle, and wish for a more indulgent path.

FIGURE 5.2 The funeral relief of C. Rubrius Urbanus, shown here in a drawing, includes an image of the deceased reclining at table, even though the verse epitaph scolds him for living too frugally. (Courtesy of the British Museum.)

Together with the other epitaphs we have surveyed, Urbanus' example helpfully highlights Flavius' professed outlook on life and death. Flavius' delight in pleasures, when read against this background, comes into focus as distinctly less odd. Embracing the goods of today in the here and now was a mainstream sensibility, perhaps most famously articulated in Horace's *Ode* 1.11, which has one poetic voice exhort another, *Carpe diem*, "Seize the day." That said, there is something more fascinating and more powerful about an admonition to eat, drink, and make love when it comes from a tombstone. The deceased, in the end, have authority because they can no longer revel in such pleasures. But whereas these other inscriptions implore readers to live it up, Flavius unites that imprecation with proud professions – his sculpture shows him drinking and crowning his head, and the epitaph mentions his beautiful bedmate. He undertook these very activities while

To Eat Is to Be? Flavius' Worldview in Perspective

alive and did not simply wish he had, as in Urbanus' relief. His monument, in other words, offers a rarer combination of do-as-I-say and also do-as-I-did messages.

Pulling back from these narrative questions, however, allows us to recognize the profound currents of dining, death, and deep thinking that appear time and again in the sources I have mentioned and that flow together to animate Flavius' monument. Sure, one might object that, in the face of death, everyone is bound to turn to the Big Questions – What is the point of it all? Did I lead a good life? What comes next? And it is not exactly controversial to contend that tipping back a cup can get people contemplating Deep Thoughts. If neither of those sides of the triangle surprises much, then the third, between dining and death, stands out. Sometimes we feel most alive when we enjoy food and drink with dear friends, and yet Roman visual culture frequently offered a striking counterpunch: a reminder of mortality, delivered at table via a drinking cup or a skeleton doll, or even offered amid the cemetery itself. The do-as-I-say message may have been a downer or perhaps even prompted revelers to turn philosophical, while the do-as-I-did message offered wisdom from beyond the grave. In either case, to a degree that we have a hard time understanding, Romans were besieged by reminders, both overt like these and more implicit, that their days were numbered.

Flavius and Flavia – An Odd Couple?

Now that we have a fuller sense of Flavius' outlook on the world, let us rejoin the last two chapters' discussion of Flavia and unite the couple in one discussion. What initially strikes us are two things: first, that the husband and wife appear to have markedly different outlooks on the world, as Flavia's links to the Isiac ethical/moral code and potential outlook on death appear to contrast with Flavius' espousing of an enjoy-life-now attitude; second, that Flavius appears to reference their disparate beliefs in his epitaph. As a reminder, after the inscription introduces Flavia and describes the length of the couple's marriage, lines 9–11 move on to the consequences of her death:

> Solaciumque sui generis Aurelium Primitivum
> tradidit, qui pietate sua coleret fastigia nostra,
> hospitiumque mihi secura servavit in aevum.

> As a comfort, she left me her son, Aurelius Primitivus,
> to tend our house/tomb dutifully; and so, herself
> released from care, she has kept a welcome for me forever.

Flavia, having passed away and handed over her son to Flavius, appears as *secura*, "untroubled," as she preserves a welcome reception for Flavius. However we parse the individual words, they contrast substantially with the kicker to Flavius' epitaph:

> cetera post obitum terra consumit et ignis.
>
> After death, earth and fire devour all the rest.

Earth and fire stand in for the two ways of disposing of the dead – burial/inhumation and cremation, which Flavius appears to have chosen. If the description of Flavia dangles the possibility of postmortem existence and action, the epitaph's final line feels like slamming shut the back cover of a book before placing it aside.

Flavia and Flavius were not alone in this contrast of outlooks. For another couple pairing of an Isis-worshipper and her less enthusiastic partner, we can turn to the Augustan-era elegist Propertius and his lover Cynthia. When the poet laments Cynthia's absence from their common bed for ten days, he blames the "dismal rites" (*tristia ... sollemnia*) of Isis for the separation. It is a clever bit of wordplay, for the ritual itself marked Isis' mourning the death of her husband-slash-brother Osiris, and the events are also sorrowful for the poet, since he goes to bed without his lady friend.[25] At the poem's close, Propertius describes Cynthia as *nimium pia*, "too devout," and says, "Let's make the journey three times" upon her return.[26]

It is helpful to compare this situation to what we encounter with Flavius and Flavia, for the differences can prove illuminating. We can start with the two men's description of their relationship. On the one hand, Propertius portrays himself almost as a life support system for a sex organ and bemoans his partner's devotion. On the other hand, Flavius' worldview has a philosophical direction, even if its cutting edge runs fairly dull. Moreover, by contrast with Propertius' poetic voice, Flavius honors Flavia's commitment to Isis through specific language and without editorial comment. Which raises a question: Whereas couples today from different faith traditions often wrestle with thorny issues (which holidays to observe, for instance, what foodways to respect, and how to raise any kids), were such "mixed marriages" even considered a phenomenon in need of reconciling in the Roman world?

For Jews and early Christians, the answer was an emphatic Yes. A flurry of ancient Jewish sources condemns the marriage of a Jew with a non-Jew.[27] And one of the earliest New Testament texts, Paul's first letter to the Corinthians (early 50s CE), wrestles with the issue, which was bound to arise in this nascent community. What should happen when one spouse follows the Christian god and the other does not? Paul's answer: If the nonbeliever is willing to live with the believer, then the believer should not seek a divorce. After all, Paul adds, believers might save their spouses. (The need for guidance from Paul suggests that some early church members in Corinth insisted the couple *must* separate.) But if the nonbeliever wishes to depart, then so be it.[28] (Divorce was not permitted between believers.) The issue was taken up and nuanced by Church fathers, such as Tertullian, who considers when one spouse converts to Christianity during the marriage.[29] In the end, what matters for us is that the issue of mixed marriages was very much in the air in the early church, and grew ever more fervent over time, with passing generations seeking to complicate what they saw as a troubling part of Paul's early writings.

Did a similar sentiment prevail outside of Jewish and Christian settings? Were mixed marriages "a thing"? Yes, but primarily along axes other than religion. Roman myth enshrined the partnering of Romans with other groups, such as the Sabines, or, still earlier, the intermarriage of Trojan Aeneas with Latin Lavinia. And yet, in Rome in 449 BCE, the Twelve Tables codified what had been a customary prohibition of marriage between plebeians and patricians, which arose partly from the two groups' religious differences in terms of deities reverenced and rituals enacted. Nevertheless, a mere five years later, a new law was promulgated that reinstated intermarriage. In fact, when a consul raised religious objections to the reversal, claiming that the offspring of plebeian-patrician marriages would cause problems in taking the auspices, the plebeians rose up in reaction, and the consul's patrician supporters capitulated.[30] In the realm of law, concern about mixed marriages did occur, but it governed spouses of different legal status – citizen and slave, for example – and not religious difference.[31] No laws barred marriage for religious reasons until the rise of Christianity in Late Antiquity – a fact that reflects Romans' previous willingness to incorporate foreign peoples and their gods into an ever-growing domain.[32]

Of course, laws are one thing and attitudes another. Indeed, suspicions about the arrivals of new deities (such as Bacchus in the second century BCE) as well as Rome's troubles in war (as during the Second Punic War) both prompted hand-wringing and fears for Rome's religious landscape, but it is hard to disentangle religious concerns from a broader xenophobia.[33] That said, in some spaces where one might expect different lifestyles to cause issues, we actually see intermarriage. In the later Roman Empire, for instance, marriage between Roman citizens and barbarians occurred frequently, and imperial legislation showed barely any concern for racial mixing, which is striking when considered against the broader background of imperial systems, which commonly express concerns about infiltration of some "other."[34] In fact, marriages across vast geographic distances (by ancient standards, at least) were leveraged for commercial ends, such as Republican-era traders at the Aegean trading center of Delos who forged connections with Phoenician merchant families through intermarriage.[35] And within a few decades of Flavius' death, we even see a long-distance, cross-ethnic marriage at the highest ranks of Roman life in the pairing of the future-emperor Septimius Severus, from Leptis Magna in modern Libya, and Julia Domna, a descendant of the Emesene dynasty in Syria and daughter of the high priest of the sun god Elagabal. In one last inadvertent sign of the empire's connectivity, the couple married in Lugdunum, modern Lyon in Southern France, where Severus was governor.[36]

In the end, for the realm of religion and worldview, it is helpful to return to Propertius' complaint about Cynthia's adherence to Isis. While it appears that he wields a divergent view and thus formed half of a "mixed" relationship, his greatest lament is not about Cynthia's choice of divinity but the degree of her adherence and its toll on his sex life. Cynthia's piety is not the problem *per se*; it is simply that she is too pious (*nimium pia*), and he too lustful. One wonders if, behind the presentation of Flavia by Flavius, something similar lurked – that, while Flavia's devotion ran deep, Flavius was simply less bound up in religious concerns. Or maybe his fidelity lay elsewhere; Flavius does invoke a god, Lyaeus – twice, in fact. I have rendered Lyaeus as "wine" by transference, but the deity represents another name for Bacchus/Dionysius.

If we take this connection seriously, then the depiction of Flavius and Flavia's outlooks might partly align, for Lyaeus derives from the Greek Λυαῖος, "the loosener, relaxer, deliverer from care." For instance, in one of Horace's *Epodes*, Lyaeus helps "to dissolve cares and fears."[37] Such a resonance parallels one of the adjectives that Flavius' epitaph assigns to Flavia, as *secura* consists of the prefix *se-* – meaning "apart" as in the English word *se-cede*, "to go apart" – and the noun *cura*, "care." Thus, Flavia herself is also described as without or free from care. Could this be coincidence, or might this be a point of alignment for our careless couple, who each in their own way found, whether in the cup or an Egyptian goddess, a degree of respite and release from worldly concerns?

Let me close this section with three thoughts. First, perhaps we see little indication of intramarriage conflict around religion because, in general, religion was a communal endeavor lived out in public, civic life and much less of a personal matter than we assume today. Moreover, in a polytheistic system, there was little expectation of exclusivity: Romans largely cultivated gods according to their need or desire at the moment – Venus for matters of the heart, for instance, or Mercury to lend a hand with commerce. And, as we have seen, even in voluntary associations such as the worship of Isis, initiates did not rule out other deities but henotheistically considered their preferred divinity supreme. Only when strictly monotheistic systems arose did the matter entail serious debate and troubleshooting.

Second, for the primary apparent difference between Flavia and Flavius – what happened after death – little orthodoxy governed Roman thinking.[38] Scholars of the ancient world are routinely asked about the Greek or the Roman view of death. And we rarely supply a satisfying answer for a simple reason: There was no single view of the afterlife. In addition to the outlooks of our two protagonists, we have encountered the emperor Hadrian's image of his playful *animula*, "little soul," which, once he dies, may encounter "pale, stern, and bare places."[39] Many of us have read about Aeneas' descent to the underworld in Vergil's *Aeneid*, which involves a rich variety of experiences: Some figures endure punishments, Aeneas vainly attempts to embrace his departed father, pleasant visions of Elysian fields abound, and reincarnation is a possibility.[40] Cicero nicely summarizes the diverse visions:

> Some think that death is the separation of the soul from the body; some believe that there is no such separation, but that soul and body die together and the soul is extinguished with the body ... Furthermore, there is much disagreement about what the soul itself is, where it is, and where it came from.[41]

Expecting unanimity in Rome, and even within one relationship, is a fool's game.

Lastly on that note, a broad principle across the Roman Empire was that cultural difference was usually accepted or at least accommodated. We usually consider folks navigating those waters, because practices and beliefs flowed from various corners of the Mediterranean and then were sloshed together in ports, sanctuaries, the military, or Rome itself – the ultimate cosmopolitan supercollider. But the example of Flavius and Flavia encourages us to imagine the phenomenon even seeping into the family unit, especially when a marriage, such as theirs, was apparently forged at a more advanced age, after both members of the couple had achieved some worldliness and maturity.

Flavius' Life Overall

As we close the section of this book dedicated to Flavius' life and move toward how others encountered his funerary monument within the necropolis, it is useful to take stock. How much can we say about Flavius' life? The outline of a biography has emerged, and we have traced his likely origin in a family of former slaves, his marriage to Flavia and welcoming of Aurelius into his household, his accumulation of resources sufficient to afford this funerary ensemble, and his fondness for dining. Obviously, we are very much reliant on Flavius' own choices in what information to present implicitly or explicitly through his epitaph, funerary monument, and tomb. And that is frustratingly typical of studying everyday Romans. Outside of extraordinary circumstances, individual members of the lower rungs of Rome's social ladder grant us little more than funerary evidence, which is bound to offer a particularly "interested" version of a person's life, a curated "highlight reel." As a result, we often miss out on much of the texture of their individual experience.

And yet what Flavius has chosen to present fascinates, nevertheless. His funerary ensemble delivers even less of a résumé than others, offering nothing by way of discussion of *negotium*, whether that be involvement in a trade, public or semipublic offices, or horizontal relationships such as guilds. Rather, he plunges visitors to his tomb and monument deep into the world of *otium*, pinning his self-presentation on a realm apart from business. It is not unlike the person whose social media shows them frolicking on the beach or at the latest hip restaurant while gliding past their hours huddled over a keyboard. I am not making the case that this view is unhelpful – rather, in Flavius we may witness something of an ideal, but one that is less visible elsewhere. His priorities come into focus, not least the importance of making a splash through his tomb – its location, exterior, and interior – as well as the monument and epitaph within. The whole must have been pricey, and that was certainly part of Flavius' point.

But we also gain a view of other priorities, which center on showcasing his fluency with matters poetic, philosophical, convivial, and even religious. Such an emphasis on lifestyle and sophistication, we must remember, was not yet mainstream (though it would grow in coming decades[42]) and potentially even rarer for someone with Flavius' recent family history. He was hardly near the senatorial class, and his family was not far removed from being someone else's property. All of which suggests that dividing the Roman population into elite and nonelite is too stark a distinction, and that a variety of different substrata or overlapping and undulating registers of standing were operative. Is a priest or rabbi a prominent individual even though, while enjoying visibility, she may not earn much money? Is a soccer player whose name is chanted by thousands of fans and who garners a hefty paycheck an elite member of society? What about someone whose wealth derives from inheritance and a family name but has little otherwise to show for themself? Even these questions about familiar ground suggest how complicated issues of rank and status can be, and we have figures like Flavius – as a member of the mob who was careful to mark his rising above – to thank for at least prompting the questions about the Roman world.

CHAPTER 6

Meeting Flavius at the Tomb

In August 2019, an Irish Priest, Father Tomás Walsh of County Cork, spoke up about what he viewed as the troubling and growing practice at his parishioners' funerals – gifts of "a can of beer, a packet of cigarettes, a remote control, a mobile phone or a football jersey" that were brought to the altar during requiem Masses. These things do "not tell us anything uplifting about the person who has died," he wrote in his parish newsletter.[1] The offenders would hardly have seemed odd to ancient Romans, however, and may have been quite familiar, for funerary monuments like Flavius' not only celebrated the joys of this life but even went one or more steps further by expecting mourners to maintain such practices well after the funeral, with the deceased partaking as well. This chapter shifts the narrative camera from Flavius' life and its commemoration to his survivors and their experiences when they encountered his funerary ensemble. We might recall that Flavius' epitaph anticipates such interactions, both in praising his stepson, Aurelius Primitivus, for piously taking tending to the tomb (line 10: *qui pietate sua coleret fastigia nostra*) and in issuing commands to visitors. To a degree that can be striking to many of us today, practices at the tomb underscore the degree to which for Romans, there was no hard-and-fast boundary between the realms of the living and the dead.

Dining with the Dead

Starting with the funeral itself, Romans regularly feasted at the tomb. If Aurelius followed standard practices, then he and others marked the day of interment with an "ancient custom" called the *Silicernium* that apparently consisted of a meal of sausage.[2] Another tombside meal nine days after interment, the *cena novendialis*, brought a family's mourning period (the *feriae denicales*) to a close as they poured wine over the deceased's bones.[3]

Meeting Flavius at the Tomb

Not done yet, Flavius' birthday likely saw Aurelius and other loved ones gather for sacrifices, meals, and the tomb's decoration with flowers. For example, one inscription devotes rent from an apartment building to tomb-side sacrifices on the deceased's *dies natalis* (birthday). The same epitaph also specifies comparable tombside celebrations on public festivals, which dotted Romans' religious calendar, such as the *Violaria*, *Rosalia*, and *Lemuria*.[4]

Aurelius would have felt the strongest pull during the *Parentalia*, which unfolded February 13–21 and saw families attend to their kinsfolks' graves.[5] Ovid comments that the *manes*, the spirits of the dead, required little on this occasion – a small garland, some wheat, a bit of salt, wine-soaked bread, and scattered violets. While the poet maintains an Augustan sense of restraint, he also concedes that larger offerings are not forbidden at the *Parentalia*.[6]

Indeed, wills and epitaphs outline more-than-substantial accommodations for the *Parentalia*. In Misenum, the city on the Bay of Naples that housed the Roman navy for the western Mediterranean, one individual details the extensive events he wanted on future *Parentalia*. In addition to ten pairs of wrestlers, he assigned money to his tomb's decoration with violets and roses, to the dousing of his bones with one pound of pricey oil, to a meal for city magistrates and others in the dining hall atop his tomb, and, finally, to a sacrifice for the deceased.[7] Other *Parentalia* celebrations marshal impressive arrangements and participants: a tombside dinner for twelve of the deceased's fellow textile dealers; statues of the gods arrayed for a feast before a husband and wife's tomb; and a meal that, the text stipulates, must include sacrificial victims *(hostiae)*. This last example also instructs that local senators receive cash distributions at the tomb on the deceased's birthday.[8]

Not surprisingly, inscriptions also stipulate accommodations – spaces and furnishings – that were commensurate with these events' grandeur. One of Trajan's freedmen provided for his wife's tomb to be equipped with an atrium (forecourt), solarium (sun room), and triclinium (dining room), which likely stood atop the tomb, as happened at Misenum.[9] In Gaul, an inscription produced a laundry list of accoutrements for a tomb: a couch and two benches (both of imported marble), rugs, and dining cushions; orchards, ponds, and gardens; and a portrait of the deceased at least five feet tall.[10] We read elsewhere of summer dining rooms, lounges, a five-room getup, and probable upper-floor dining areas. Alongside are water supplies ranging from cisterns to basins, channels to wells, and even pools.[11] Foodstuffs might come from orchards or vineyards within the tomb complex.[12] One individual wanted the wine from a one-third-acre vineyard

FIGURE 6.1 Romans regularly flocked to tombs to pay their respects to the deceased and to eat and drink alongside them. This tomb at the necropolis of Isola Sacra hosted revelers on a biclinium in front of the tomb door. (Digital image courtesy of the American Academy in Rome, Photographic Archive.)

to be poured on his remains each year – no less than fifteen pints of wine, he adds (the equivalent of about ten bottles today).[13]

Obviously, these examples stand near the peak of Mt. Everest, socially speaking, yet Romans of a lower range, such as Aurelius, also provided extensive arrangements for tombside feasting. Amid the tombs of Isola Sacra – a cemetery between the mouth of the Tiber and Rome's port – ovens appear, presumably for baking bread and heating food. So too do wells, which offered water for cleaning, drinking, or the flowers that honored the dead. The most obvious remnant of dining at tombs, however, are biclinia – "couches" constructed of sloped masonry that are often accompanied by masonry cubes that likely supported tables (Fig. 6.1). Both structures even appear alongside so-called *cassone* burials, in which the deceased was entombed in a humble box shaped like a steamer trunk.[14] Placing dining facilities outside a tomb put them on display, so onlookers could not only check out who was partaking when a banquet was underway but could also spot the potential for such events even when the tomb was quietly shut tight. If you could not afford anything on such a scale, a pipe or broken amphora neck at the earth's surface allowed revelers to offer a drink to the dead.

All this adds up to a serious point: Tombside dining and drinking formed substantial parts of funerary ritual, ones into which Romans sank significant resources and devoted meaningful time, not only right after a loved one's death but in future days, months, and years across the calendar. Consequently, when anyone walked among the house-tombs on the Via Cornelia and looked through its iron grate to spy Flavius Agricola's funerary monument, they did not merely see a man drinking at table while crowning his head with a wreath but understood his act as one fitting for a funerary setting. And if passersby read the epitaph, they could have made out the name of the figure responsible for maintaining the tomb and the various expected rites. Perhaps the words spurred Aurelius on, pushing him to live up to the praise that Flavius lavished upon him, or perhaps Aurelius continued his pious cultivation for fear of the judgment of other readers if his work fell short.

Drinking with Flavius

That wining the dead occurred near in Flavius' tomb is clear from the holes cut into its floor, whereby the ashes of the deceased were nourished by poured libations.[15] Tomb S's tight dimensions offered little space for dining within the structure, though substantial room was available in front when it was first built.[16] Circumstances were ripe for festivities, as Aurelius and fellow diners needed only to walk twenty-five meters to draw water from a well in the forecourt of Tomb H. Both at that tomb and two others nearby (Tombs F and O), surviving staircases led to upper floors where revelers/mourners could partake in al fresco dining atop the tomb. Unfortunately, Constantine's construction of the first St. Peter's scraped away those structures.

Given these provisions, what experience might Aurelius and other visitors to Flavius' tomb have had if they heeded his admonition and raised a glass here? How should we imagine the scene? One inscription from late third century North Africa captures both ideal and realistic circumstances about what could have played out. The epitaph marks a daughter's commemoration of her mother, as both the content and the first letters of each line make clear. They form an acrostic spelling *fili(a) dulcis(s)imae matr(i)* (a daughter [gave this] to her sweetest mother):

> To the memory of Aelia Secundula: We all have already spent much, as is right, for the burial and, what's more, for the altar holding our mother Secundula. We were happy to add a stone table at which we may recall the many terrific things she did, while the food, the cups, and the coverlets are set out, so as to heal the vicious wound that gnaws at our hearts. As the hour draws late, we gladly revisit stories about our virtuous mother, and our praises of her, while the old lady sleeps . . .[17]

Though this example arises from a different context – a Christian burial across the Mediterranean – it likely represents a continuation of ancient ways. Revelers create the table, perhaps even atop the altar, and adorn it with linens. And anecdotes and memories pour out in honor of the deceased, as the proceedings continue deep into the night.

Some events became raucous, or at least that is the impression given by a provision in Rome's oldest law code, the Twelve Tables, which outlawed tombside drinking bouts (*circumpotationes*).[18] And the persistence of traditional means of feasting the dead met the frequent censure of early Church Fathers. Tertullian laments the expense of "the dantiest banquets" and individuals who offer provisions for the dead but return home drunk.[19] In a similar mood, Augustine writes:

> I know that many people are worshippers of tombs and pictures. I know that there are many who drink abundantly over the dead, and who, as they produce feasts for the corpses, bury themselves over the buried, and regard their gluttony and drunkenness as religion.[20]

If Augustine's words here would condemn revelers' actions, he elsewhere seems to shrug at the inevitability of these feasts – even in a Christian context at martyrs' tombs. He appears willing to endure them, provided "they be not sumptuous beyond what is becoming respect for the memory of the departed, and that they be distributed without ostentation, and cheerfully to all who ask a share of them."[21] Even if we do not take these authors at their word about the *degree* of these events (with people stumbling home tipsily), what Christian sources outline about their *nature* is nevertheless revealing. When family, friends, stepsons, or others came to pay their respects by drinking and dining with Flavius and the others entombed in his structure, they stepped into a jolly occasion akin to an al fresco picnic, where, as the wine flowed and dusk crept in, stories circled

Meeting Flavius at the Tomb

around the fire, and the air filled with plucked notes or bellowed songs. Some commemorations, such as celebrations of Flavius' birthday, likely saw a huddle of well-wishers around his tomb alone, but days of wider appeal like the *Parentalia* witnessed neighboring revelers trying to outdo one another with elaborate dishes and furnishings that they were reticent to share tomb to tomb.

Dead or Alive?

This was not just a matter of Aurelius' partying at Flavius' tomb. To a degree that may be hard for us to grasp, Romans considered these meals to extend to the deceased's participation. One epitaph from Rome puts it directly, addressing the departed couple, "Friends and parents, may you come here in good health to the funeral feast, and enjoy yourself with everybody else."[22] With a still more jocular tone, the dead could issue invitations, as another tomb from Rome does: "Stranger, the buried bones of a man request you not to piss at this tomb, but, if you are an agreeable man, mix a drink, drink it, and give me some."[23] These examples involve the dead partaking with the living, but another Roman flipped the script. He so wanted to ensure his presence that he, while still alive, celebrated a burial rite in his own honor on a daily basis, complete with wine, a funeral feast, and a procession to his cubiculum amid the applause of his eunuchs and their singing, to musical accompaniment, of "he has lived his life, he has lived his life!"[24] Flavius' appearance and epitaph anticipate his readiness to partake.

Buy-in for this practice was not universal. Perhaps no document states the skeptical sentiment more directly than a bilingual inscription from Rome. The Latin portion lays out a man's wishes for his wife's tomb, while the shorter Greek portion addresses the reader:

> Do not pass by my epitaph, dear passer-by. Stop. Read and learn, and when you understand, go on: There is no Charon waiting on a boat in Hades; no judge named Aeacus; no dog called Cerberus. All of us who've gone dead down here are now no more than rotting bone and ash. I've told it as it is and have no more to say. Now, passer-by, go on and know I keep the rule of dead men: tell no tales. This tomb's just stone. So bring no myrrh or garlands. Do not waste money on a fire. If you want to gift me something, you should have done it when I was still alive. If you mix wine with ash you just get mud. Besides, the dead do not drink wine.
>
> Just sprinkle some soil. Say: what I was before I was, I have become once more.[25]

Seems like a fun guy. Though this epitaph may involve some self-irony, in that the deceased here does, in fact, tell tales, it nevertheless expresses a sharply cynical view that has much in common with Lucian's *De Luctu*, which has a dead man ask: "(What good to me) is the garlanded stone above my grave? What's the point of your pouring out pure wine? Do you really imagine that it will somehow trickle down to where we are?" As for offerings of food, they do not "do the tiniest bit of good for those of us in the lower, and the ash that remains is useless, too. Unless, that is, you believe we can eat dust."[26]

Even as these contrarians voice their opinions, they underscore the mainstream thinking, namely that the dead partook in meals and expected someone like Aurelius to "pour one out" for them as well. Some evidence pushes further, even raising the possibility that the deceased served as hosts of such banquets. The professional dream interpreter Artemidorus, for instance, recalls a client's reports of being approached in a dream by some friends who told him, "Receive us and give us dinner." Artemidorus understood this as "the custom for companions to go to the dwelling (i.e. tomb) of deceased members (of a funerary association) and to dine there, and the reception was said to have been given by the deceased because of the honors paid to him by his fellows."[27] Fellow diners, whether they envisioned the deceased offering the food, ran the risk of mistaking them for the living, to judge from a fragmentary stele from Dyrrachium, a city in modern Albania opposite Italy's heel. Showing a woman half-reclining, half-lying on a couch, the marker offers a verse imprecation to the reader: "Friend, do not be amazed because you see me like this, reclining on a couch or sleeping – I am dead."[28] All of this points out the degree to which, for Romans, though legal restrictions kept the lands of the living and the dead spatially apart, they hardly existed in true separation. Rather, the deceased were still widely believed to continue to exist, to partake in, and even to host tombside activities.

In Flavius' sculpture and epitaph, we see how this dichotomy not only falls apart but could have its slippage actively toyed with. First is physical verisimilitude (Fig. 6.2). Flavius' overall monument measures nearly six feet in length; were Flavius to stretch out in front of the *lectus*, it appears as though he would come close to its length. Aurelius and other visitors to this sector of the Via Cornelia necropolis would see large-scale stucco figures decorating other tombs but nothing as large as Flavius' portrayal. Additionally, Flavius' depiction emphasizes lifelike actions. His eyes are open; his face looks straight out; his propped-up posture and extended hand imply alertness and even engagement; and he is shown in motion, not

Meeting Flavius at the Tomb

FIGURE 6.2 A reconstruction of the sculpture, cinerary urn, and epitaph of Flavius Agricola's funerary monument illustrates how lifelike the deceased's appearance could be. Depicted life-sized, alert, in action, and with an inscription that brought his words to light, Flavius toyed with the boundary between life and death. (Drawing: Elijah Greene.)

resting his hand on his forehead but placing or removing his crown. We can recognize these aspects as intentional choices when we examine similar monuments. Some that depict life-sized figures on couches show the deceased as asleep (or even peacefully dead). And those that clearly show figures as awake have them looking away from viewers – as was the case, for example, with the girl from the Getty and Julia Attica's husband in Chapter 1 (Figs. 1.3, 1.5).[29] The immediacy of the deceased is a broad theme in *kline* monuments, but Flavius' pushes proximity as far as possible.

Now – despite how the gaze, actions, and scale of Flavius' statue rendered him lifelike – Aurelius and other visitors to his monument quite obviously would recognize that he was dead. After all, they were standing in a necropolis, staring at a marble statue, and likely also seeing a cinerary urn at the figure's feet. Yet when they read Flavius' epitaph, matters blurred. For one thing, we need to recognize that, when ancient readers made their way through a text, they seem to have read aloud, in effect giving voice to the words.[30] As one literary epitaph puts it: "Hey traveler, do you want to know that a poet lives even after death? Check it out: What you are reading I am speaking – your voice, to be sure, is mine."[31] While playing on the same writer-reader relationship, some inscriptions draw out the contrast between the form of the physical inscription and its auditory presence. Two lines of one epitaph have the reader, through the stone, "giving voice" to the deceased: "Because this writing entrusted to the stone preserves my voice, it will live by your voice, whoever you are that reads this inscription."[32] And an Ostian headstone drew attention to the disparity between the vocalized words and their petrified form: "Here am I who, though lacking a voice, speaks from the cut marble."[33] Flavius' words filled the air when they were read.

> Tibur mihi patria, Agricola **sum** vocitatus
> Flavius, idem ego **sum** discumbens, ut me **videtis**,
> sic et aput superos annis, quibus fata <u>dedere</u>,
> animulum <u>colui</u> nec defuit umqua Lyaeus.
> 5 <u>Praecessit</u>que prior Primitiva gratissima coniuncx
> Flavia et ipsa, cultrix deae Phariae casta,
> sedulaque et forma decore repleta,
> cum qua ter denos dulcissimos <u>egerim</u> annos.
> Solaciumque sui generis Aurelium Primitivum
> 10 <u>tradidit</u>, qui pietate sua <u>coleret</u> fastigia nostra,
> hospitiumque mihi secura <u>servavit</u> in aevum.
> Amici, qui **legitis**, **moneo**, **miscete** Lyaeum
> et **potate** procul redimiti tempora flore
> et venereos coitus formosis ne **denegate** puellis;
> 15 cetera post obitum terra **consumit** et ignis.

In Flavius' epitaph the present-tense verbs (in bold) are principally in the first- and second-person and appear predominantly at the beginning and end of the text. Past tense verbs (underlined) are in the third person (except one) and dominate the inscription's middle section.

The first-person sections of Flavius' epitaph likewise emphasized his speech and brought it to life. In fact, the verbs' tenses and moods heightened the effect. Most notably, when the epitaph uses the first person in the first and third sections, the verbs are in the present tense, and the majority of the second-person verbs in those sections are in the imperative. The verbs of the expository second section, largely in the third person, take past tenses. In other words, this statue made introductions and barked orders in the here and now while replaying narrative in the perfect and imperfect. Then there is *what* he "spoke." As Flavius was dispensing wisdom, or what passed for it, he of course was also partaking in acts that chimed with learned conversation at banquets, where anything from history and literature to philosophy and fantasy could be discussed.[34] The realism is amplified because his inscription's content is consonant with his convivial context.

Meeting Flavius at the Tomb

If playfulness surrounding the funerary realm feels odd or far-fetched, that may be more a reflection of our culture's attitudes than those of the Romans. In Western cultures today, generally speaking, we often see death as largely a thing to be reverenced, solemnly memorialized, or kept at a distance, while the preceding pages make clear, I hope, that a different spirit animated many ancient attitudes. Still more obvious examples illustrate visual punning in commemorations. The funerary marker of M. Modius Maxximus, the head priest of Magna Mater (*archigallus*) at Ostia, for example, contained a double pun for his name and position, for it showed an overturned grain measure (*modius*) surmounted by a rooster (*gallus*). Meanwhile, Atistia – the wife of the prominent baker Eurysaces, whose whole tomb trumpeted the source of his riches – had her ashes contained *in hoc panario*, "in this breadbasket."[35] Given the lifelike nature of Flavius' monument, one wonders if the circular cutting by the figure's feet not only held a cinerary urn but, in the spirit of M. Modius Maxximus and Atistia, one in the form of a vessel fit for a convivium, like a krater for mixing wine and water, which is well-documented in the material record.[36] What better way to commemorate a life of pleasures and jocularity than one last riddle, Flavius may have figured.

To wrap up this chapter, let us consider a final piece of funerary art which, like Flavius' funerary monument, also greeted visitors to a tomb. Around the same time that Flavius was breathing his last, another tomb was constructed across Rome, along the famed Via Appia. When visitors stepped within it and looked down, they encountered a striking mosaic (Fig. 6.3).[37] Picked out in white and black tesserae, it depicted a skeleton reclining at table in a near-identical posture to Flavius' sculpture: weight on the left side, buttressed by pillows, torso facing the viewer, legs crossed. The most notable difference is the figure's right hand, which points toward the Greek caption below, the Delphic maxim γνῶθι σαυτόν, "Know yourself." In many ways, its medium and message parallel Flavius': Below the deceased, an inscribed imperative gave voice to a philosophical outlook of the sort fitting for convivial discussion. I want to make two points about this figure. First, scholars discussing the *Totenmahl* motif hotly debate whether reclining figures are shown dining in life or partaking in the funeral meal. The example of Flavius showcases how this need not be an either-or situation, as he equally commemorated his lifestyle and joined in his survivors' revelry, to the degree he could, postmortem. Here again, at the threshold of the living with their dead, funerary decoration plays with the boundaries between the two realms, most obviously in having the dead address living visitors. Second, the skeletal figure and his *sententia* amplify

FIGURE 6.3 The floor mosaic in a tomb along the Via Appia in Rome plays on philosophy, dining, and death by portraying a reclining skeleton issuing the famed Delphic maxim "Know thyself." (Photo: author. Courtesy of Ministero della Cultura – Museo Nazionale Romano.)

the message of Flavius, who was as lifelike as marble would allow. When delivered by a skeleton, the words of wisdom have a different tenor: If you are being fully honest with yourself, then you know that *this* is what you will become, and so enjoy life's pleasures while you still can. Know thyself, to someone living, means coming face-to-face with your own mortality and recognizing that your days are numbered.

• • •

In this book's Introduction, I spelled out a goal of considering individuals' particular experiences and making sense of them within a broader nexus of social and cultural practices. In Part I, I hope to have done precisely what I prescribed with respect to Flavius Agricola's life and funerary monument. As we delved into this individual, we have witnessed many aspects of his life course: marriage, worldview, lifestyle, background, and more. For students whose image of the Romans is dominated by statesmen parading around in pristine white togas delivering orations, Flavius offers a helpful corrective. His name suggests a humble background, and yet his funerary monument, poetic epitaph, and tomb location cry out that he had "made it." Along the way, his life course varied from what we might normally expect. First, we read of none of his own children but learn of his marriage to a woman who appears to have brought her own offspring to their household. Likewise, his self-presentation revolves not around the speaker's platform or the battlefield, nor around (at least so far as we can discern) the realm of work to which many ordinary Romans appear to have staked their identity. Rather, Flavius' monument focuses on the triclinium and the world of life's joys.

I want to close Part I with a few reflections – the first is about methodology. The richness of an ancient individual's life comes into focus because we deploy the full range of a classicist's toolkit. Unlike almost any academic discipline we can name, Classics is defined less by a certain methodology and more by a time and place. The field's broad umbrella spans religion, economics, sexuality, hydro-engineering, you name it. And so examining one person like Flavius requires us to "walk all the way around" his life, not seeing him from only one disciplinary perspective or from one specific angle. And to gain access to many vantage points, we have employed many approaches, from the topographical to the philosophical, from material studies to Latin literature, from demography to epigraphic conventions. Flavius escapes simple definitions because we have donned many methodological hats. These are both the challenges and the rewards of "doing Classics."

Next, reveling in Roman relationships to death inevitably should lead to considering our own cultural outlook. Many modern readers will conjure different ideas of relating to those who have died. And yet, in private moments, some visit graves to share thoughts, pray, or perhaps place flowers on anniversaries of births, deaths, and weddings. Collectively we attend parades and fire off blanks on national days of remembrance, and many Mexican and Mexican-American communities celebrate Día de Muertos on November 1 with private altars at which gifts of flowers, food, and drink are offered to the departed. (And that is leaving out the anthropologically-rich turf of Halloween.) My point in offering these comparisons is double: on the one hand, when we begin to survey contemporary practices – individual, national, or sub-cultural – then similarities to the Romans begin to emerge, and what can initially seem oddly foreign might begin to feel more familiar. On the other hand, that current also runs the other way, as modern Western customs, when held up against Roman ones, might start to bleed into unfamiliarity. Studying another culture offers a window into that time and place, complete with its frameworks and customs. Yet it also involves holding up a mirror to what we might take for granted and thus urging us to probe familiar habits more deeply, from a remove, and with something of an outsider's perspective. It was little more than a century ago that many Americans and British people, like Romans, attended to the deceased on their own, receiving visitors who expressed condolences in the deceased's dwelling. The funeral parlor/parlour's arrival both reflects and shapes our changing relationships to dead family and friends.[38] This example goes to show how delving into Rome gets us outside ourselves and invites us to ponder why we do what we do.

Finally, a note on unresolved issues with the ancient material. Flavius' example makes the point that, like the meter in his epitaph, an individual's life was often much more complicated and richer in practice than we might imagine. In fact, Flavius' inscription offers a glimpse of not one but three different lives, none of which we might initially conjure in our mind's eye as we summon an image of a typical Roman. Beyond Flavius, we have met the (perhaps) widowed and re-married Isis devotee and the pious step-son attending to his stepfather's tomb. In this one family, then, we see differences in religious outlook, parentage, and, not least, gender. For instance, Flavius could enjoin friends to live it up at the dining table and in the bedroom, which many would have considered inappropriate if Flavia had voiced it. As this one example makes clear, their situation entailed a number of potential tension points: how did Flavia's veneration of Isis, which frequently involved belief in an afterlife, jive with Flavius' imprecations to enjoy the gifts of this life, since after death all else goes up in smoke or heads underground? While Aurelius is described as acting with piety, how did he really feel about Flavius? What drove Flavia to Flavius in the first place – a desire for security, his charm, his chiseled abs, or something else?

As Part I has expanded from one life to others, such as Flavia and Aurelius, it has drawn on wider patterns in Roman life to help make sense of Flavius' situation. Such contextualization enriches our understanding, as it explains the broader dynamics of Roman society and culture. And yet it also threatens to obscure the essential point of this project, namely that this constellation of issues and circumstances were particular to our cast of characters. This was the reality they lived out. Even if it shared some contours with other members of Rome's non-senatorial ranks, they had to find their own means of making their way through life and then commemorating that existence.

This fundamental tension – between the particular and the general, between the individual and the overall population – lies at the heart of doing social history of any period, yet may be most profound for less-well-documented periods such as Roman antiquity. How are we, as scholars, to explain an individual's particular life course (and to fill in the inevitable gaps in our evidence) without drawing on a broader set of examples? But, at the same time, does doing exactly that threaten to mask the individuality of someone's experience? As a result, even if the preceding pages have explained some aspects of Flavius' and his family's lives, many are bound to go unexplained, sometimes because we do not have the evidence at our fingertips to make sense of them, and sometimes because they were simply the perpetual problems or issues that any individual or family has to reconcile. Consequently, the example of Flavius suggests that not everything has to be ironed into smooth complicity, but could be messy because that is the way life often is.

A measured perspective has not always governed the reception of Flavius' sculpture and epitaph. As we have seen, the inscription was carved off by offended papal authorities, with important knock-on effects. Not only did this step obviously prevent further inspection of the epitaph, but it also intellectually separated the artwork and the text for about three-hundred years; only in the twentieth century would scholarly detective work reunite the two.[39] This example makes the point that the past rarely comes down to us unfiltered. And yet too often scholars of material culture concentrate on the endpoints – an artifact or artwork's original context and its present-day exhibition – without recognizing the "many middles" between these bookends, which piled their own meanings onto ancient material and even, as in the case of Flavius' ensemble, physically altered what passed from one generation and from one century to the next. What we encounter today is not just the product of antiquity, but of multiple other "pasts" between the ancient world and today. Part II of this book explores how different eras have received, understood, displayed, packaged, repackaged, materially transformed, and heaped layers of meaning on Flavius' monument.

PART II

The Many Afterlives of Flavius Agricola

The Many Afterlives of Flavius Agricola

In 1967, the French literary critic and theorist Roland Barthes published the influential essay "La mort de l'auteur," or "The Death of the Author." Barthes' argument ran counter to much literary criticism at the time, which typically understood a text's meaning to derive from its author's intent and life. "What did the author mean?" was the traditional question. Barthes shifted focus, contending that the meaning of a work derives from the impressions of readers. As Barthes puts it, "A text's unity lies not in its origin but its destination."[1]

One way of thinking about Barthes' argument is to recognize that a literary work, absent its author, takes on a life of its own. To take an example familiar to some of this book's audience, Vergil's *Eclogue* 4 promises a new age ushered in by a child's birth. Over the millennia since its composition between 42 and 37 BCE, the poem has experienced many divergent receptions. Here are two. Constantine and other early Christians interpreted *Eclogue* 4 as prophesizing the birth of Christ. The emperor apparently even gave a sermon at the Council of Nicaea in 325 CE that offered an extended Christian explanation of the poem.[2] Sixteen hundred years later, a postage stamp issued in 1937 by Benito Mussolini's fascist government of Italy deploys line 7 of *Eclogue* 4. On a banner strung between two Roman standards appears: *iam nova progenies caelo demittitur alto* (now a new generation is sent down from high heaven). Vergil's words are sandwiched between reminders of Augustus, as the 2,000th birthday of the princeps is recorded at the stamp's top, and the bottom cites a line of Augustus' *Res Gestae*.[3] This was far from a one-off, as the fascists continually aligned themselves with Roman antiquity and sought to portray themselves as its rightful heirs and descendants, not least by conducting massive excavations in Rome, Pompeii, Herculaneum, and elsewhere.[4]

What does this have to do with Flavius Agricola and his funerary monument? Just as texts like Vergil's are deployed and redeployed across different contexts and for different ends, a similar process occurs for artworks and artifacts. Some examples are well-known, such as Mussolini's excavation of the Ara Pacis and its reinstallation alongside the Mausoleum of Augustus as part of the Piazza Augusto Imperatore in Rome. Or, in a different vein, we might consider the so-called Euphronios krater, an Athenian red-figure vase of the sixth century BCE that was illegally taken from an Etruscan tomb in Italy in 1971, sold to the Metropolitan Museum of Art in New York, and then repatriated to Italy in 2008. What did this punch bowl mean to the Etruscan who wanted the ancient import entombed? How was it viewed by dealers both Italian and American? What justified its $1 million price tag to Met officials, given its shady provenance? And what drove Italian officials to seek its return?[5]

We have so far considered Flavius' biography as well as the impression of that life (and those of Flavia and Aurelius) that he intended to impart. This process has shared similarities to the critical lens Barthes pushed against. The remainder of this book now adopts a more Barthesian focus on the reception of Flavius' monument. What follows could be called an "object biography" of Flavius' sculpture. Such approaches, in the words of a pair of scholars, "address the way social interactions involving people and objects create meaning" and seek to understand how these connotations "change and are renegotiated through the life of an object."[6]

Flavius Agricola's monument was once ensconced whole in a purpose-built tomb in a sunny necropolis on Rome's periphery. It now stands in the Indianapolis Museum of Art, absent its inscription, lacking its cinerary urn and lowest quarter, minus struts that secured the position of its right arm and foot, and plus some reconstruction of its fingers and cup. Concentrating exclusively on these two bookends, as happens frequently in archaeology, would mean missing out on the many intervening periods. Successive generations often attach new meanings to an artwork, deploy it for their own ends, and dress it up in different intellectual and cultural clothing. This process may seem fairly innocuous, akin to a snowball rolling downhill and picking up all manner of material as it grows ever larger. But acts of writing, erasing, and reframing an object's meaning are much more complex, and can have a serious impact on the bookends.

Though the monument was tailor-made for Flavius, the removal of its inscription at the command of papal authorities rendered it anonymous. Only in the mid twentieth century would scholarly sleuthing reunite the

Part II The Many Afterlives of Flavius Agricola

sculpture, the inscription, and their famous findspot.[7] Absent those links, the monument (or should we call it a sculpture at this point?) proved symbolically malleable. Though clearly showing an individual, the artwork contrasted with freestanding sculptures and busts through its size and incorporation of furniture. Yet Flavius' portrait – with its cup, crowning, and clearly convivial context – presented a narrative direction that invited comment, concern, and other responses. Finally and importantly, though its sizable footprint meant that it took up space, it could still be transported with relative ease, which facilitated its movement, initially across Rome but later across Europe, the Atlantic, and beyond.

Part II of this book tells the story of Flavius' monument's travels. Where did it go? How was it passed along? Why and in what ways was it valued? What meanings were attached to the piece? And what do the sculpture's travels reflect about the ways that antiquities have been viewed, valued, deployed, manipulated, and shuttled around?

CHAPTER 7

Flavius Agricola in Early Modern Rome

Mounting Suspicion and the Inscription's Destruction

Complicated circumstances enmeshed Flavius Agricola's monument from its very discovery, which in turn shaped its physical form. Let us recall that the tomb was revealed in 1626, as workers dug at the intersection of St. Peter's transept and nave in preparation for the foundations of the baldacchino, designed by superstar architect Gianlorenzo Bernini, that would rise over the high altar. Pope Urban VIII and other Vatican officials believed the tent-like structure would stand immediately atop the bodily remains of the basilica's titular head, the first pope, and the rock on which Christ said he would build the church. This was *a* ground zero (and *the* ground zero for many) in Christendom.

To understand the prevailing atmosphere, it is helpful to consider the years leading up to the monument's unearthing. Several projects had recently broken through the floor of the Renaissance church. Just a decade earlier, church officials sought to modernize the *confessio* – an area for Mass immediately in front of Peter's purported resting spot. Beforehand, only a small passageway through the subterranean grottoes permitted access to the apostle's remains. Work between 1615 and 1617 opened a much larger space in the Renaissance floor, surrounded it with a balustrade, and offered access to the *confessio* via a double staircase.[8] We should take two things from this – first, though Peter's tomb was already the focal point of the church's entire construction (itself a deeply considered response to the Protestant Reformation), seventeenth-century construction endeavored to spotlight Peter's tomb all the more; second, excavating the "modern" *confessio* offered the opportunity to dig into earlier chapters in the church's life.

Vatican officials were prepared and eager to look back into history, for they were intimately familiar with the *Liber Pontificalis*, a collection of papal biographies. It stated that many of Peter's nearest apostolic successors, such as Popes Linus and Cletus, were buried near him.[9] So, when the project exposed tombs, an interpretation was already at hand. One canon of St. Peter's – a clergy member closely associated with the church – was present at the excavation and describes the scene:

> Many tombs of saints were found there ... including a Pope of imposing stature wearing a chasuble and a Pallium. He was not touched, however, as by high orders he was immediately covered. Many other corpses were found bandaged with stripes an inch wide ... In another one, the inscription "Linus" was found, yet another one gave out an odor that everyone present considered miraculous.[10]

Others likewise believed that history was coming to light. Pietro Paolo Drei, a worker of the Fabbrica di San Pietro (the body tasked with the construction and maintenance of the basilica), produced a plan of the tombs and bodies, captioned in part: "These Pontiffs, marked with fasces and crosses, are Saints Linus, Cletus, Anacletus, Euaristus."[11]

Early seventeenth-century diggers' awareness of the past triggered both fear and enthusiasm at the prospect of further soundings for Bernini's baldacchino. According to letters and other documents in Vatican archives, some folk voiced concern about nearing the sacred spot of Peter's tomb, while others cheered the possibility.[12] The former camp, led by the Pope's expert Christian archaeologist, Nicolò Alemanni, spelled out three dangers: doubts about the actual presence of Peter's body, possible mixing of the saint's remains with other burials, and potential damage to Peter's tomb.[13] Despite their diverse opinions, everyone surrounding the Vatican, from workers and acolytes to cardinals and the pope, shared deep anticipation of the project.

When digging began on June 30, 1626, workers immediately encountered more tombs than expected. Work slowed as the Pope summoned Alemanni to assess them. His ruling that they belonged to pagans and not to "saints" expedited the project. Yet ominous signs soon appeared: Alemanni fell ill and died forty days later, and Urban VIII's poor health led St. Peter's canons to consider interrupting work. Practical matters worried some as work progressed. Ugo Ubaldi, one of the basilica's canons, in recognizing that the ground was pocked with these tombs, expressed deep anxiety about the building's overall physical integrity. Its pavement, he noted, was a mere 11 cm thick and occasionally hovered above a void. Urban VIII nevertheless ordered the work to proceed but to be shrouded with maximum security: Laborers were under constant surveillance; only certain canons were permitted to open graves and handle bones; and both a notary and a draftsman began to monitor proceedings.[14] The holes for the baldacchino's foundation grew deeper, medieval burials were brought to light (their occupants having desired eternal rest near Peter), and, at a depth of almost five meters below the Renaissance floor, workers came across Tomb S and, within it, Flavius Agricola's monument. A report from Ubaldi, dated one month later, describes the piece, noting its furniture, posture, clothing, and state of preservation before coolly stating that it "was placed among the other marbles of the *fabbrica*." The salacious inscription receives no mention.[15]

This understated reaction was, to put it mildly, not typical. The site was essentially placed on lockdown. One cleric of St. Peter's – whose family had placed a pope on Saint Peter's throne a generation earlier and who would otherwise have enjoyed full run of the basilica – had to write a letter asking permission to visit the excavations twelve days after Flavius Agricola's tomb was uncovered.[16] Why? This discovery did not bring about the physical collapse of Saint Peter's tomb but could hardly have been worse symbolically, since the monument – with its boozy protagonist, mention of an Egyptian goddess, imprecation to make merry in both the dining room and the bedroom, and apparent denial of an afterlife – was deemed utterly incompatible with the veneration owed to this most holy spot. Beyond the topographical symbolism, embarrassment also increased because of the church's ongoing battle with Protestant rivals, as the Thirty Years War was being prosecuted at the very same time, largely along Catholic-Protestant lines in the prolonged wake of the Reformation.

And so Urban VIII took action. One account produced soon after the pope's death in 1644 offers our nearest account of what happened.[17] According to the document, the verses were "first denied, hidden, and hushed up by him [i.e. the pope] and by others under threat of most severe penalties and most rigid excommunication." The text continues, "Most horrible threats on the part of the pontiff were called for and made against those who dared to speak of such verses." The pope ordered the verses immediately plastered over and the statue secretly taken away to a "most unknown place" in order to "destroy its memory forever." Rumors even circulated that the statue was hurled into the Tiber.[18]

Neither the marble yard nor the Tiber's tawny waters hosted Flavius Agricola. Rather, the memoirs of Cassiano Dal Pozzo relate the discovery of the monument and report that the inscription "was broken, and the statue conserved and carried to the garden of Cardinal Barberini at the four

Flavius Agricola in Early Modern Rome

fountains."[19] This was property belonging to the Barberini clan, where their grand palace, the Palazzo Barberini, would soon rise tall. I will address the garden momentarily. For now, it is enough to note that Dal Pozzo was Rome's premier antiquarian, served as secretary to the very same Cardinal Barberini (Francesco, Urban VIII's nephew), and commissioned a drawing of Flavius Agricola's monument (Fig. 7.1).[20] So, this information is nearly as firsthand as possible. And whereas the canon studiously avoided mention of the inscription, Dal Pozzo not only discusses it but adds the detail of its removal from the monument. We do not know who cut it away, but inspection of Dal Pozzo's drawing together with the sculpture's remains is suggestive. The sketch displays a blank space where the inscription's letters would have been carved, while the physical sculpture, in its current form, shows a diagonal cut down and away along the front edge, but nothing similar on the sides or back.[21] Presumably the angled cut removed the material into which the letters were carved, basically leaving a blank panel at the monument's base and making the ensemble appear much like Dal Pozzo's drawing while on display in the Palazzo Barberini. Only in the twentieth century would scholarly detective work reconnect the epitaph and sculpture.[22]

FIGURE 7.1 A drawing of Flavius Agricola's funerary monument was commissioned by Cassiano Dal Pozzo soon after the piece made its way to Barberini property in 1626. It illustrates the sculpture as it likely appeared in the Barberini gardens and later within the Palazzo Barberini. (Courtesy of the Royal Collection Trust / © His Majesty King Charles III.)

Let me conclude this section with the obvious point that the contexts of the monument's discovery have shaped what we encounter today. Namely, offense taken by papal authorities led to the artifact's physical alteration. The inscription's removal, moreover, had knock-on effects somewhere down the line, as an apparent sense of "incompleteness" on the fractured front was remedied by lopping off the piece's lowest quarter altogether.[23] Meanwhile, subsequent publications of the inscription illustrate lingering misgivings about its content. A 1702 catalog of Latin inscriptions characterized the epitaph as "Epicurean impiety" that "this fool has mixed with … a barbaric style."[24] A few decades later, a compendium of Latin inscriptions inserted dashes in place of the final two lines, since "we are fearful that decent histories may cause offense if one were to consult them."[25]

This "long tail" of suspicion points up just how remarkable it is – given all the buildup to the monument's accidental unearthing, the threats surrounding the inscription's publication, and the general red-faced-ness provoked in the pontiff – that the sculpture survived at all, let alone passed to the pope's nephew. That said, the inscription's removal helped to dampen anxieties. As we remarked, the epitaph's last four lines did correspond closely with the figure's posture and gesture. Yet the two textual elements without a visual analog were likely the ones considered most offensive by church authorities: Flavius' encouragement of lovemaking and apparent denial of an afterlife. Stripped of these aspects, the monument granted its possessors greater latitude in its symbolic framing and redisplay, and therefore made it palatable for a cardinal's art collection.

Cardinal Barberini, The Palazzo Barberini, and the Continued Appeal of Antiquity

Cassiano Dal Pozzo's mention of the statue's movement to the *garden* of the cardinal is meaningful, since in 1626 the Palazzo Barberini was taking shape more on an architect's drawing board than in stone. Urban VIII had only recently been elected pope, and the Barberini, as relative newcomers to Rome's scene, had not yet meaningfully imprinted themselves on Rome's cityscape. The family of wealthy merchants had relocated from Florence and, by the late sixteenth century, began acquiring influence in Rome, often holding church offices and operating businesses simultaneously, despite regulations prohibiting that very thing. Their center of operations was the so-called Casa Grande on Via dei Giubbonari, not far from the Palazzo Farnese and Palazzo Spada in the center of Early Modern Rome's action. Though large, the structure lacked much ornamentation, as custom stipulated it must (since the Barberini had not reached the highest echelons of Rome's pecking order), with minimal trimming around windows and portals.[26]

Cardinal Maffeo Barberini's election as Pope Urban VIII on August 6, 1623, launched the family into the stratosphere of power. The new pontiff showered the cardinalate on his brother and two nephews, including Francesco Barberini – who was named Vatican secretary of state. Meanwhile, Urban VIII consolidated secular power in Francesco's younger brother, Taddeo, through several offices, notably head of the papal army and de facto mayor of Rome. Nepotism was endemic to Renaissance and Baroque Rome, but the shameless Barberini version offended even contemporaries. One Englishman, John Bargrave, wrote, "Upon the elevation [of Urban VIII], his kindred flew from Florence to Rome like so many bees (which are the Barberini's arms) to suck the honey of the Church, which they did excessively."[27] The clan required a palace befitting their new status, which permitted them to entertain visiting dignitaries in appropriate style. They selected a parcel on Rome's northeast whose previous owners, the Sforza clan, had built a relatively modest structure amid gardens and vineyards. As the agrarian sensibility suggests, the location was perched on the edge of the city's built-up area. Yet the spot boasted a line of sight directly westward to St. Peter's and the Vatican apartments of Urban VIII, a topographical connection that proclaimed Barberini dominance over the city.

Before the ink on the purchase contract was even wet, the Barberini were lining up a who's who of Rome's leading architects to design the palace. Carlo Maderno, Francesco Borromini, and Gianlorenzo Bernini began sketching plans for a monumental structure.[28] The end product bridged two existing models of elite residence: The new Palazzo Barberini enfolded the existing Sforza structure into an H-shape that, in pairing a luxurious building with a landscape of leisure, drew on models of rural villas. And yet, in its striking three-story elevation, the Palazzo Barberini was every bit an urban palace, even if it did not stand with block-like solidity as a looming presence over an urban piazza, as other palazzi typically did (Fig. 7.2).[29]

The palazzo's façade made clear Barberini ambitions as Rome's new emperors. Its use of superimposed arches framed by engaged Doric, Ionic, and Corinthian columns mimicked the Colosseum's exterior. And its first-floor metopes "quoted" the Temple of Vespasian in the Roman Forum. For anyone who missed the messages, the architects quarried travertine from those very same ancient buildings and redeployed it here.[30] After the family moved in around 1632, Taddeo Barberini and his nuclear family occupied

FIGURE 7.2 The façade of the Palazzo Barberini cited ancient structures and was created using stone quarried from them. The northern wing (left) housed apartments for the family's secular branch, while the southern wing was occupied by the cardinal nephews. Grand reception spaces opened between the two wings. Visible in this etching are also an ancient obelisk (left foreground), a Roman inscription (far right), and Bernini's Ponte Ruinante (right), all of which showcase an aesthetic of attractive disrepair on the Barberini grounds. (Image: Wikimedia Commons; etching by Giambattista Piranesi, Rijksmuseum.)

the palazzo's northern wing and Cardinal Francesco took up residence in the southern wing. Grand reception spaces formed the crossbar of the H between them. An imposing double-height *salone* was intended to host grand events, and its ceiling received an elaborate fresco, painted illusionistically to give the impression that the ceiling was not present, and that viewers were looking into the heavens. Nary a saint, Christ, nor Virgin appear, however. Rather, Roman historical figures, a host of personifications of virtues, and pagan deities frame the ceiling's central scene, where Divine Providence showers her favor on the Barberini coat of arms.[31] From their palace's architecture to its permanent decoration, then, the Barberini saturated their surroundings with motifs evoking the ancient world.

Enter Flavius' funerary monument. The Palazzo Barberini, like other Roman palaces, drew power not only from the built environment but from an overwhelming array of other cultural goods. A library, a stunning set of tapestries, a cadre of intellectuals supported in-house, a science museum,

Flavius Agricola in Early Modern Rome

a theater fit for opera, an assemblage of paintings by leading artists, and a botanical collection of rare specimens – these all signaled Barberini preeminence.[32] And their collection of antiquities constituted another key tool in expressing the clan's position. By the mid seventeenth century, the Barberini possessed hundreds of pieces of ancient sculpture, architectural fragments, and the like, which they displayed throughout the palace and its grounds.[33] Such a collection expressed manifold messages – about power, prestige, erudition, and much more.

To understand this situation, it is helpful to take a step back. The active preservation, curation, and display of antiquities in Rome was less than two centuries old. Throughout much of the Middle Ages, discovering an ancient statue or architectural fragment meant happening upon a useful raw material, since the marble could be burnt to produce mortar to fuse building materials. Toponyms in Medieval Rome and Ostia menacingly pinpoint *calcaria*, lime kilns.[34] By the middle of the fifteenth century, however, the situation was changing, as active collecting of classical antiquities increased.[35] Soon, displays of ancient art on the Capitoline and at the Vatican shaped Roman sensibilities. At the former location, Sixtus IV (1471–1484) gifted to the Palazzo dei Conservatori (the seat of magistrates governing the city) and "to the Roman people" a series of bronze statues, such as the famous bronze She-Wolf, that had stood at the pope's Lateran Palace and had been central to Roman identity. The next half-century saw papal munificence continue along similar lines, with the addition of, for example, the equestrian bronze of Marcus Aurelius. Even though Pope Julius II (1503–1513) owned only one statue, the famed Apollo Belvedere, it took center stage in a niche-lined sculpture court within his Belvedere villa in the Vatican.

The prestige enjoyed by the displays on the Capitoline and at the Vatican spurred private collectors, and thus began a furious competition for ancient sculptures that included the papacy and Rome's leading families.[36] For example, once Pope Paul III (1534–49) filled the final niches in the Belvedere courtyard, he and his nephews concentrated on their private collection in the Palazzo Farnese. Papal workers were deployed to Farnese property to excavate sculptures from the Baths of Caracalla; there they recovered two monumental sculptures that we still call the Farnese Bull and the Farnese Hercules.[37] Pliny's mention of the former sculpture garnered attention on par with the celebrated sculpture of Laocoön and helped, together with the numerous other antiquities in the family's hands, to put the Farnese assemblage on a level with ensembles belonging to the papacy and city.[38]

An arms race for this cultural material was underway, as the sculptures both symbolized power/prestige and also offered, amid Renaissance Rome's feverish devotion to classical heritage, a through-line between antiquity and the present day. To have a sculpture, in other words, did not only mean that you had access and taste but that you had learning and pedigree. The next decades would see Rome's private collections mushroom as social aspirants – especially families arriving from Florence, Umbria, and other parts of Italy without such ready access to antiquities – sought out ancient sculptures and the cachet they brought.[39] Some individuals, such as Vincenzo Giustiniani (the scion of a Genovese banking family), amassed huge arrays and sought to broadcast that fact by producing illustrated booklets that could showcase their holdings to audiences across Europe. By the time of Flavius' unearthing, collecting had spread widely, but the choicest pieces were concentrated in the hands of power-broker families like the Farnese, Borghese, Medici, and Ludovisi, who displayed them within both urban palaces and suburban villas for Rome's citizens, foreign visitors, scholars, and many other audiences.

Let us return to Flavius' monument at the Palazzo Barberini. The sculpture was likely very welcome, since the Barberini were relative upstarts on the Roman scene and had much ground to make up, antiquities-wise, on other families. Cassiano Dal Pozzo's memoir, we recall, locates the sculpture in Cardinal Francesco Barberini's garden. He does not give a precise placement, since the space was a construction site in 1626. Despite several sizable inventories of the palazzo's artworks, the monument does not seem to reappear in the documentary record until 1738.[40] Why? In all likelihood we can dismiss the possibility that the taint of its history lingered and precluded its being listed. After all, how many people had seen the sculpture in its original location? And how many would have recognized it, absent its context and inscription? Perhaps it was taken elsewhere. Or, more prosaically and more likely, the large scale of the Barberini collection might have meant that the sculpture was simply missed. No wholesale inventories of the garden post-1626 survive, so the simplest answer was that it remained outdoors on display within the Barberini grounds.[41]

An exterior display did not mean relegation to the margins, for palazzo owners concentrated attention on gardens, even if they wanted those surroundings to appear natural. Often owners displayed sculptures in palace courtyards and other outdoor settings in a seemingly casual manner, as though in the circumstances of their discovery. An "informal" grouping of sculpture in the courtyard of the Palazzo Santacroce, for example,

Flavius Agricola in Early Modern Rome

actually reveals a curated pyramidal structure like a temple pediment. Fragmentary statues, altars, and other antiquities lay along garden paths without plinths or stands of any type at the Palazzo Cesi.[42] At the Palazzo Barberini, an even more pronounced version of this aesthetic of attractive disrepair or studied carelessness encompassed artifacts and architecture alike. An etching by Giovanni Battista Piranesi shows an obelisk lying in pieces in the palace's forecourt. Discovered in the late sixteenth century, it was moved here by Urban VIII in 1633. Visible on the far right is a huge inscription from an arch of Claudius, which the Barberini mounted on a wall.[43] And furthering this patina of antiquity is an architectural fantasy created by Bernini in the right middle distance. The *Ponte Ruinante* took the form of a bridge connecting Cardinal Francesco Barberini's apartment to the garden, yet, as its name suggests, it took the form of a bridge that was in the process of falling. Half of one arch looks as though it has collapsed, and a block of a second arch looks as though it were in the process of slipping. Made with spoliated remains, it intentionally looked like an ancient Roman remain that had fallen into disrepair – an artificial ruin.[44]

If Flavius' monument began its postantique life as the flashpoint of controversy, it became, once its inscription was removed, a more innocuous marker of Roman-ness. Though we cannot know for certain what display it partook in, the sculpture would have contributed to, and drawn meaning from, the environment of the palace's grounds. They dripped with classical references – from the structure's very stone through to its form, decoration, adornment, and even the operas it hosted. But there was a difference between evoking antiquity and owning/collecting/displaying a piece of it. The former conveyed classical heritage, but the latter required something tangible and therefore signaled wealth, power, and more. It is not surprising, then, that an ascendant family – aiming to proclaim their magnificence and to fill the ample grounds and rooms of a new palace – jumped to add another piece, particularly one as unique as Flavius Agricola's.

Flavius Agricola Helps Tell the Barberini Tale

When the monument next raises its head in the documentary record, it helped to bear a rather more specific message. Thanks to a 1738 inventory of the Palazzo Barberini that labels rooms, lists their sculptural contents, and estimates each artwork's monetary value, we can identify the location of Flavius' sculpture and understand the prestige in which it was held. The record lists the artwork in the northern wing's first *anticamera* on the *piano terreno* (ground floor), which we can identify as the room scholars name

B20; it values the piece at fifty *scudi*.[45] This spot was very prominent, since it offered the most direct access from the forecourt to a suite of rooms occupied by the family's secular branch during the summer months (Fig. 7.3). For visitors it helped set the scene – one that highlighted the Barberini clan's history and ambitions.

Room B20 worked together with the preceding room to establish a distinctly imperial tone. Portraits of Roman emperors and empresses predominated: Colossal busts of Hadrian and Trajan, for example, stood

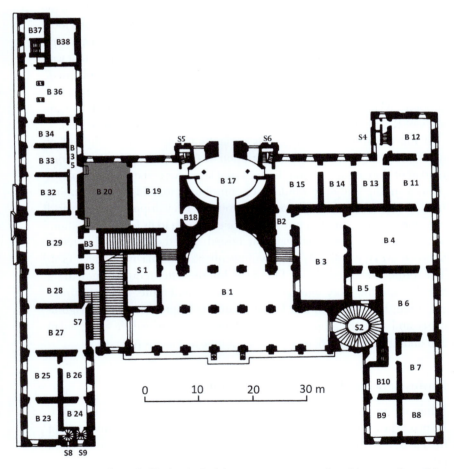

FIGURE 7.3 In 1738, Flavius Agricola's monument was cataloged in room B20 of the Palazzo Barberini, whose post-1679 plan is seen here. In that location, it offered the cultural cachet of antiquity and also shared space with more modern works that lent it new shades of meaning. (Drawing: Elijah Greene.)

out in room B19, while one of Vespasian shared B20 with Flavius. Also appearing were Augustus, Domitian, Lucius Verus, Julia Domna, Lucilla, and others. Across the two rooms and their nineteen artworks, only four are distinctly nonimperial. The décor of the following room, B29, underscores the programmatic display – it held ten sculptures, nine of which represented divinities. The first two rooms, then, armed with such distinguished historical figures, participated in a centuries-long tradition of depicting cycles of *uomini famosi*, "famous men," in palaces and civic buildings, which ultimately traced back to the display of ancestral portraits (*imagines*) within ancient Roman households.[46] In a way, including these individuals was, like the palazzo's façade, claiming an ancient lineage and tacking the Barberini clan onto it. Such ancestor creation was common in Early Modern Rome, as various clans sought out homophonic precursors of their family name in Republican history – the Massimo family, for instance, associated themselves with Fabius Maximus Cunctator, hero of the Second Punic War.[47]

Why was Flavius included here, then? Three immediate and related possibilities emerge: First, his representation, though not a bust like most other statues in his room, was distinctly a portrait and thus was consistent with the representation of individuals. Alongside emperors and empresses, Flavius became a pseudoancestor of the Barberini, another *uomo famoso*, even if no one knew who he was. Second, the sculpture was considered valuable: With an estimated worth of fifty *scudi*, it was the second-most prized piece in its room, and, of the 115 sculptures in this set of apartments, only 14 were considered more highly valued.[48] Third, his monument was rare for its scale and form, occupying more space and lending more heft than the busts that dominated the Barberini collection. Sometimes in the case of antiquities, size mattered.

Several other more recent artworks decorated B20, and they spotlighted crowning moments of Barberini triumph in the seventeenth century.[49] I would like to suggest a fourth reason for Flavius' inclusion – its content echoed Barberini-produced spectacles in Rome and thus aided in evoking more recent Barberini family history and tying it to Rome's imperial past. Three huge paintings on the walls of B20 immortalized show-stopping ceremonies:

* a nearly six-by-fifteen-feet canvas showed Urban VIII investing his nephew Taddeo as Rome's prefect (essentially, the mayor) in the Cappella Paolina within the Quirinal Palace on August 6, 1631;

* a similarly large painting depicted Urban VIII presiding over the canonization of the Jesuit order's founder, Saint Ignatius, at the Jesuits' primary church, the Gesù, in 1641;

* and another megalographic depiction commemorated Carnevale festivities being celebrated immediately outside the Palazzo Barberini in 1656, soon after the arrival of Queen Christina of Sweden in the Eternal City (Fig. 7.5). (In a major coup for the Roman church, the queen had abdicated her throne, converted to Catholicism, and moved to Rome.[50])

Within a palace trumpeting the Barberini, it is not surprising to see so much celebration of the family. That said, the visitors who place these paintings in the same room as Flavius also remark that no other paintings in this wing of the palace depicted contemporary events; all the others are religious in theme. Thus, the décor of B20 presents an autobiographical highlight reel of Barberini moments of glory.

The most valuable sculpture in Flavius' room lent additional commentary on the Barberini family story, with knock-on effects for how Flavius' sculpture was viewed. Estimated at 300 *scudi*, the sculptural group shows three figures in sorrow: the life-sized goddess Latona with her offspring, Apollo and Diana, both depicted as toddlers (Fig. 7.4). Cardinal Francesco commissioned the marble group from Florentine artist Domenico Pieratti, who executed it between 1629 and 1635.[51] It depicted a specific episode in Latona's life when, after bearing Jupiter's children, she endured exile at the hands of a jealous Juno. Amid her wanderings, she and her children were thirsty and came upon a pond, yet some uncivil peasants stirred up the mud to stifle the deities' quest for a drink. In revenge, Latona lifted her hands to the heavens, cursed the peasants, and had them turned into frogs.[52] Pieratti's sculpture captures this final scene.

Whatever the sculpture's original attraction, it took on special meaning in the following decades because of its parallels to the Barberini clan's experiences. After Urban VIII's death, the rival Pamphili family and the Roman mob, angry at Barberini excesses, drove Francesco and Taddeo Barberini into exile. They remained in Paris for nearly a decade before coming back and resecuring a place in Rome's hierarchy. In Latona's story, the Barberini saw a parallel for their own restoration, and they promoted the myth extensively. In a series of fabulously expensive tapestries that retold Urban VIII's pontificate, for example, one work featured the story and visually quoted Pieratti's statue group.[53] In other words, the sculpture helped to reframe the Barberini's postexile story as one of rightful restoration after a temporary setback.

Flavius Agricola in Early Modern Rome

FIGURE 7.4 Domenico Pieratti's sculpture of Latona, Apollo, and Diana (1635) occupied the same room in the Palazzo Barberini as Flavius' monument. Together with other artwork in the room, the two sculptures helped to frame the Barberini clan's story for visitors. (Photo: author.)

In room B20 of the Palazzo Barberini, Flavius' monument – amid the *uomini famosi* and the paintings – likely assumed new meanings just as the Latona group had done. The sculpture, with one hand clasping a wine cup and the other crowning his head, struck a distinctly convivial pose and signaled celebration. In this way, he represented a welcome nod to the Barberini's carefully cultivated reputation for hosting grand banquets. In the theatrical spirit of Baroque Rome, prominent families endeavored to outdo one another in public displays combining theater, music, and processions. As one example, 1634 saw the Barberini mount the seventeenth century's most expensive spectacle, a *giostra del saracino* (a 'Saracen' joust) in the Piazza Navona in honor of a Polish royal. When the theatrics and subsequent parade were concluded, Donna Anna Colonna Barberini, wife of Taddeo, hosted a sumptuous banquet.[54] Similarly elaborate events welcomed Queen Christina of Sweden for Carnevale in 1656 (following the "carousel" represented in B20's painting; see Fig. 7.5) and the ambassador for King James II in 1687, when the household crafted a series of sugar-paste sculptures that wove together English and Barberini imagery. One depicted Constantine's famous *in hoc signo vinces* (by this sign you will conquer) on its base, since the Roman emperor was born in Britain.[55] We know these details because pricey books were published by Rome's leading families when they produced such grand spectacles; the printed version disseminated into Europe's courts each foray in this game of one-upmanship. And so, Flavius' unabashed advertisement of conviviality could only strengthen evocations of past Barberini feasts and fetes. If Flavius' statue stood opposite the Latona group, as their listing in the inventory suggests, then the two

FIGURE 7.5 Filippo Lauri and Filippo Gagliardi's *La Giostra dei Caroselli* commemorates Carnevale festivities held at the Palazzo Barberini in 1656. Queen Christina of Sweden is portrayed looking on from the lower balcony projecting from the palace (halfway along palazzo at right). The balcony was accessible from a room adjacent to where Flavius Agricola's monument was displayed. (Image: Wikimedia Commons; Museo di Roma.)

would have formed a pendant pair, the one a mournful marker of exile and a record of revenge, the other a celebration of Barberini munificence and magnificence.

Visitors and Viewers

All this artwork in B20 – painting and sculpture – was intended to ensure a striking first impression for formal visitors. Hosts at a Baroque palace signaled the status of visitors through a well-known ceremonial practice linked to the architecture. Key was a sequence of rooms – first came a guard room (*sala dei palafrenieri*), then a series of two or three anterooms (*anticamere*) before the audience hall (*camera d'udienza*), where the host would actually sit with the guest. Basically, the shallower into this series you made your way as a visitor before being greeted by the host, the greater your standing. A visiting cardinal would be met in the guard room, an ambassador from a lesser state in the inner anteroom.[56] They would then proceed with the host to the audience hall, with seats arrayed to articulate respective ranks. The sensitivity of the diplomatic choreography is clear from one story. Once, when the Grand Duke of Tuscany visited Cardinal Francesco Barberini, the chairs were positioned equally in a nod to equivalent statuses. Twice the duke adjusted his chair in a sign of deference, and twice the cardinal moved to recreate parity.[57] First, second, and third impressions were extremely important for visitors. In this route charged with hierarchical overtones and anticipation, everyone had to pass through B20, whose decoration offered an overture for what was to come.

B20's impact was not felt by diplomats and VIPs alone. Rather, visitors of many sorts could view this assemblage and the broader Barberini collection, since Roman palaces were becoming increasingly open, prefiguring the institutional museum. By 1600, artworks "were no longer simply the private possessions of individuals, demonstrated by their owners to interested visitors," but anyone who presented themselves appropriately could essentially make their way into reception spaces that were not in use.[58] In fact, so many visitors made their way to the grand second-floor *salone* in the mid-1600s that the caretaker there, Mattia Rosichino, grew tired of being asked about the fresco scheme. And so he interviewed the painter's iconographic advisor and then penned a short pamphlet that allowed visitors to walk themselves through the program.[59] A remodeling of the Palazzo Barberini in the 1670s saw most residential suites moved upstairs to the *piano nobile*. The ground floor was reserved primarily for works of art, yet the Barberini maintained the traditional sequence of rooms to grant the illusion that you were visiting a private person's collection.⁶⁰ In the same set of rooms as Flavius' sculpture, viewers could marvel at famed paintings by Caravaggio, Raphael, Titian, Poussin, and others.⁶¹ As other palaces likewise accommodated visitors, guidebooks mushroomed in number, and families often deployed an erudite individual (called a *letterato*) to highlight the collection and thus impress especially notable visitors, as we know the Barberini did for the British ambassador in 1687.⁶² A similar figure likely explained the collection to Queen Christina on her visit, and we know she passed through this suite of rooms on her way to soak in the Carnevale festivities on the Barberini grounds (see Fig. 7.5).

...

Let me conclude. In 1704 what could fairly be called Europe's first "art book" was published in Rome. Entitled *Raccolta di Statue Antiche e Moderne* (Collection of Ancient and Modern Statues), it consisted of engravings by Domenico de Rossi and text by noted antiquarian Paolo Alessandro Maffei.⁶³ Interestingly, the volume was not organized by theme or date but by the sculptures' location in Rome, which reflects two facets of antiquity collecting in the Baroque era. First is the rise in the importance of visitors. As guidebooks to Rome's treasures proliferated, word and fame spread to audiences local and abroad, to high French society, and especially to members of the British aristocracy, whose young men undertook the Grand Tour that traced the roots of Western culture. Ancient statues were no longer merely a sign of elite luxury but of public munificence, as collections occupied different spaces, the architecture was reshaped and doors were opened in order to grant access to visitors – scholars, guests, and some members of the general population.

Second, the organization of artworks by location reflects the persistently fierce competition for these markers of taste. Tellingly, de Rossi and Maffei's book includes only a handful of pieces that did not appear in a similar list some seventy years earlier.⁶⁴ Thus, the corpus of accepted masterpieces was well established, which only tightened the market and increased the prestige of known pieces. And so, in answer to the question of why Flavius' monument made its way into the Barberini household and assumed such a prominent spot despite its scandalous discovery, one answer is that it was another addition to the collection that signaled power, prestige, learning, and culture. Stripped of its inscription, Flavius' sculpture bore no lingering stigma. In fact, its combination of form, size, portraiture, and activity boasted a novelty that made it attractive and a specificity that granted it a narrative direction. When situated within the right architectural and artistic context, it became more than just an oddity of ancient art and vague claim of status; it helped tell a rather more precise story about its owners and their clan's history.

CHAPTER 8

Flavius in the Modern World

Carving away the inscription from Flavius' funerary monument made it possible for the now anonymous statue not only to nestle comfortably into the bevy of delights – musical, horticultural, architectural, intellectual, and artistic – on display at the Palazzo Barberini but also to enjoy pride of place in Barberini self-presentation. Over subsequent decades, as political and financial power shifted within Europe and globally, the sculpture rode those tides as it moved from Rome to Paris to New York and, ultimately, to Indianapolis. Following Flavius can be challenging at times, as the trail grows colder, and as less detail is available than we might wish. Nevertheless, as Flavius' sculpture was moved from Roman palazzi to the pages of the *New York Times*, it took on – or, rather, was laden with – additional meanings by each context it confronted. This chapter traces those travels, the physical alterations that the sculpture underwent, and the ways that the artwork was adapted to the demands and desires of each setting. Flavius' sculpture sheds light on issues surrounding antiquities, their movement, and their study.

The Politics of Art in Late Nineteenth-Century Italy

Barberini standing did not persist. An intermarriage with another noble family, the death of a Barberini heir, and a dispute about the inheritance ultimately saw the colossal Barberini collection divided in 1812. After much legal wrangling, half the art remained in the Palazzo Barberini and half moved with another branch of the family to the Palazzo Sciarra along the prominent Via del Corso.[1] Flavius Agricola's sculpture was among the pieces that made the short trek. Within a century, it would feel the brunt of the eroding old order.

Just as they had done when the collection was in its former home, guidebooks lured visitors to the Palazzo Sciarra with lists of its ample artworks.[2] Nineteenth-century scholars also started documenting these and other holdings, and it is here that we can pick up our story of Flavius Agricola's monument, for it appears both in a French guidebook and in a massive German inventory of ancient sculpture in Rome published in 1881.[3] Intriguingly, the author of the latter work's preface thanks all who, when faced with his request for access, showed "open minds and that genuine Roman liberality." He laments the only exceptions, writing that he could not check his work at the Palazzo Sciarra and the Villa Giustiniani, in effect raising questions about their owners' hospitality.[4]

Though the German scholar does not name the illiberal man in question, it was Prince Maffeo Barberini Colonna di Sciarra, very much a public figure in late nineteenth-century Rome – a politician, pioneering newspaperman, and patron of the arts. Financially profligate, he displayed a special talent for sinking money into speculative investments that never panned out. When fiscal crises swept through the late 1880s, Prince Maffeo felt the financial heat and got desperate. Among other efforts, he started liquidating the family's art collection. The French guidebook claims that all the marbles in the second room of the Palazzo Sciarra were for sale, and we know that he sold off an ancient sculpture of Aesclepius and three Baroque busts to Danish buyers.[5] In an effort to grease the skids for a potential sale of his most famous paintings, he deployed the presses of his newspaper, *La Tribuna*, to produce a fifty-page illustrated booklet advertising "Ten Paintings of the Galleria Sciarra."[6] A year later, the Prince sold the paper.

By 1893, matters would grow still worse. The Banca Romana imploded, and examination of its papers embroiled the prince in charges of corruption. In light of this mess, word spread about Prince Maffeo's plans for his collection, which law required to pass undivided to his eldest son. Englishman August Hare's 1893 *Walks of Rome* (the thirteenth edition of this venerable guide) grumbles that "no ordinary visitor has looked" upon the art of the Palazzo Sciarra for a year, and then produces a list of "six celebrated gems of the gallery now believed to be taken out of Italy."[7] The state intervened in the affair, as inspectors from the Ministry of Public Instruction noted several paintings missing from the Palazzo Sciarra. Popular tumult ensued, and Italy's Chamber of Deputies enacted legislation governing the disposal of artworks and their potential purchase by the state.[8]

In the meantime, Prince Maffeo offloaded his collections widely across Europe. Members of the phenomenally wealthy Rothschild family in Paris acquired at least three paintings illustrated in the *Tribuna* supplement, while several other artworks and at least one ancient sculpture were moved to Paris as well.[9] Ancient works, such as what scholars have called the Sciarra bronze and the Sciarra Amazon – a very rare fifth-century BCE Greek sculpture and a Roman marble emulation of a famous Greek original, respectively – were also sold, the bronze in 1892 after being smuggled out of the country in a suitcase, the marble in 1897.[10] They both passed through the hands of German-scholar-turned-art-dealer Wolfgang Helbig and ultimately into the collection of the Ny Carlsberg Glyptotek in Copenhagen, along with eight other ancient sculptures from the Sciarra collection. As we shall see, Flavius Agricola's sculpture was likely marketed alongside these pieces but next pops up in the documentary record in Paris. While I can find no explicit documentation that Flavius Agricola's funerary monument headed France-ward in the 1890s, the lack of comment should not be surprising. After all, the paintings – with sky-high profiles thanks to their presumed artists: da Vinci, Raphael, Titian, Caravaggio, and the like – were what attracted popular and political attention.

The artworks' sale both speaks to changing fortunes and also shows how art, both ancient and more recent, was taking on new meanings for the general public. In short, its movement abroad roiled Rome. A usefully polemical guide is Costantino Maes, a Rome-born librarian and activist who produced a weekly pamphlet entitled *Il Cracas*. The periodical's backstory encapsulates Maes' proclivities: also known as the *Diario di Roma* (Journal of Rome), it reprised a long-running Roman work (1716–1848), and its title page regularly listed the year both AD and AUC (*Ab Urbe Condita* – from Rome's supposed foundation in 753 BC). Mixing editorials about current events with well-researched pieces on long-standing Roman customs, such as the origins of holiday foodstuffs, *Il Cracas* screamed that the publication was intended for Maes and his fellow *Romani di Roma*, dyed-in-the-wool Romans from Rome.

Soon after the Sciarra controversy broke out, Maes and *Il Cracas* weighed in through an intriguing rhetorical appeal and line of argument. Rather than make a purely ethical or moral argument, Maes instead turns to matters statutory and patriotic. He cites laws against the exportation of artworks, requests the nullification of their sale, and proclaims multiple times that "what matters the most is our National interests and honor."[11] He names legislation and royal decrees by chapter and verse, reproduces court rulings against Sciarra, and offers additional commentary on these documents. Maes' remarks are as learned as they are emphatic, drawing on ancient Roman law in the original Latin while deploying an arsenal of boldface type, capital letters, and pointy fingers that both highlight his main points and anticipate today's emoji-speak. In this "giant artistic disaster" of Italian patrimony, he notes the irony that the Campidoglio (that is, the Capitoline Hill), where the world's spoils were brought in ancient times, can no longer witness "works of our very own hands."[12] For Maes, the means of argument offered the message: He quotes Dante (the Italian poet par excellence); imagines Roman jurists Ulpian and Papinian encountering a modern lawyer in the Forum, addressing him in Latin, and then having him beaten; and reprints a letter that ponders an Italian selling to a German "a piece of the fatherland" (*un pezzo di patria*).[13]

In the end, we can view these changes from two vantage points: those of the populace and those of once-great families. The invocation of national pride might initially strike us as odd, since Italy was only declared a nation-state in 1861 (and would require another decade for full consolidation). In the decades surrounding Italy's *Risorgimento*, however, artwork was no longer a private concern, but – through British "walks," German compendia, and the opening of once-shuttered palazzi – increasingly entered the public domain and conscience. The standard expectation was that art was open and available. Yet, with the rise of institutional museums outside of Italy, Rome's streets saw any loss of their artistic heritage as a mark against Rome, Italy, and their honor. Moreover, since Romans were preternaturally armed with a gift for historical memory, Napoleon's campaigns in Italy and French invasions of the Eternal City could only have lent extra sting to the Parisian destination of much of the Sciarra collection.

If, through the seventeenth and eighteenth centuries, classical artworks like Flavius Agricola's sculpture had distinguished grand families, then the dissolution of that old European order signaled a broad shift in art's meaning for those houses. What was once a storytelling prompt and an emblem of exclusivity became a cash cow, a source of liquidity in the face of financial straits. The Barberini were hardly alone, as the Borghese clan likewise sought to sell off their artworks.[14] Financial forces may have outweighed symbolic value for these families, but as Maes and *Il Cracas* demonstrate, artworks both more and less ancient were gaining as markers of identity for the nascent Italian state, whose influence and importance were overshadowing Rome's old order.

Making the Rounds of the Art Market

Once Prince Maffeo started offloading the Barberini/Sciarra artworks, Flavius Agricola's sculpture disappears from the documentary record for a couple of decades. Insinuations of a wholesale movement of Sciarra holdings to members of the Rothschild family appear in *Il Cracas*, but that contention speaks most vividly to Maes' anxieties and antisemitism.[15] When the sculpture and its trail are regained, they reveal an odyssey through the hands of some fascinating characters on the international art market, who showcase broader twentieth-century economic, political, and military movements.

The piece resurfaces when it was offered for sale, with over 100 other artworks over the years, to the Ny Carlsberg Glyptotek in Copenhagen. We know this thanks to Frederik Poulsen, the museum's director, who supplied photos of the pieces to a mammoth German encyclopedia of ancient sculpture, which then published the images in 1947 (Fig. 8.1).[16] The photo shows the sculpture's condition in the early twentieth century and, by comparison with the seventeenth century Dal Pozzo drawing (Fig. 7.1), it also illustrates the changes the sculpture experienced. The figure's left hand and part of the cup have been damaged, and its base (where the

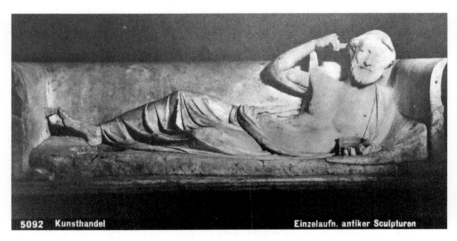

FIGURE 8.1 This photograph of Flavius Agricola's funerary monument was sent to the Ny Carlsberg Glyptotek in Copenhagen at an unknown date before 1936. It shows the piece without its base, in a damaged condition (note the fractured hand with the cup), and with the original struts still intact. (*Photographische Einzelaufnahmen antiker Sculpturen* (Arndt et al. 1893, vol. 17B, no. 5092).)

inscription was once carved) has been removed, leading some people to identify it mistakenly as a sarcophagus lid. We also see that struts (which the artist of the Baroque drawing chose not to display) were deployed in antiquity to stabilize the right arm and the right foot.

The photo proves that Flavius Agricola's sculpture was being shopped around by the 1930s, but otherwise it is challenging to pin down exactly when, since Poulsen submitted photos of sculptures that were offered to the Glyptotek over a span of decades. The most likely possibility is that Flavius Agricola's sculpture was dangled before the Danes in the 1890s when the museum acquired the Sciarra bronze and Amazon. The sculpture's next certain date – its sale in Paris in 1936 to a New York dealer – presents a *terminus ante* quem (latest possible date) for its move to France and identifies its next certain owner after the Sciarra-Colonna clan: Demotte Inc., an art dealer with bases in both Paris and New York. It is, of course, also possible (but less likely) that it was Demotte Inc. that offered the sculpture to the Glyptotek.[17] Other possibilities exist as well, and in this predicament we find ourselves in largely the same hazy situation that often confronts art historians and museums as they seek to establish an artwork or artifact's chain of possession. Much that we wish were preserved does not seem to have been saved or is occasionally even intentionally obscure.

At whatever point Flavius Agricola's sculpture was moved to Paris and into the Demotte family orbit, it undeniably plunged into what *Time* called a "tragi-comedy," which is both juicy and also relevant for our understanding of Flavius' sculpted form.[18] Belgian-born George Joseph Demotte founded and ran the company. By the early twentieth century, he had leveraged an especially strong reputation in dealing French medieval art into an empire spanning Paris and New York. But in January 1923, Demotte announced a plan to give away vast swaths of his holdings to American institutions, claiming to be shutting down his New York gallery after growing weary of mounting losses and the arrest of his New York representative.[19] This seemingly rash decision unfolded amid intensifying disputes on both sides of the Atlantic. In the USA, Demotte had recently sold an enameled bronze statue of the Virgin and Child to a New York collector; when the latter died, his estate's executors called in Sir Joseph Duveen, a superstar British art dealer, to assess the holdings. Duveen labeled the Virgin and Child statue a fake, and so Demotte fired back with a half-million-dollar lawsuit for slander. In return, Duveen vowed to spend that same amount proving the piece's falsehood.[20]

Meanwhile, Paris was consumed with media reports that Demotte sold a number of inauthentic artworks to the Louvre. Attention focused especially on a pair of high-relief figures known as the Parthenay Kings, after their discovery in a town by that name. As displayed in the Louvre, the sculptures appeared full length, from their crowned heads to their bare feet, just as Demotte had sold them in 1914. The front page of the May 22, 1923, edition of *Le Matin*, however, noted that photos of the torsos – without legs – had been published a half-century before. "Un Miracle au Musée du Louvre," an ironic headline screamed, sardonically noting "the dead statues that are born again."[21] The most likely artisan of the legs – Emile Boutron, the chief sculptor at Demotte's Montparnasse workshop – could not have been the source of the story and old photo. Though he bragged that he was "the only living sculptor to have his works in the Louvre," he had died three years earlier under mysterious circumstances, shot in the head while working alone in his accustomed studio.[22] The controversy surrounding the Louvre quickly spilled to the New York art world and especially the Metropolitan Museum of Art, as the *Times* ran story upon story about dealers of whom Demotte had run afoul.[23]

Even if Demotte's choices did catch up with him, these events show both Demotte's ability to gauge what rendered an artwork sellable and his workshop's predilection for "improving" something deemed incomplete.[24] Correspondingly, Flavius Agricola's statue, like a house that gets a kitchen renovation, underwent an upgrade, as photographs "before" and "after" Demotte's possession show significant interventions. The struts have been removed, and reconstructions rendered both hands as well as the cup whole again. Though we do not see the wholesale fabrication of any major parts, it is important to recognize that, when inspecting any artwork or artifact that does not come directly from the ground, we are often looking not at an original whole but at a literal (if also skilled) construction of the past. Even the famed ancient statue of Laocoön dug up in Rome in Early Modern Rome was, it turns out, incorrectly restored and displayed in the Vatican for more than four centuries. Only the chance discovery of a missing segment of Laocoön's right arm in 1906 corrected the fault.[25]

Back to Demotte. For drama only his death could match his life. On September 3, 1923, the first day of the hunting season in France, Demotte spent the day at the chateau of fellow Parisian dealer and long-time friend Otto Wegener. Just after lunch, according to court records, Wegener fired a shot to prove that his gun had been recharged, but the recoil jarred loose the firearm, which fell to the ground and fired a second shot. This one struck Demotte in the chest, killing him in short order. A devastated Wegener reportedly tried to kill himself on the spot but was restrained.[26] Demotte's son Lucien, though only seventeen, ran the galleries in the wake of his father's death before his own untimely passing from pneumonia in 1934. At this point,

FIGURE 8.2 An object card from the Brummer Gallery archive, with small (and reversed) photograph of Flavius Agricola's sculpture, shows the artwork as it appeared upon its arrival stateside in 1936. Note also the stamp later designating it for sale at auction. (© Metropolitan Museum of Art. Image source: Art Resource, New York.)

the elder Demotte's widow, Lucie Demotte Marcus, conducted some business for the firm.[27] She was likely the agent in Flavius Agricola's next move.

From Demotte's collection, Flavius Agricola's sculpture passed into the hands of Joseph Brummer, a major figure in the early twentieth-century Manhattan art world. The Metropolitan Museum of Art in New York possesses the Brummer Gallery records and has helpfully digitized the archive and posted it online.[28] According to the records, the sale occurred on October 15, 1936. Correspondence between Joseph and his brother Ernest describes the purchase of a lot from Demotte's gallery for 38,500 francs. While the archive does not offer an individual purchase price for Flavius Agricola's sculpture, the portrait receives the highest individual valuation by some margin on one checklist.[29] We do not know what motivated the transaction, though the rising threat of Hitler's Germany, its violation of the Treaty of Versailles, and retaking of the Rhineland in March 1936 could only have added urgency in Demotte's Parisian showrooms. Indeed, the sculpture's processing and shipment to New York are strikingly speedy; after passing through a Saint-Ouen warehouse, it arrived less than six weeks later (Fig. 8.2).[30] The threat was real, for an artwork

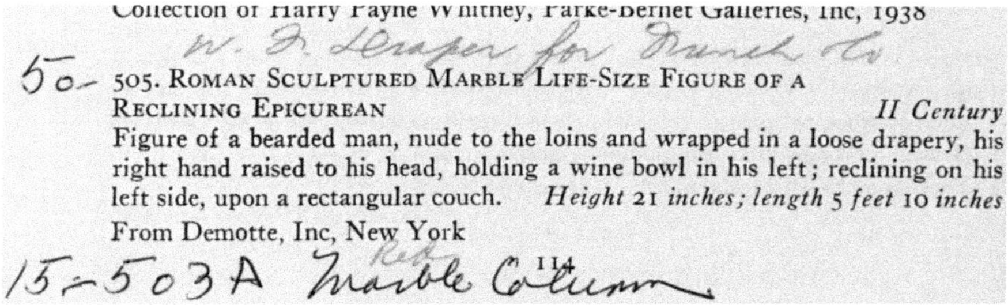

Flavius in the Modern World 137

> Collection of Harry Payne Whitney, Parke-Bernet Galleries, Inc, 1938
>
> *W. J. Draper for French & Co*
>
> 50— 505. ROMAN SCULPTURED MARBLE LIFE-SIZE FIGURE OF A
> RECLINING EPICUREAN   *II Century*
> Figure of a bearded man, nude to the loins and wrapped in a loose drapery, his right hand raised to his head, holding a wine bowl in his left; reclining on his left side, upon a rectangular couch.   *Height 21 inches; length 5 feet 10 inches*
> From Demotte, Inc, New York
>
> *15-503A Marble Column*

FIGURE 8.3 Handwritten annotations in the Parke-Bernet auction catalog of June 8–9, 1949, record the purchase of Flavius Agricola's sculpture by French and Company.

purchased by Brummer in 1937 was confiscated by Nazis soon after their invasion of Paris.[31]

Brummer's rise to prominence in New York put Flavius Agricola's sculpture before the eyes of leading American industrialists. Originally, Brummer intended to become a sculptor and traveled from his native Hungary to Paris to study with luminaries such as Matisse, Rodin, and Rousseau. Selling others' artwork began as a side hustle but turned into a business, as Brummer and his brothers opened a Parisian gallery in 1912. The threat of World War I sent them to New York, where they added a Manhattan gallery to the family holdings. By the time of Joseph's death in 1947, the business was a powerhouse that brokered important purchases for some of New York's biggest names and institutions. The Lansdowne Amazon, for example, he purchased in 1930 for more than $140,000; it then passed to John D. Rockefeller Jr. before landing at the Metropolitan Museum in New York. In this golden age of collecting, more than 400 works in the Met can be traced through Brummer.[32]

Joseph Brummer's death triggered his gallery's dissolution. Flavius Agricola's sculpture was sold at a massive three-day auction sale in 1949 at Parke-Bernet, the preeminent Manhattan auction house. A copy of the auction catalog in the Met's library has been scanned and posted online.[33] Handwritten annotations appear above and below the entry for Flavius's sculpture; they were likely scrawled by someone representing the Met at the auction (Fig. 8.3). The same handwriting appears throughout, but in two different shades of blue: one apparently for preparatory notations, the other for on-the-spot jottings. Some annotations are mysterious, yet one right above the listing for Flavius' piece gives a name, "W. J. Draper for French Co." Sure enough, Flavius Agricola's sculpture next pops up with French and Company, another New York art dealer with a clientele as prestigious as Brummer's. Names like Getty, Hearst, Morgan, Vanderbilt, and Rockefeller appear, as well as further connections to Fricks, Mellons, and Astors.[34] This who's-who of robber barons and industrialists echoes the words of George Demotte's nemesis, Sir Joseph Duveen. In describing his business model, he famously quipped, "Europe has a great deal of art, and America has a great deal of money."[35]

That was hardly truer than in the case of Mitchell Samuels, the principal founder of French and Company, who specialized in tapestries. Interestingly for our story, he executed the remarkable reassembly of a group of thirteen known as the "Constantine Tapestries." Designed by Rubens, they constituted a gift from Louis XIII of France to none other than Cardinal Francesco Barberini in 1625, the year before Flavius Agricola's funerary monument would cause a stir in his uncle's court and soon end up in his own garden.[36] The works, ancient and Baroque, though separated for centuries, were reunited in Manhattan for American clients.

These connections invite some stocktaking. Though Flavius Agricola's sculpture passed among characters embroiled in worldwide affairs and at the pinnacle of the American art scene in the early twentieth century, it only moved several blocks throughout this time (Fig. 8.4). A half-hour stroll along Manhattan streets would take you past the showrooms of Brummer, French and Company, and the Hartman Galleries (more on them shortly). Demotte's New York gallery and the Hartmans' future location were nearby too. In these spots, in front of leading collectors and museum agents, Flavius Agricola's sculpture did not sell.[37] Why? Its quality is good; its substantial size probably a positive too. But there were downsides. Though it once boasted a remarkable findspot (under St. Peter's) and pedigree (Barberini ownership), that information had been temporarily lost to history. The artwork did not take a famous form, like a bust, however, nor did it represent a famous person, such as an emperor. And, as for its content, an older man lying about drinking may have hewed too closely to mid twentieth-century stereotypes of Romans, when films like *Caesar and Cleopatra* (1945), *Quo Vadis* (1951), and *Ben-Hur* (1959) found traction in moralizing sensibilities. Perhaps a rebrand was necessary.

"At the Edge of a Hollywood Pool ... "

If French and Company hoped to turn a quick profit, they were disappointed, for eight years later, the midtown art dealers featured the sculpture

Flavius in the Modern World 139

FIGURE 8.4 Flavius Agricola's statue hardly moved within Manhattan for the better part of four decades as it traveled from the Brummer Gallery (1936–1949), through the Parke-Bernet auction house (1949) and French and Company's galleries on 57th Street (1949–1959?) and Madison Avenue (1959–1968) before changing ownership to the Hartman Galleries (1968–1972). Hartman Rare Art and the Demotte Gallery illustrate the close proximity of many Manhattan dealers. (Drawing: Elijah Greene.)

in a nearly half-page ad in the Sunday *New York Times* (Fig. 8.5). The front page of the November 10, 1957, edition detailed the search for an aircraft lost between San Francisco and Honolulu and updated readers on Cold War relations with three articles featuring Russian topics. On page 108 of the 356-page "Late City Edition," French and Company's advertisement pictured Flavius' monument under an all-caps header "GET UP, LUCULLUS ... COMPANY'S COMING!" The same font appears below the photograph (highlighted in a mod curving cutaway) to announce a "HEROIC 'BARGAIN BASEMENT' SALE."

On the first count, French and Company play up what had been the downfall of Flavius' monument at its discovery, namely a keen zest for life's pleasures. In calling the figure Lucullus, the ad not only granted a name but affixed a particularly charged one at that. Lucius Licinius Lucullus was

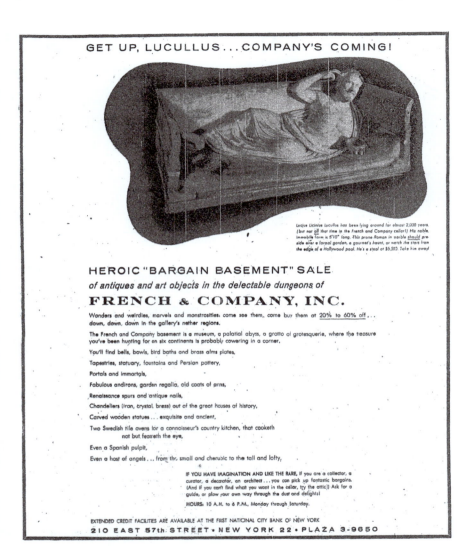

FIGURE 8.5 French and Company used Flavius Agricola as the poster boy for a classy yet breezy lifestyle in a 1957 advertisement in the *New York Times*. (Courtesy of French and Company.)

a Late Republican figure known both for his military acumen as well as the extravagant lifestyle that flowed from his battlefield successes. Two centuries after his death, Lucullus' reputation remained strong enough to merit a biography from Plutarch. When turning to Lucullus' lifestyle, Plutarch begins, "In the life of Lucullus, just as in an ancient comedy, one reads in the first part of political and martial matters, and in the later part of drinking bouts, and banquets, and all-night revels, and torch-races, and all manner of frivolity."[38] After the pivot from valor to luxury, Plutarch sticks to the latter topic, describing innovations in fish raising and vast villas chock full of artworks and libraries.[39] But Plutarch devotes the most space to Lucullus' tastes for dining in style: "Not only with his dyed coverlets, and beakers set with precious stones, and choruses and dramatic recitations, but also with his arrays of all sorts of meats and daintily prepared dishes, did he make himself the envy of the vulgar."[40] In addition to food, then, Lucullus' banquets offered a full array of extravagance.

Now, the connection to Lucullus likely had several intended resonances for readers of the ad. First, even as the adjective *Lucullan* was increasingly used during this period, Lucullus was no household name, except perhaps among those with classical educations.[41] *Lucullus*, for this reason, offered an imprimatur of traditional standing even if you did not know what it really meant. It looked old and signaled classy classicism. Second, for anyone who did know about Lucullus' luxurious lifestyle, there may have been some slippage surrounding who was being addressed. The second-person imperative of "GET UP, LUCULLUS ... COMPANY'S COMING!" sounds like it is admonishing the reader: "You've got guests arriving, Mr./Mrs./Ms. Fancy, and you need to spruce up your pad!" – in other words, buy this sculpture. Third and most obviously, Lucullus offered a handy shorthand for the unashamed pleasures that the sculpture's protagonist was involved in. It personalized the piece, wrapping a potential acquisition in an ancient tradition of luxury and – when the next line weighs in – heroism.

The small print advances the sensibility:

> Lucius Licinius Lucullus has been lying around for almost 2,000 years. (but not <u>all</u> that time in the French and Company cellar!) His noble, immobile form is 5'10" long. This prone Roman in marble <u>should</u> preside over a formal garden, a gourmet's haunt, or watch the stars from the edge of a Hollywood pool. He's a steal at $6,500. Take him away!

Beyond allowing us to track Flavius' monument from one subterranean space in Rome to a "delectable dungeon" in Manhattan, the caption shifts the frame, over the course of a few sentences, from the sculpture's content to its physical form and, ultimately, its potential for a buyer. The purchaser, like Lucullus, would have fancy entertainment spaces, resplendent food and drink, and a spot to take a dip like a screen idol. Are the "stars" actual constellations or does the ad's new "epigraph" help the sculpture evoke a realm of hospitality where he might "preside" over a cocktail party featuring John Waynes and Marilyn Monroes? In other words, the presentation of Flavius' portrait here is largely as a piece of decoration that is simultaneously fun, classy, sociable, and upwardly mobile. There is virtually nothing about its art historical value, beauty, or value for students of ancient Rome.

Stripped of its original archaeological and epigraphical context, and therefore appearing as nothing but content, Flavius Agricola's sculpture was slapped with a new identity. When French and Company ran this ad, scholars had not yet reconnected Flavius' epitaph with the remainder of his funerary monument. If they had, would their campaign to market the sculpture as a decorative piece have been feasible, given the inscription's saucy finale? Independent of that, the advertisement seizes on Flavius' posture and activity, making him the pitch-man for a life of time-honored opulence and refinement, even as it reduces the sculpture to an objet d'art.

Such a characterization can partly be explained by panning out and looking at the page on which the ad ran, since its menagerie of content declares its presumed readership. A long vertical Sak's 34th ad traces the left side of the page, proclaiming, "This is the bra to wear under your Chemise." Other corners are plastered with ads for the Macy's beauty salon ("Unika removes unwanted hair forever"), a Yonkers interior design concern (" ... our salesmen are decorators in their own right ... taking a keen personal interest in her decorating problems"), and a midtown hairdresser ("Oil Paintings and Hair Color: Neither is squeezed from tubes. Artists creat [sic] both."). Shoehorned among these is a wealth of engagement and marriage announcements. In fact, betrothals and nuptials stretch between pages 89 and 123, no doubt fueled by the upcoming wedding season for New York's socialites. This context very much pinpoints the clientele that French and Company had in mind: female, wealthy, and interested in the latest happenings of New York society.

As the ad's context and content suggest, the larger realms of the art world and contemporary American social dynamics played a role in Flavius Agricola's presentation. By 1957, French and Company were in the midst of restructuring their business, largely to make over a crusty reputation. (One critic jokingly called them the "High Priests of the Gothic and the Renaissance.") French and Company records, housed at the Getty Research Institute in Los Angeles, reveal what was happening behind the scenes.[42] An in-house document reports that 80 percent of sales in the art market were in contemporary art and laments that French and Company had missed the boat.[43] The firm bought a block-long four-story building and

Flavius in the Modern World   143

constructed atop it a fifth-floor gallery that broke the company's mold. Strident in its minimalism, the top-floor space was hailed by one critic as "the city's most extravagant showcase for contemporary art." To signal the change, the abstract expressionist Barnett Newman inaugurated the gallery with twenty-nine paintings.[44]

But before the new could come in, the old had to go out. The sale at the old property was intended to generate capital, clear out stock so it would not need to be moved, and free up space for a different type of inventory.[45] Yet the task was not simple due to the firm's reputation and their gallery's castle-like façade. To broaden the clientele, the advertising campaign adopted what company memos call a "lighter note" designed to strip away the solemn severity and thereby to improve foot traffic for the special sale.[46] Hand in hand with a recognition of the old ways' dissolution was the realization that different people, especially women, were making ever more decisions about domestic affairs for a growing middle class in postwar America. The firm labeled this group the "young-rich," carefully distinguishing them from nouveaux riches, the latter being obsessed with trappings of standing, such as old master paintings.[47] This marketing campaign aimed to "steer clear of the just-looking-thanks crowd while at the same time attracting thousands of new luxury item customers."[48] Or, as the firm's patriarch Mitchell Samuels put it, "We wanted to reach the increasing number of Americans with constantly improving tastes and the money with which to indulge them."[49]

Amid engagement announcements and ads for upper-range department stores, the picture of Flavius Agricola's sculpture was seen by people who imagined themselves along very much the lines that French and Company envisioned. And its pitch sought to thread the needle, balancing a playful tone and relaxed content – a reclining figure, not a staid portrait – with a patina of antique dignity that, together with the price tag, made clear that lookie-loos would not be reaching for their checkbooks. As one memo put it, the ad campaign steered clear of "come-and-get-it approaches" while still appealing to the growing number of upper-middle-class art buyers in America.[50] Old art needed to be repackaged for an emerging demographic, and Flavius/Lucullus was just the man for the job.

From New York to Indianapolis

Efforts by French and Company to reshape their business model and recast their image did not take root. Working through the firm's archives is akin to watching a car crash in slow motion: The company's board wrestled with a challenging balance sheet, real estate deals were struck that brought unintended consequences, and, in a cash-raising effort, the firm sold shares to people outside its founding family. Most notable among these is City Investing, which took control of the company after Mitchell Samuels' death in 1959 and held it until 1968, when French and Company's holdings were divested. (Parke-Bernet hosted a series of auctions of former French and Company inventory through late 1968 and early 1969.[51]) The firm's name and much of its inventory passed to Martin Zimet, who held it until his death in 2020. A portion of the building and the remainder of its contents were bought by Alan and Roland Hartman, who moved the headquarters of the Hartman Trading Company into the structure and recast their business as the Hartman Galleries.

Alan and Joan Hartman would donate Flavius Agricola's sculpture to the Indianapolis Museum of Art in 1972. The statue does not appear in auction catalogs, and this Roman material does not chime with the Hartmans' overriding focus on European and Chinese art and furniture, so all evidence points toward the sculpture's passing to the Hartman Galleries and then its donation to the Indianapolis Museum of Art. Joan Hartman served the museum in a variety of capacities: as a visiting specialist for the Wilbur D. Peat Program in Oriental Art, as curator of an exhibition of Chinese jade, and as a trustee.[52] The Hartman family – first Alan and Joan, and then (following a divorce and remarriage) Alan and Simone – would give nearly three-dozen artworks to the museum between 1972 and 1976. Flavius Agricola's sculpture is one of a handful that does not originate from Asia. That is, the large Roman piece stands very much as an outlier in the Hartman family's gifts and expertise. The museum valued the sculpture at $30,000, which constituted a substantial portion (if not all) of the donation that typically accompanied an invitation to join the museum's board of trustees.[53]

Conclusion

These days Flavius Agricola's sculpture is exhibited in a newly configured gallery in Indianapolis (Fig. 8.6). Previously, it had occupied a small room that was mostly stuffed with mummies and Greek pots. It now stands at the endpoint of an exhibit dedicated to visions of the body across cultures and millennia. Sprawled out against the backdrop of an enlarged Japanese print, Flavius has been repackaged once again. This new context encourages museum visitors to consider what the sculpture's posture, material, and scale reflect about the culture from which it arose.

Flavius in the Modern World

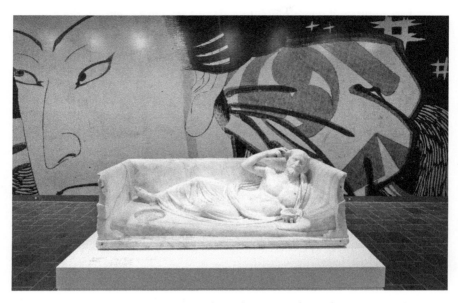

FIGURE 8.6 At the Indianapolis Museum of Art, Flavius Agricola's sculpture is currently exhibited as the culmination of a gallery dedicated to representations of the human body across different cultures. (Courtesy of the Indianapolis Museum of Art at Newfields.)

In this location, art lovers, school groups, and the occasional Classics student or scholar view Flavius' sculpture. Knowing the artwork's colorful history, however, might tempt us to consider who else cast eyes on the sculpture. The list likely includes some heavy hitters of history: a toga-clad Constantine as he made plans for the original St. Peter's basilica; a mitered Barberini pope and one of Italy's greatest architects as they sought to highlight an apostle's reputed resting place; a resplendently dressed Queen Christina of Sweden as she was feted around Rome after abdicating the throne, converting to Catholicism, and moving to the Eternal City; any number of Parisian Rothschilds; and leading art dealers and their top-hat donning customers with names now emblazoned on hospitals, libraries, museums, and universities across the United States. Flavius Agricola desired visibility, but this audience far outstrips the travelers along the Via Cornelia that he ever imagined impressing.

Alternatively, we might turn the question around and consider where the sculpture has traveled: Rome, Paris, Manhattan, and now Indianapolis; an ancient necropolis, the underbelly of the heart of Catholicism, palazzi full of antiquities, elegant French and American showrooms, not-so-stylish basements, and now a museum gallery. Across these settings, the funerary monument, from the beginning of its postantique life, has been treated largely as a token or a symbol in various disputes – sanctity versus profanity, Christian versus traditional Rome, Italian versus outsider. Especially after it was literally stripped of its name, it offered a canvas onto which diverse meanings could be projected – totem of classical refinement, emblem of Italian-ness, money-making opportunity, cheeky *bon vivant*, and so on. The sculpture offered a flashpoint at various moments, yet it is just as interesting to consider how Flavius Agricola's monument was subject to remarkable swells and tides in history: the Christianization of Rome, the Counter-Reformation, the dissolution of the old European order, the rise of the modern European nation-state, worldwide military threats, the growing wealth of American industrialists and their desire for traditional trappings of status, and the growth of the upper-middle class and women's increasing financial pull in postwar America.

The story of Flavius Agricola's artwork, then, bears lessons for our study of history. At the end of Part I, I argued for care in seeing too much of the present in the past or vice versa. Tracing the afterlife of this funerary monument, however, complicates that dialogue and suggests that the past that we encounter, even in physical form, is hardly unfiltered but can even have a different physical shape because of the ways that it has been confronted, and thus treated, in the past. Most obviously, the content of Flavius' epitaph led to its removal from the monument's sculpture. Even for a sculpture that bore a close relationship to its inscription, the physical and long-standing intellectual separation of the two enabled different readings of the sculpture. It could not be a Barberini ancestor or Lucullus if it were Flavius.

If this chapter has largely chronicled what happened to Flavius' sculpture, absent his epitaph, then what happened to the monument's words, absent the sculpture? Though their primary place of publication, the *Corpus Inscriptionum Latinarum*, mentions the inscription's findspot and connection to the sculpture, that thread quickly wore thin. The words were essentially reduced to raw text in collections of inscriptions, floating free of those original contexts. One result has been that Flavius' final words have frequently been reproduced as stand-alone sentiments, which obviously lose much of their meaning when disconnected from a life-sized statue and from their contrast with Flavia's portrayal elsewhere in the inscription. At the Indianapolis Museum of Art today, the object label quotes Flavius' initial self-introduction and then jumps to his closing sentiment, omitting any mention of Flavia or Aurelius. This selection makes a fair amount of

Flavius in the Modern World

sense, since these lines have the most bearing on what visitors see. Yet it also undercuts Flavius' original intention, which was to memorialize his wife and her son on nearly equal epigraphical footing to himself.

Such a separation of husband and wife has much in common with treatments of the inscription, as scholars have tended to focus on Flavius' words-to-live-by or Flavia's adherence to Isis. (Aurelius receives minimal scholarly discussion.) What is lost in such bifurcated approaches? For one, the two spouses are treated as freestanding individuals, with little mention of their marriage or relationship. More importantly, without that connection, they are essentialized as *bon vivant* and Isiac devotee, largely studied in turns by those interested in tombside philosophizing and women's participation in Romano-Egyptian religion. They are not husband, widowed and remarried wife, stepfather, mother, devotee of Lyaeus, hardworking beauty, or widower. And, correspondingly, potential tensions and possible resolutions in their relationship have slipped through the cracks.

Such treatment is partly fallout from the papal order to destroy the inscription, yet also partly results from the conventions of Classics. Too often different categories of evidence are relegated to different sources – *this* is where to find sculpture, *here* is where you go for inscriptions, *over there* for tomb architecture, and so forth for grave goods, frescoes, stuccowork, and other raw material from the ancient world. And so, even after Flavius' sculpture and his inscription's text have been reconnected, scholars of Isis today frequently cite the inscription and then assign it to the third century CE, even though the sculpture and tomb to which it belongs can be confidently dated to a century earlier. My goal is not to critique other scholars for failing to undertake the tasks that interest me; rather, I want to point out that what was once intended to be a unified whole has been split into categories studied by different camps of specialists.

In the end, unlike the wooden tablets that inadvertently recorded Venidius' biography at Herculaneum (see Chapter 2) – whose survival amid Vesuvius' pyroclastic material was lucky – Flavius' monument and epitaph come to us not due to freak natural causes but despite many cultural and archaeological barriers. By the same token, we must rely on (and be thankful for) the antiquarian impulses of seventeenth-century scholars for the transcription of the inscription. The same goes for the inventory takers in Baroque palazzi and the archivists who have thought to preserve documents from various art concerns as they were being bought out or going under. For every Brummer Gallery where detailed records exist, there seems to be a Demotte Gallery where all that seems to survive is a smattering of photographs.

Overall, the situation offers a reminder that even the physical remains of the past are subject to much interference by previous centuries, their interests and anxieties and ways of organizing what survives. That is, we both ought to be aware of how to interpret what happens to come down to us, and we should also recognize that the predilections of the past shape what we see. There is simply much that we do not have because it did not appeal or because it offended, and many questions that have not been posed because the organization of the evidence does not prompt them.

Witnessing the different ways that Flavius Agricola's reception has morphed with the times should give us pause, yes, and encourage us to ponder how we, as products of our own time and place, may be seeing him and the rest of Roman antiquity in certain lights, perhaps even ones of which we are not fully aware. Yet history is not just a dialogue between past and present. It is wrapped up in all the pasts that were once the present, all the moments that shaped (and were in turn shaped by) an artifact, archaeological site, historic personage, or past phenomenon. In other words, it is necessary not just to be mindful of what we bring to the study of the past but what others have as well.

Epilogue

In the Introduction, I referenced a coin minted under the emperor Titus (Fig. E.1). On one side appeared the figure of the emperor sitting amid a heap of weapons, a reference to his roles in the Jewish War, the capture of Jerusalem, and the construction of the building depicted on the coin's opposite side, the Flavian Amphitheater. The coin adopts an unusual perspective, showing the Colosseum's façade while also permitting a glimpse into the building. We spy the columns tracing the uppermost reaches of the interior and a few heads peeping out between them. Lower down two more rings of spectators are visible, the lower one pierced by an entrance and split into wedges by staircases. When we last examined the coin, we remarked about how only one individual appeared – the emperor – while everyone else was merely an undifferentiated head.

FIGURE E.1 Though ordinary Romans are rendered as undifferentiated dots within the Colosseum on this coin, the study of Flavius Agricola offers a reminder that they led distinct and complicated lives. (Courtesy of the British Museum.)

After the preceding chapters, it is now helpful to revisit this coin. For one thing, as Flavius Agricola has come into focus, we can now put a face on someone who might have taken his place in the amphitheater. Or perhaps three faces, for, to a lesser extent, we have also learned about Flavia Primitiva and Aurelius Primitivus. We have witnessed some of their aspirations, recognized some of their struggles, seen how they wrestled with life's big questions, and unpacked the legacy that they hoped would remain after their deaths. In studying these individuals, my goal has not been to pretend to put faces on all the spectators, but, by delving as deeply as possible into one example, to tell an interesting story about Romans who were, both proverbially and literally, on the other side of the coin from the emperor.

In trying to piece together Flavius' life, we have drawn on the remarkably diverse toolkit of ancient studies. Among other approaches, we have considered the formal visual properties of his sculpture, weighed the literary "sampling" of his epitaph, considered the specific language of the transfer of Aurelius Primitivus from Flavia to Flavius, pondered the intersection of philosophy and religion, analyzed the shape of Flavius' cup and its presence or absence in silver hoards, sized up the funerary monument within its tomb and the tomb within its necropolis, deployed sociology to understand the experiences of Isiac worshippers, and delved into inscriptions to understand female roles in the cult. Unlike any other department on a college or university campus, Classics or Ancient Mediterranean Studies is defined by a time and place, not a methodology. It encompasses and accommodates everything from literary analysis to underwater archaeology. Parachuting into each of these subdisciplines brings challenges, since they all have their own technical vocabulary, internal debates, and deep reservoirs of bibliography. And yet these manifold approaches are both useful and necessary.

Useful because they have allowed us to walk "all the way around" Flavius, to consider his experiences from multiple perspectives. While any one of those subdisciplinary inquiries would have been interesting and compelling on its own, only an orchestrated effort from multiple angles yields a three-dimensional vision. Flavius emerges as a drinker, a thinker, a man of letters, the descendant of someone perhaps once in fetters, a loving husband and generous stepfather, a striver, and a man simultaneously heroic in body and serious in disposition.

To return to the coin, one thing to note is that, while all the heads look alike, they occupy different positions, some relegated to "obstructed view seats" on the tier with the columns, others occupying the two visible rings closer to the action on the arena floor. Since seating was assigned according to legal status – the lower your rank, the higher you were in the

Epilogue

amphitheater – what we see on the coin are the three humblest tiers of spectators. This was not just a practice, as in our sporting arenas; instead, Roman law spelled out who could sit where. And to judge by our sources, interlopers occasionally took spots to which they were not entitled, and the Roman equivalent of "bouncers" sometimes intervened to set matters straight.[1] We do not know where Flavius would have sat if he secured a spot at a gladiatorial combat, but the effects of such a hierarchy-obsessed society definitely pervades his funerary monument. From its location amid tombs constructed by fancier folk to its verse epitaph, size, costly material, and leisure-forward content, so much of Flavius' presentation in death was intended to suggest that, even if he would have been seated toward the top of the Colosseum, he deserved to be closer.

Flavius was of course not alone in such a complex life nor in such striving. Though it can be a challenge to do so, we must remember that every dot in the amphitheater's crowd represented an individual who, like this book's protagonists, conducted a life full of goals, setbacks, struggles, and joys across all manner of different realms of life. We may be tempted to paint the ancient world with broad strokes, segmenting populations along different lines (legal status, gender, occupation, land of origin, urban and rural, etc.) and studying those categories. The lives of Flavius, Flavia, and Aurelius, however, urge us to recognize the diversity and complexity of individual experiences, particularly at the intersections and amid the tensions of those categories. Everyone looking on in that structure, as well as those who laid its stones, those hoisting its awnings, those fighting in its arena, those who fashioned the fighters' armor, those wrangling animals, those blaring their bronze instruments as accompaniment to the events, those hawking snacks, and those dragging away the dead – they all had names, faces, dreams, disappointments, scars from run-ins with disease or violence or accidents, distinct gaits, verbal accents, and personal turns of phrase. Even as this book has concentrated on the story of one individual, I hope it has opened the door for readers to consider, explore, and revel in the diversity of Roman lives in all their details, both within and beyond the amphitheater. Many more distinct stories remain to be told.

A multipronged approach to Flavius has been necessary because there simply is not substantial data for individuals beyond the Caesars and Constantines of the Roman world. As we move higher into the Colosseum's upper tiers, the evidentiary air becomes both thinner and more clouded by caricatured representations emanating from those closest to the action. Few of the folks taking the uppermost seats had the time, means, literacy, or inclination to document their experiences actively. If they did record something in a customary genre, it has rarely survived the manuscript tradition that saw medieval monks and others copy and recopy ancient texts, winnowing the corpus of classical literature according to the outlook of their own time.

This explains the prominence of *physical* things in this book, both as evidence for Flavius Agricola and also for putting his experiences and presentation in context. Everybody leaves behind garbage (though some more than others), and some scribble on walls, hand over a sack of coins for an engraver to chisel an inscription, or shovel still more for a carving above the incised words. And yet – as a historian trained in material culture, as an archaeologist who has spent summers on excavations, and as a scholar who digs through archives – I am painfully aware of what gets recorded and cataloged on a site, what gets tossed in the dump heap, what is left exposed to the elements, what gets covered and what makes its way into a museum, what is put on exhibit and what remains sequestered in storerooms. The last two chapters of this book document how, even for someone as well-off and as intentional about shaping his legacy as Flavius Agricola, the filtering of the past extends from literature to physical objects: what survives, what gets noticed, and what gets published. Without intrepid seventeenth-century antiquarians puzzling out letters by torchlight – despite threats of punishment – we would have Flavius' fascinating sculpture but not his verse epitaph. Similarly, clever scholarly sleuthing in the twentieth century reunited the sculpture with its inscription, and we should salute those efforts as well.

All of this suggests the degree to which we today are very much at the mercy of previous generations as we seek to locate scraps of the past, puzzle them out, and stitch them back together. Back to the coin again. Even its best-known feature, the Colosseum, looks different from what we encounter in Rome today because of interventions over the millennia: Statues decorate its arches, for instance. The amphitheater certainly commands our attention today, but it is not the only building visible on the coin. Two other structures squeeze into the curved space to its sides. The identity of the double-decker portico at right is not immediately clear – it could offer an architectural shorthand for the hulking public baths that Titus constructed on the amphitheater's north side – but the distinctive conical form allows the building at left to be recognized as the Meta Sudans. *Meta* most commonly denotes the conical turning posts at the ends of the Circus Maximus' spine, where chariots attempted to make hairpin turns. *Sudans* means "sweating," a reference to the water that emanated from the top of the cone at this monument, which likely functioned as a type of crowd-

Epilogue

cooling device like the misters sometimes found today in city parks, at music festivals, and on football sidelines. Here in the Colosseum valley, where Nero's megalomaniacal Domus Aurea had monopolized Rome's urban core only a decade earlier, the Meta Sudans took its place alongside the amphitheater, baths, and other offerings as part of the Flavians' endeavor to turn a private pleasure palace inside out and to return the space to the populace. That common link among public amenities presumably stood behind the Meta Sudan's inclusion on the coin: the Flavians wanted to show their full suite of offerings.[2]

The Meta Sudans was well-known enough to inspire imitations in Rome's provinces, yet you would have to tote an excellent guidebook or visit Rome with a knowledgeable topographer to identify this once-prominent monument today.[3] After its classy exterior had been stripped away over the ages, the masonry core of the Meta Sudans nevertheless stood into the twentieth century to a height of almost ten meters, about half of its original stature. In fact, it features prominently in paintings of the area over the ages. But under the Fascist government headed by Benito Mussolini, the above-ground portions were demolished to make way for the Fascists' preferred parade route among more attractive remnants of Rome's imperial domination. A bit more than a half-century later, excavations again revealed the fountain's foundations, which now lurk ankle height amid heavy grass within a pedestrian plaza.[4] Again we see the susceptibility of monuments, even those funded and celebrated numismatically by someone sitting in a special arena-side seat, to history's selective process of manipulation and exclusion.

• • •

This book has entailed two goals: to shed light on individual experience among the Roman lower classes through the lens of one monument and the lives it reflects, and to illustrate how that evidence has itself been shaped by the centuries since the monument's unearthing. Implicit in both goals is an effort to push readers to recognize how much they are products of their own time and place. In the first half of the book, Flavius' life points up Roman ways of life – such as dining with the dead, dining while dead, or being represented simultaneously in youth and old age – that can strike modern readers as odd. Yet at the same time close examinations of another culture might also prompt questions about our own oddities, such as rampant celebration of youth, dressing up as the characters in movies we are going to see, and snapping photos of ourselves in front of famous artworks.

The second half of the book, by illustrating how the past's physical remains have been packaged and repackaged over the centuries, should likewise prompt questions. How much are our methods for approaching the past themselves products of the discipline's history? To a great degree, I would wager. Here are just a few ways. There is little chance that this book, with its focus on the lived experience of an individual beyond the halls of power, would have been written even a half-century ago. Ever since the 1960s, as Classics has sought to become less classist, it has brought a broadening interest in the history of the masses and the recovery of marginalized lives. Additionally, as material evidence has been increasingly deployed to write social history, all manner of "artifacts" – finds, art, buildings, even whole cities – have been understood not only as passive data *reflective* of the past but as active *agents* in their own time. Titus' coin, in this view, not only documents what we are now missing from the Colosseum and its surroundings but also, we now recognize, shaped the perceptions of Rome's citizenry in the first century. And such a concentration on ancient viewers and ancient lives has extended to the so-called somatic turn, which has focused scholarly attention on the lived and embodied experience of historical figures, adding flesh, bone, noses, fingertips, and tastebuds to the names of people like Flavius, Flavia, and Aurelius. And the second part of this book – in tracing the trajectory of Flavius' sculpture and elucidating the various relationships it has had across various times, spaces, and societies – has also engaged in an approach known as "object biography," which emerged less than forty years ago. Its own trajectory as a methodology has been hastened by the digitization of archives and their posting online.

Voltaire famously wrote, "History is nothing but a pack of tricks we play on the dead." The case of Flavius Agricola seems to me both to prove his point and to make us consider what we have up our sleeves next.

Notes

1 The Monument, The Epitaph, and Their Setting

1. Visitors: www.statista.com/statistics/1137402/vatican-museums-attendance/.
2. Several other ancient graveyards stand on Vatican grounds. They permit fewer visitors to less pleasant surroundings; one, for example, rests underneath a parking garage rather than the largest church in Christendom: Liverani and Spinola 2010, esp. ch. 4.
3. For a history of the church, see McKitterick et al. 2013.
4. For a general introduction in English, see Toynbee and Ward-Perkins 1956.
5. Indianapolis Museum of Art inv. 72.148.
6. Wrede 1981, 103; Roller 2006, 43; Zanker and Ewald 2012, 153.
7. CIL 6.20383. On this sculpture: Wrede 1977, 403–405; Giuliano 1981, 159–160; Fejfer 2008, 130–131. Museo Nazionale Romano inv. 125829.
8. A survey of twenty-five cinerary urns with circular bases – predominantly cylindrical in shape – shows an average height to diameter ratio of 1.35. The diameter of Flavius' cutting is about 24 cm, which would suggest a height of approximately 32–33 cm. The examples range between ratios of 1.09 and 1.49, which would yield heights of 26–36 cm.
9. CIL 6.17895a = CIL 6.34112 = CLE 856.
10. Only in the twentieth century would a scholar reconnect the epitaph with the sculpture: Pucci 1968–1969. See Chapter 7 for many more details about the reaction that the inscription provoked.
11. For example, The Walters Art Museum inv. 23.180.
12. For additional examples of inscription-image connections in Roman funerary contexts, see Davies 2007 (esp. 46–49 for discussion of Flavius Agricola's monument).
13. For the fullest discussion of this drawing, see Claridge and Dodero 2022, vol. 2, 526–528, n. 306.
14. Several examples of the text's location: Musei Capitolini inv. 1999 (Wrede 1977, 395); Museo Vaticano Chiaramonti inv. 1565 (Wrede 1981, 99–100); Getty Villa inv. 73.AA.11 (Wrede 1990).
15. "[I]n lettere bellissime erano scolpiti i versi seguenti." The document was found in the nineteenth century among the records of G. Manzi,

a functionary in the Barberini library, and published in Melchiorri 1823, 163–167.
16. Regardless of their artist, drawings in Dal Pozzo's collection reveal a scrupulous attention to proportion (Vermeule 1966, 6; Claridge and Dodero 2022, 1.96–98), and this rendering of Flavius Agricola's sculpture is accurate, in terms of length and height, to within 2 percent.
17. Getty Villa inv. 73.AA.11, on which see Wrede 1990.
18. For example, 1.54 cm per character for *CIL* 6.9956 (from Palazzo Altemps inv. 174), 1.51–1.60 cm per character for *EphEp* 9.573 (from Castel Porziano Antiquarium).
19. The Circus enjoyed a relatively short lifespan, as excavations have shown that at least one tomb occupied part of its track by the last decades of the second century CE: Humphrey 1986, 545–552; Liverani 1999: 21–28; Gee 2011/2012.
20. Topography and history of the Vatican plain: Castagnoli 1992; Liverani 1999; Liverani and Spinola 2010, 11–22; Gee 2011/2012.
21. For much of the mid twentieth century, Tomb R was identified as Flavius' findspot, and scholars have used records relating to one tomb in discussions of the other. The result has been to take an already confusing situation – with records in seventeenth-century Latin and Italian that, while detailed for their time, were working through an extremely complex archaeological circumstance – and to pile on additional knots and jumbles. Castagnoli (1992, 87) reproduces the text of a document in the Vatican archive, which could not be clearer in identifying Tomb S as Flavius' proper home: "Excavating the foundation for the bronze column, namely the first on the left of someone facing toward the altar and praying at the *confessio* of St. Peter ... A very fine marble tomb was discovered with a reclining marble statue, half-nude, with the following inscription ... ." The document then offers a transcription of Flavius' epitaph.
22. Toynbee and Ward-Perkins 1956, 33–35; Liverani 1999, 139–144; Gee 2003, 38–39.
23. Tomb of St. Peter: Euseb. *Hist. Eccl.* 2.25; *Lib. Pont.* "Peter" 6. *Scavi Vaticani*: Appollonj Ghetti et al. 1951; Toynbee and Ward-Perkins 1956, esp. 127–134. "Old St. Peter's": McKitterick et al. 2013; Liverani and Spinola 2010, ch. 3. Nero and St. Peter: Gee 2011/2012, 72–75.
24. Appollonj Ghetti et al. 1951, 76, and fig. 52. A travertine threshold block remains in place, yet later interventions stripped away the accompanying doorjambs (likely also in travertine). The jamb-less opening stands about 1.2 m wide; its height was likely around 1.3 m.
25. For the excavation, see Chapter 7.
26. Appollonj Ghetti et al. 1951, 71. The decoration on the interior was divided into lower- and upper-zones. The former, occupying roughly the first meter above the pavement, consisted largely of the *arcosolia*; panes of yellow and purplish paint occupied the remaining areas. A simple cornice ringed the interior, above which were positioned a series of niches alternating between rectilinear and apsidal. They likely circled the entire interior of the tomb.
27. Interior dimensions: Appollonj Ghetti et al. 1951, 71.

28. The monument's width may have squeezed within the *arcosolium*, but even without accounting for any feet underneath the surviving portion of the sculpture (as are depicted in a seventeenth-century drawing), it would not have fit vertically, as the top of the *lectus* would not fit within the *arcosolium's* curve. Appollonj Ghetti et al. (1951, 74–75) report another simple sarcophagus under that *arcosolium*, but it is known only from Baroque-era records, and thus might be misassigned to Tomb S.
29. Now, there is admittedly a degree of circularity in this argument, since scholars have drawn on stylistic features of Flavius' sculpture to date the structure that housed it. The common assumption, almost certainly correct, is that they were imagined in relationship with one another. In any case, all the evidence, both architectural and sculptural, suggests that the artwork and building were constructed within a short time of one another.
30. A major break in Flavius' monument appears on the front left corner of the piece, where the upright of the couch was at some point cleaved off and then repaired. We cannot confirm that this break occurred when Baroque workmen sought to lift the artwork from deep below the basilica's floor, but – just like when you try to pivot a couch around tight quarters today – that front corner would have been the toughest angle in the extraction process.

2 The Person, A Life, and Its Presentation

1. Hartnett 2017a, 247–255.
2. Wrede 1981, 107; Liverani and Spinola 2010, 134; Zanker and Ewald 2012, 153–155.
3. The *cognomen* Agricola is well attested in the imperial period, with seven members of the senatorial class holding the name, and sixty-two other examples of individuals: Kajanto 1965, 82–84, 321.
4. Individuals who were granted citizenship followed a similar pattern. For more on naming conventions, see Solin 2016.
5. We simply cannot know for sure that Flavius was not a freedman himself, since during the second century freedpeople were dropping the habit of designating that status epigraphically, no longer using *l[ibertus]* or *lib[ertus]*, "freedman." The *cognomen* Agricola, "farmer," does not offer resolution either. Kajanto (1965, 83) notes that 77 percent of the uses of occupational *cognomina* come from the free population under the empire. Yet there are exceptions of using Latin job titles for enslaved peoples: for example, *Mensor*, "surveyor" (*Dig.* 23.2.57a), and *Custos*, something like "warden" (*CIL* 10.557) At least three confirmed enslaved people with the name *Agricola* are attested: C. Helvius Agricola: *CIL* 6.19256; Agricola Pompei Valentis servus: *Dig.* 48.18.1.22; Agricolae Caesar. N. ser.: *CIL* 6.8533.
6. Cic. *De Or.* 2.263, *Phil.* 5.19; [Cicero] *In Sall.* 19; Catull. 44; Hor. *Ep.* 1.8.12, *Od.* 2.6.5; Mart. 4.79; Juv. 11.65–74.
7. For the attractions of Tibur in the late first century, see Stat. *Silv.* 1.3.

8. Little evidence connects the Flavians to Tibur other than the completion of work on a tunnel for the Aqua Claudia near Tibur: *ILS* 3152. On the Albanum Domitiani: Darwall-Smith 1994.
9. *AE* 1945, 136: *monumentum mihi faciatis ... ex IS III n(ummum).*
10. Duncan-Jones 1982, 78–79 and 126–127 (discussion), 93–99 and 162–163 (raw data).
11. Subsistence: Hopkins 1978, 66–67. Legionary pay: Speidel 1992.
12. Refurbishment: *CIL* 14.2115 (Lanuvium). Paving: *CIL* 11.6127 (Forum Sempronii); *AE* 1919, 64 (Velitrae). Endowment: *CIL* 14.2793 (Gabii).
13. Stat. *Silv.* 5.1.228–231: *nil longior aetas / carpere, nil aevi poterunt vitiare labores: / sic cautum membris; tantas venerabile marmor / spirat opes.*
14. Von Hesberg 2002, esp. 47–48.
15. Titus Aelius Tyrannus: *AE* 1945, 134; Titus Matuccius Pallas: Appollonj Ghetti et al. 1951, 43; Tullia Secunda: *AE* 1987, 154; 2010, 168; 2018, 113; 1987, 148.
16. Liverani and Spinola 2010, 77–83, 92–108, with notes.
17. *C(aius) Valerius Herma fecit et Flaviae T(iti) f(iliae) Olympiadi co(n)iugi et Valeriae Maximae filiae et C(aio) Valerio Olympiano filio et suis libertis libertabusque posterisque eodem*; Liverani and Spinola 2010, 101–103. For more on this phenomenon, see Borbonus 2014; 2021.
18. Appollonj Ghetti et al. 1951, 71.
19. Appollonj Ghetti et al. 1951, 71–75.
20. Fejfer 2008, 122–125. Tomb H has two life-sized marble portraits: Liverani and Spinola 2010, 92–108 (with previous bibliography).
21. Liverani and Spinola 2010, 134.
22. For example, Mayer 2012 to be read with Wallace-Hadrill 2013.
23. Petr. *Sat.* 37, 76.
24. Hackworth Petersen 2006, 1–16.
25. Petronius has Trimalchio boozily describe his desired tomb after a notable preface: "It is silly for a man to deck out his house while alive, but to neglect the one where he must dwell far longer." Petr. 71: *Valde enim falsum est vivo quidem domos cultas esse, non curari eas, ubi diutius nobis habitandum est.*
26. *CIL* X.1030: *Naevoleia L(uci) lib(erta) Tyche sibi et C(aio) Munatio Fausto Aug(ustali) et pagano cui decuriones consensu populi bisellium ob merita eius decreverunt hoc monimentum Naevoleia Tyche libertis suis libertabusq(ue) et C(ai) Munati Fausti viva fecit.* On this tomb: Hackworth Petersen 2006, 65–68; Laird 2015, 53–68.
27. Bücheler 1895–1897. A number have been reproduced with commentary and English translation by Courtney (1995).
28. Milnor 2014.
29. Schmidt 2014, 764.
30. For parallel patterns in epigraphic meter, see Adams 1999. My thanks to Matthew Gorey for puzzling through the epitaph's meter and for the reference.
31. *Rhet. Her.* 4.18, citing Ennius frag. 108.
32. For example, Ovid deploys polysyndeton to capture how thoughts flit through Daedalus' mind (*Met.* 8.215–216): *hortaturque sequi damnosasque erudit artes et movet ipse suas et nati respicit alas.*
33. Ov. *Tr.* 4.10, *Met.* 5.494. For more, see Fairweather 1987. Cf. Ov. *Tr.* 3.3.73–74.

Notes to pages 32–37

34. Hor. *Carm.* 1.7. Plancus was consul in 42 BCE, supporting M. Antony before reading the winds and swapping allegiance to Octavian in 32 BCE. He proposed granting the name *Augustus* to the latter. His mausoleum rises triumphantly above Gaeta, where his epitaph (*CIL* 10.6087) lists his accomplishments.
35. Hor. *Carm* 1.7.17–22: *sic tu sapiens finire memento / tristitiam vitaeque labores / molli, Plance, mero, seu te fulgentia signis / castra tenent seu densa tenebit / Tiburis umbra tui. Teucer Salamina patremque / cum fugeret, tamen uda Lyaeo / tempora populea fertur uinxisse corona.*
36. SHA, *Hadrian* 25.9–10.
37. "Forty-Three Translations of Hadrian's 'Animula, Vagula, Blandula,'" coldewey.cc, http://coldewey.cc/post/17072720047/forty-three-translations-of-hadrians-animula.
38. Flavius' description of Flavia as *gratissima coniuncx* copies, in both word order and metrical position, Jupiter's address of Juno in *Aeneid* 10.607. Similarly, Flavius' idiosyncratic and emphatic phrase *idem ego sum* of line 2 mimics Ovid (*Epistulae ex ponto* 4.3.11–18), which has three consecutive couplets beginning with *ille ego* or *ille ego sum* before switching to *idem ego sum* followed by a second-person verb, as in Flavius' epitaph. Some editions have *ille ego sum* in line 17.
39. *CLE* 1111 = *CIL* 6.10097 with Courtney 1995, 330–331: *quondam ego Pierio vatum monimenta canore / doctus cycneis enumerare modis, / doctus Maeonio spirantia carmina versu / dicere, Caesareo carmina nota foro.* See also Koortbojian 1996, 227–230.
40. Milnor 2009.
41. *CIL* 14.292: *decurioni col(oniae) Ost(iensis) fla(mini) divi Vespasiani, patrono fabrum navalium Ost(iensium).*
42. For example, Wallace-Hadrill 1994, 143–147. For histories and critiques of the notion, see Hackworth Petersen 2006; Mayer 2012, 168–170.
43. Joshel 1992; D'Ambra 1988; 1998, 46–48.
44. Dunbabin 2003, 103–140; Roller 2006, 22–45; Davies 2007.
45. Zanker and Ewald 2012, 185.
46. For communal feasting across multiple social registers, see Donahue 2004. Examples of *lectisternia* (feasts for gods): Livy 5.13.6–8, 22.1.18–20; *CIL* 5.5272. Meal for a dedication: *CIL* 10.1450. Multiple meals for a religious guild: *CIL* 6.10234. Lower-class group meal: *CIL* 14.2112.
47. Ellis 2004.
48. Hartnett 2017b.
49. Grain distributions: Aldrete and Mattingly 1999. *Sportulae*: Mart. 8.49.10; Juv. 3.249; Duncan-Jones 2008.
50. Roman couches: Mols 1999, 35–52, 124–129; 2007–2008.
51. Musei Capitolini inv. 2108; Roller 2006, 28–38. Handsome servers: Petr. *Sat.* 74; Philo *de vit. cont.* 50–52; Sen. *Ep.* 119–114; Juv. 5.56–62; Mart. 12.70.9.
52. Roller 2006, 27–30 (quotation on 30).
53. Joshel 1992.
54. Cic. *De Or.* 1.27: ... *ut dies inter eos curiae fuisse videretur, convivium Tusculani.*

55. Mart. 14.135: *Nec fora sunt nobis nec sunt vadimonia nota: hoc opus est, pictis accubuisse toris.*
56. Veyne 2000; Mayer 2012; Courrier 2014, esp. Part II.
57. Hallett 2005, 297–299; see also Davies 2018.
58. Polyb. 6.53.
59. Verism: Hallett 2005, 279–287; Fejfer 2008, 263–269; Rose 2008; Pollini 2012, 13–68; Maschek 2022, esp. 186–191.
60. Hallett 2005, 46, 57.
61. Hallett 2005, 216.
62. Fejfer 2008, 200–207; Zanker and Ewald 2012, 186.
63. Hallett 2005, 292.
64. Hallett 2005, 296.
65. For another treatment of the cup of Flavius' monument, see Bender 2020.
66. Bronze parallels: Tassinari 1993, 1.55, 2.98–109 (fifty-eight examples); silver: Museo Archeologico Nazionale di Napoli inv. 145518 (found amid the silver treasure of the Casa del Menandro, Pompeii, 1.10.4).
67. Tassinari 1993, 1.51–61, 1.232, 2.93–141; Allison 2004, 56–58.
68. Tassinari 1993, 1.232.
69. For an overview and further bibliography, see Painter 2001, 14–15.
70. Tomb of Vestorius Priscus: Clarke 2003, 185–203.
71. Wrede 1981, 247–248, cat. 139.
72. Wrede 1981, cat. 121–158.
73. Wrede 1981, 260–261, cat. 174, pl. 24.5. IG 14.1990: ΣΑΤΟΡΝΕΙΝΟΣ ΕΓΩ ΚΙΚΛΗΣΚΟΜΑΙ ΕΚ ΔΕ ΜΕ ΠΑΙΔΟΣ ΕΙΣ ΔΙΟΝΥΣΟΥ ΑΓΑΛΜ ΕΘΕΣΑΝ ΜΗΤΗΠ Ε ΠΑΤΡ Ε. Zanker and Ewald 2012, 198–199. Portraits in the guise of Dionysus/Bacchus in literature: Stat. *Silv.* 2.7.124–131; Ov. *Tr.* 1.7.1–4; Apul. *Met.* 8.7.
74. On this phenomenon: Wrede 1981; Hallett 2005, 199–204; Fejfer 2008, 127–130; Zanker and Ewald 2012, 195–199; Borg 2019, 191–290.

3 Flavia Primitiva: Wife, Mother, *Casta Cultrix*

1. *CIL* 14.2298.
2. For some general characteristics of Roman slavery and "social death": Bradley 1994 (esp. ch. 2). Freedman reliefs: George 2005; Borg 2012; Mouritsen 2011 (esp. ch. 2).
3. *CIL* 6.10230 = *ILS* 8394: *Quibus de causeis quom omnium bonarum feminarum simplex similis- que esse laudatio soleat, quod naturalia bona propria custodia servata varietates verborum non desiderent, satisque sit eadem omnes bona fama digna fecisse, et quia adquirere novas laudes mulieri sit arduom, quom minoribus varietatibus vita iactetur, necessario communia esse colenda, ne quod amissum ex iustis praecepteis cetera turpet, eo majorem laudem omnium carissima mihi mater meruit, quod modestia, probitate, pudicitia, obsequio, lanificio', diligentia, fide par similisque cetereis probeis feminis fuit.* Translation of Lindsay 2004, which offers a strong resource on the inscription.
4. Cf. *CIL* 6.1527 = *ILS* 8393 (the "Laudatio Turiae"). See Riess 2012.

5. Thuc. 2.45.2: εἰ δέ με δεῖ καὶ γυναικείας τι ἀρετῆς, ὅσαι νῦν ἐν χηρείᾳ ἔσονται, μνησθῆναι, βραχείᾳ παραινέσει ἅπαν σημανῶ. τῆς τε γὰρ ὑπαρχούσης φύσεως μὴ χείροσι γενέσθαι ὑμῖν μεγάλη ἡ δόξα καὶ ἧς ἂν ἐπ' ἐλάχιστον ἀρετῆς πέρι ἢ ψόγου ἐν τοῖς ἄρσεσι κλέος ᾖ.
6. Pomeroy 1995, 229.
7. *OLD* s.v. 1–3, 11.
8. *OLD* s.v. 6. For a similar use, see *AE* 1998: 1576–1578 (Tunisia).
9. Architectural definition: *OLD* s.v. 3–4. Cf. Cic. *Phil.* 2. Metaphorical sensibility: *OLD* s.v. 7. Cf. Val. Max. 5.1.ext.1.
10. *Solacium* describes a source of relief, comfort, or consolation in the face of a misfortune (cf. *OLD* s.v. 1, which spells out circumstances such as the death of a friend: Cic. *Div. Caec.* 7; Ov. *Met.* 5.191), even carrying with it the sense that a *solacium* helps to make up for the loss (*OLD* s.v. 2a).
11. *CIL* 6.9499 = *ILS* 7472: *vero plus superaque parens*.
12. Lelis, Percy, and Verstraete 2003.
13. Treggiari (1991) is the classic treatment.
14. On widows in Rome: McGinn 1999; 2008, esp. ch. 2. Kraus (1994, 73) suggests that as many as 30 percent of adult women in the Roman world were widows. For American women in 2022, the figure is closer to 8 percent: 'Marital Status of the United States Population in 2022, by Sex,' statista, www.statista.com/statistics/242030/marital-status-of-the-us-population-by-sex/.
15. Evans Grubbs 2002, 198–202, for sources and discussion.
16. On the Augustan marriage legislation: Suet. *Aug.* 34; Cass. Dio 54.16.1–2, 56.1, 56.10; Tac. *Ann.* 3.25, 28. For more, see Treggiari 1991, 37–80; Evans Grubbs 2002, 83–87.
17. See *BGU* 1052 for an example of a marriage contract from Roman Egypt that spells out similar circumstances, detailing how Apollonius "will furnish Thermion, as his wedded wife, with all necessities and clothing according to his means."
18. *CIL* 6.18817: *obligati amori pariter*.
19. Huemoeller 2020 on the monument and the phenomenon more broadly.
20. Adoption: Lindsay 2009. In general on Roman families: Dixon 1992, esp. ch. 1.
21. Classic studies of Greco-Roman Isis: Witt 1971; Takács 1995. Isis' arrival and resistance in Republican Rome: Apul. *Met.* 11.30; Tert. *Ad Nat.* 1.10; Cass. Dio 40.47, 42.26; Val. Max. 1.3.4. Bacchus: Livy 39.8–19.
22. Pfeiffer 2018. Important intervening episodes: Cass. Dio 47.15.4, 53.2.4–5, 54.6, 66.24.2; Tac. *Ann.* 2.85.5; Jos. *AJ* 18.66, 19.3.70–80; *BJ* 7.4.
23. Adherence to Pharian Isis in Rome is implied by Tib. 1.3.23–32. On Isis Pharia, see Bricault 2019, 160–167. *Pharia* also parallels the circumlocution of Lyaeus deployed twice by Flavius. It functions as both an alternative name for Bacchus/Dionysus and a proxy for wine.
24. On religion in Rome, see Beard, North, and Price 1998; Rüpke 2007; 2016; 2018; Mackey 2022.
25. On this altar: Dobbins 1992.
26. Plin. *HN* 28.11.
27. Macr. *Sat.* 3.9.7–8.

28. Met. 11.2: *quoquo nomine, quoquo ritu, quaqua facie te fas est invocare: tu meis iam nunc extremis aerumnis subsiste, tu fortunam collapsam adfirma, tu saevis exanclatis casibus pausam pacemque tribue.*
29. Met. 11.5: *En adsum ... rerum naturae parens, elementorum omnium domina, saeculorum progenies initialis, summa numinum, regina manium, prima caelitum, deorum dearumque facies uniformis.*
30. Met. 11.5: *Aethiopes utrique ... Aegyptii caerimoniis me propriis percolentes appellant vero nomine reginam Isidem.*
31. On henotheism and Isis, see Mazurek 2022, 72–76.
32. OLD s.v. 1–2. Generic descriptor: Malaise and Veymiers 2018, 495.
33. In addition to those discussed below: CIL 8.9050, 11.4631; AE 1920, 105. Examples of *cultrices* of this sort in non-Christian literature: Stat. *Theb.* 12.30; *Silv.* 5.1.191.
34. *Sacerdotes*: RICIS 501/0162, 704/0401, 501/0174 (*pastophorus*), 501/0183 (*melanep-(h)ore*: cf. Plut. *Isis and Serapis* 39 [366D-E]), 605/0103 (*ornatrix*). In general, see Malaise and Veymiers 2018, 495–496.
35. It is difficult to know what to make of a woman from Capena named Varia Italia, who was honored by the city's town councilors, Augustales, and others as a *sacerdos et cultrix Cereris et Veneris*: AE 1954, 166. Why the two titles, when one would seem to supersede the other, unless Varia was a priestess in one cult and only a devotee of the other? An inscription listing thirty-eight individual *cultores* of Jupiter Latius includes at least three women, which suggests that *cultor/cultrix* was something of a catch-all: CIL 11.6310. Similarly vague are the terms *sacrorum* and *Isidis sacrorum*, which are applied more to women than men: Heyob 1975, 107–108.
36. Bubastis: RICIS 503/1113, 501/0169. Memfiana: CIL 6.11271.
37. Hor. *Od.* 4.5.21–24.
38. Williams 1999, 96–124.
39. Juv. 6.487–491; Ov. *Ars Am.* 1.77–78; Mart. 11.47.3–4. See also Ov. *Amores* 2.2.24–25; *Ars Am.* 3.633–637; Juv. 9.20–25; Josephus, *Jewish Antiquities* 18.65–80.
40. Apul. *Met.* 11.19: *quod enim sedulo percontaveram difficile religionis obsequium et castimoniorum abstinentiam satis arduam cautoque circumspectu vitam, quae multis casibus subiacet, esse muniendam.*
41. Plut. *Isis and Serapis* 2: σώφρονι μὲν ἐνδελεχῶς διαίτῃ καὶ βρωμάτων πολλῶν καὶ ἀφροδισίων.
42. Prop. 2.33a.1–6: *Tristia iam redeunt iterum sollemnia nobis: / Cynthia iam noctes est operata decem. / atque utinam pereant, Nilo quae sacra tepente / misit matronis Inachis Ausoniis! / quae dea tam cupidos totiens divisit amantis, / quaecumque illa fuit, semper amara fuit.*
43. Prop. 2.28.59–62. Other poets share similar gripes, even riffing on one another: Tib. 1.23.23–34; Ov. *Am.* 3.9.33–40.
44. Ov. *Am.* 1.8.70–85; Prop. 4.5.33–34. The connection between abstaining from sex (and sometimes also food) and Isis worship extends further afield to Greco-Roman novels, Neoplatonic philosophy, and even early Christian authors, who found in Isis worshippers models of religious chastity: Xen. *Eph.* 3.11.2–5, 5.4.5–7; Porph. *De Abst.* 4.6–9; Tert. *Ad Uxor.* 1.6 (cf. *Castit.* 13, *Monog.* 17, *Ieiun.* 16).

45. *CIL* 6.32458 = *IG* 14.1366 = *SIRIS* 433 = *RICIS* 501/0174: [*Hic iacet Ogygii Bacc*] *hi dei nota [sacerd]os [pastophorus]quae deae Nilo[tidis usque pu]dica.* Cf. the poetic epitaph of Sidonia Felix, who "had been a priestess of the rattle-shaking goddess of Memphis" before she died at 19 as a *virgo: ILA* 2.809 = *SIRIS* 789 = *RICIS* 704/0401: *Memphidos haec fuerat divae sistrata{e} sacerdos.* For another *virgo*, Volumnia Isiaca, see *CIL* 6.36589 = *SIRIS* 450a = *RICIS* 501/0176.
46. *CIL* 14.343 = *SIRIS* 539 = *RICIS* 503/1119. The father is named as Cornelius Victorinus Isiacus here; elsewhere (*CIL* 14.4290 = *SIRIS* 538 = *RICIS* 503/1118) he appends *Isiacus et Anubianus* to his *tria nomina*. See also *ILS* 9442 = *SIRIS* 586 = *RICIS* 512/0101: *Memphi, glegori*. This inscription pertains to a situation like Flavia's, where another mother favoring Isis is linked with her offspring. On this sarcophagus from Ravenna, however, Tetratia Isias was buried with her daughter and is hailed as a "most chaste spouse," *coniugi castissimae*. On the side of the sarcophagus, two figures appear, with one apparently anointing the other's eye; above them, the Latin transliteration of Greek words, "Memphius, be watchful," appear. An explanation of the scene's meaning derives from a Greek poem transliterated into Latin script that appears on the sarcophagus. It explains that the husband has prepared his wife – the Isiac initiate – for death, salvation, and mystic visions. Accordingly, she has taken on a new name still more evocative of the goddess. Here, then, we have a motherly figure deeply engaged with Isis whose chastity is celebrated prominently.
47. *CIL* 14.352 = *SIRIS* 536 = *RICIS* 503/1115.
48. Apul. *Met.* 11.6: *Quodsi sedulis obsequiis et religiosis ministeriis et tenacibus castimoniis numen nostrum promerueris, scies ultra statuta fato tuo spatia vitam quoque tibi prorogare mihi tantum licere.*
49. The connection between *casta* and *sedula* is in fact tightened by the use of the enclitic *-que* to join them, by contrast with the *et* that links *sedula* and the description of Flavia's appearance. I thank an anonymous reviewer for this astute point.
50. Apul. *Met.* 11.23: . . . *decem continuis illis diebus cibariam voluptatem coercerem neque ullum animal essem et invinius essem.*
51. Apul. 11.15: *Nec tibi natales ac ne dignitas quidem, vel ipsa, qua flores, usquam doctrina profuit, sed lubrico virentis aetatulae ad serviles delapsus voluptates curiositatis inprosperae sinistrum praemium reportasti.*
52. Ov. *Ep. ex Pont.* 1.1.51–54: *Vidi ego linigerae numen uiolasse fatentem / Isidis Isiacos ante sedere focos. / Alter ob huic similem priuatus lumine culpam / clamabat media se meruisse uia.*
53. A funerary inscription found on the Via Latina in Rome (*RICIS* 501/214) mentions an *aretalogus Graecus*, presumably a singer of aretalogies in Greek.
54. Maroneia aretalogy, ll. 24–26 (αὕτη τὸ δίκαιον ἔστησεν, ἵν' ἕκαστος ἡμῶν . . . ζῆν ἀπὸ τῶν ἴσων εἰδῆι), 29–31 (αἱ πόλεις εὐστάθησαν, οὐ τὴν βίαν νομικὸν ἀλλὰ [τ]ὸν νόμον ἀβίαστον εὑροῦσαι).
55. Cyme aretalogy, ll. 25, 26, 29, 30, 35, 37.
56. Morgan 2007.
57. Apul. *Met.* 11.21: *nam et infernum claustra et salutis tutelam in deae manu posita, ipsamque traditionem ad instar voluntariae mortis et precariae salutis celebrari, quippe cum transactis vitae temporibus iam in ipso finitae lucis limine*

constitutos, quis tamen tuto possint magna religionis committi, silentia, numen deae soleat elicere et sua providentia quodam modo renatos ad novae reponere rursus salutis curricula.
58. Apul. *Met.* 11.23: *Accessi confinium mortis et calcato Proserpinae limine per omnia vectus elementa remeavi.*
59. Gasparini 2016.
60. *IGUR* 2.836 = *RICIS* 501/0164: [ἦλθε]ς, τέκνον γλυκύτατον, ἀθάνατον [εἰς δῶ]μα, ἀείζων, Μάρκε Ὀρτώριε Ἐλεύθερε, [ἐτῶν] δέκα, μηνῶν τριῶν, ἡμερῶν τριῶν. [νῦν δ]οίη σοι Ὀσείρις τὸ ψυχρὸν ὕδωρ.
61. Gasparini 2016, 128–133 (quotation on 132). Similar phrasing appears numerous times across epitaphs in Greek and Latin, in Rome, North Africa, and Palestine.
62. *I. Métrique* 52: σοὶ δὲ Ὀσείριδος ἁψνὸν ὕδωρ Εἶσις χαρίσαιτο. *IG* 14.2098 = *IGUR* 2.1042 = *RICIS* 501/0196: εὐψύχι μετὰ τοῦ Ὀσείριδος.
63. For a similar sentiment about a life course approach to Roman social history, see Harlow and Lawrence 2002.
64. *Met.* 11.24.
65. *Met.* 11.25: *Tu quidem sancta et humani generis sospitatrix perpetua, semper fovendis mortalibus munifica, dulcem matris adfectationem miserorum casibus tribuis.*

4 Flavia Primitiva, Experience, and Community in the Iseum Campense

1. Mart. 7.34.4–5: *Quid Nerone peius? Quid thermis melius Neronianis?*
2. Thuno 2015.
3. Lembke 1994a, 65–73; 2018, 30–36.
4. Domitian and the Iseum: Pfeiffer 2018.
5. The Iseum Capitolinum and Iseum Metellinum are well-evidenced, while the Regionary Catalogs (fourth-century listings of Rome's monuments according to each of the fourteen regions) name two other shrines, to Isis Patricia and Isis Athenodora. For more on all of these, see *LTUR* 3.107–115.
6. *Met.* 11.26: *raptim constrictis sarcinulis … Romam versus profectionem dirigo, tutusque prosperitate ventorum ferentium Augusti portum celerrime pervenio ac dehinc carpento pervolavi, vesperaque, quam dies insequebatur Iduum Decembrium, sacrosanctam istam civitatem accedo. Nec ullum tam praecipuum mihi exinde studium fuit quam cotidie supplicare summo numini reginae Isidis, quae de templi situ sumpto nomine Campensis summa cum veneratione propitiatur. Eram cultor denique adsiduus, fani quidem advena, religionis autem indigena.*
7. Stanford Digital Forma Urbis Romae Project, https://formaurbis.stanford.edu/.
8. Lembke 1994a, n. D55; Sorek 2010, 75–88; Pfeiffer 2018.
9. Lembke 1994a, ns. D3–5.
10. Steps: Clausen 2015, 131–135.
11. Lanciani 1883; Lembke 2018, 35.
12. Clausen 2015, 159, and the following diagrams: B8a (chronological distribution), B8b (stylistic distribution), B9 (material distribution). On Egyptian art in Roman contexts: Swetnam-Burland 2015; Pearson 2021.
13. Brenk 2022.

Notes to pages 66–75

14. Heinemann 2018.
15. Foucault 1986.
16. This is particularly true for the Campus Martius, which has been inhabited continuously since antiquity, even when the city shrunk from its ancient high of one-million-plus inhabitants to fewer than 50,000 in the Middle Ages: Krautheimer 1980; Dey 2021.
17. For reflections on reconstructions of this sanctuary (and more generally), both digital and virtual, see Mol 2018; 2020.
18. Lembke (1994a) offers the go-to resource for the elements of the Iseum Campense and their current location. Statues of Nile and Tiber: Lembke 1994a ns. E1 and E2. Capitoline lions: ns. E10 and E11. Domitian's obelisk: n. D55. Marble foot: n. E6.
19. Apul. *Met.* 11.7–11.
20. Lucius continues: "Some shaped like creatures represented compressed expressions of profound concepts, in others the tops and tails of letters were knotted, coiled, interwoven like vine-tendrils to hide their meaning from profane and ignorant eyes." Apul. *Met.* 11.22: *profert quosdam libros litteris ignorabilibus praenotatos, partim figuris cuiusce modi animalium concepti sermonis compendiosa verba suggerentes, partim nodosis et in modum rotae tortuosis capreolatimque condensis apicibus a curiositate profanorum lectione munita.*
21. Apul. *Met.* 11.23: *Quaeras forsitan satis anxie, studiose lector, quid deinde dictum, quid factum; dicerem, si dicere liceret, cognosceres, si liceret audire. Sed parem noxam contraherent et aures et lingua ... ergo quod solum potest sine piaculo ad profanorum intellegentias enuntiari, referam.*
22. Tib. 1.3.23–32: *Quid tua nunc Isis mihi, Delia, quid mihi prosunt / Illa tua totiens aera repulsa manu, / Quidve, pie dum sacra colis, pureque lavari / Te— memini— et puro secubuisse toro? / Nunc, dea, nunc succurre mihi—nam posse meder / Picta docet templis multa tabella tuis—, / Ut mea votivas persolvens Delia voces / Ante sacras lino tecta fores sedeat / Bisque die resoluta comas tibi dicere laudes / Insignis turba debeat in Pharia.*
23. Lembke 1994b.
24. Lembke 1994b; 2018.
25. For the fullest treatment of these paintings, see Miller 2018.
26. Apul. *Met.* 11.22.8 and 11.23.1 (purchases), 11.24.4 (*epulae, convivia, ientaculum*), 11.27.4 (*epulae*). Cf. Tert. *Apol.* 39.5–6. For more, see Graf 2017.
27. More on the sensory experiences of Isis sanctuaries and in religious settings more broadly: Nuno, Ezquerra, and Maza 2021.
28. Important works along these lines: Durkheim 1912; McGuire 2002.
29. The sculpture was discovered in the Middle Ages underneath the church of Santo Stefano and interestingly gives its name to the church – Saint Stephen of the Baboon/Macaco, later corrupted to simply del Cacco. It thus stood in the southern section of the Iseum: Lembke 1994a, 238.
30. AE 1977, 15; 1994, 104.
31. Swetnam-Burland 2015, 60–63. CIL 6.857 (as reconstructed by Swetnam-Burland): *[locus] adsi[g]natus A. Caelio / [et] ... iliano Maximo / [curatoribus] aed[ium] sacr[arum |operumque] pu[blicorum] ded[icatum] / ... [k] sept[embris] Quintillo [et] Prisco co[n]s[ulibus].*

32. Vittozzi 2006, 71–73; Swetnam-Burland 2018.
33. Cohen 1985.

5 To Eat Is to Be? Flavius' Worldview in Perspective

1. Zanker 1995, esp. ch. 5.
2. Elsner 2007, 216–224.
3. See Cic. *Fam.* 4.5.4, *Att.* 9.7.1; Sept. *Poet.* 17. For a meaning closer to "spirit" as separate from the body, see *CIL* 10.3969.
4. 1.1: πρῶτον δὲ πάντων τέτακται τὸ περὶ τοῦ φιλοσοφεῖν παρὰ πότον.
5. Barraco 2020.
6. Dunbabin 1986, 196–199.
7. Petr. 34.10.
8. Dunbabin 1986, 224–230.
9. The butterfly is labeled as ψυχίον, a version of ψυχή, "soul." "Life is a stage": σκηνὴ ὁ βίος.
10. εὐσεβοῦ σκύβαλα.
11. Dunbabin 1986, 228–229.
12. *CIL* 6.18131: *quod edi bibi, mecum habeo, quod reliqui perdidi*.
13. *CIL* 6.15258: *balnea, vina, venus corrumpunt corpora nostra; sed vitam faciunt balnea, vina, venus*. For the broader theme and more texts, see Kajanto 1965.
14. Museo Archeologico Nazionale di Napoli inv. 109982, discovered in a tanner's workshop at 1.5.2.
15. Frier 2000; Scheidel 2009.
16. Garnsey 1988; James 2020.
17. Tac. *Ann.* 15.18.
18. Garnsey 1988, 222–225.
19. Floods: Aldrete 2007. Fires, real and in the imaginary: Barrett 2020; Closs 2020. Other urban dangers: Juv. 3.
20. Duncan-Jones 1996; 2018. Cass. Dio 72.14–15.
21. Beckmann 2011.
22. Auguet 1994, 195.
23. Bohak 2015; Faraone 2018.
24. Dunbabin 2003, 1–4 (translation and discussion). *CIL* 6.25531 = *CLE* 1106: *Qui dum vita datast, semper vivebat avarus, heredi parcens, invidus ipse sibi. Hie accumbentem sculpi genialiter arte se iussit docta post sua fata manu, ut saltem recubans in morte quiescere posset securaque iacens ille quiete frui. Filius a dextra residet, qui castra secutus occidit ante patris funera maesta sui. Sed quid defunctis prodest genialis imago? Hoc potius ritu vivere debuerant.*
25. Prop. 2.33a, on which see Miller 1981–1982.
26. Prop. 2.33a.21–22: *at tu, quae nostro, nimium pia, causa dolore es / noctibus his vacui, ter faciamus iter*. Some debate circles around the text of this line. For *nimium pia*, see Shackleton Bailey 1956, 129.
27. Cohen 2011.
28. I Corinthians 7: 12–16.
29. Tert. *Ad Uxorem* 2.3–7.

Notes to pages 87–94

30. Livy 4.6.
31. Weaver 1986.
32. On this issue, see Cusmà Piccione 2017, esp. ch. 2.
33. Bacchus: Livy 39.8–19. Second Punic War: Livy 25.1.6–12.
34. Mathisen 2009.
35. Baslez 2002; Broekaert 2012.
36. Birley 1971.
37. Hor. *Ep.* 9: *curam metumque ... iuvat dulci Lyaeo solvere.*
38. Most recently on Roman conceptions of the afterlife: King 2020.
39. SHA, *Hadr.* 25.9: *in loca pallidula, rigida, nudula.* See also Chapter 2.
40. Verg. *Aen.* 6.608–617, 698–702, 743–751.
41. Cic. *Tusc.* 1.9.18: *sunt enim qui discessum animi a corpore putent esse mortem; sunt qui nullum censeant fieri discessum, sed una animum et corpus occidere, animumque in corpore extingui ... quid sit porro ipse animus, aut ubi, aut unde, magna dissensio est.*
42. Zanker and Ewald 2012.

6 Meeting Flavius at the Tomb

1. Of many news stories the newsletter generated: Roisin Burke, *Irish Examiner*, August 5, 2019, www.irishexaminer.com/breakingnews/ireland/beer-doesnt-tell-us-anything-uplifting-about-the-person-who-died-funeral-gifts-come-under-fire-from-priest-941873.html.
2. "Ancient custom": Varro, Sat. Men. 303 (Non. P. 48, 6-9M). Sausage: Festus-Paulus 377L.
3. Mourning period: Cic. *Leg.* 2.22.55. Examples of these *cenae*: Tac. *Ann.* 6.5; Petr. *Sat.* 65–67.
4. *CIL* 6.10248 = *ILS* 8366. The inscription also requires the deceased's freedmen to light lamps and burn incense in the tomb three times monthly.
5. On the *Parentalia*: Dolansky 2011.
6. Ov. *Fasti* 2.535–554. He adds an admonitory tale of explanation – though he also claims that he does not believe it: When the *Parentalia* was once neglected when Rome was at war, the ancestral souls rose from the ground amid the quiet of the night and heinous ghosts then wandered the streets and countryside howling. Similar fears: Apul. *Met.* 8.9; Porph. on Hor. *Epist.* 2.2.209. Planning for the *Parentalia*: Petr. *Sat.* 77–78.
7. AE 2000.344b.18–26: D'Arms 2000; Dolansky 2011, 140–142.
8. Textile dealers: *CIL* 11.5047; gods' statues: *CIL* 5.5272; birthday cash and grill: *ILS* 6468. For more examples of food and flowers at the tomb, see *ILS* 7213, 7258, 8369–8374; *CIL* 3.703, 754; 5.2072; 12.4015. See also Champlin 1991, 164–165.
9. AE 1977, no. 31.
10. *CIL* 13.5708.
11. *CIL* 3.2279; 6.15594, 26942, 29959; 11.3895; 14.396.
12. *CIL* 5.2176; 6.10237; 12.3637; 13.2494.
13. *CIL* 12.1657. Cf. *CIL* 13.2465.

14. Graham 2005; Gee 2008. At the Via Laurentina necropolis different priorities governed Ostians' choices, for they constructed three-couched structures, triclinia, which they located within the tombs.
15. They likewise appear in Tombs C and F: Gee 2003, 57, and 120–121.
16. When Tomb S was finished, none of Tombs R, T, or U had been constructed, which left plenty of space nearby for tombside revelry. Since excavation has not proceeded much to the south – that is, in front of Tomb S – we do not know how much more space was available beyond the two meters currently visible, which would permit at least a small party.
17. CIL 8.20277: *Memoriae Aeliae Secundulae. / funeri mu[l]ta quid(e)m condigna iam misimus omnes, / insuper ar(a)equ(e) deposit(a)e Secundulae matri. / lapideam placuit nobis atponere mensam, / in qua magna eius memorantes plurima facta, / dum cibi ponuntur calicesq(ue) e[t] copertae, / vulnus ut sanetur nos rod(ens) pectore saevum, / libenter fabul(as) dum sera red(d)imus hora / castae matri bonae laudesq(ue), vetula dormit.*
18. Cic. *Leg.* 2.24. Cicero says the prohibition is only right, adding that the law would not have existed if they were not occurring.
19. Tert. *Resurr.* 1: *et tamen defunctis parentat, et quidem impensissimo officio pro moribus eorum, pro temporibus esculentorum, ut quos negant sentire quidquam etiam desiderare praesumant.* De Test An. 4: *Vocas porro securos, si quando extra portam cum obsoniis et matteis tibi potius parentans ad busta recedis aut a bustis dilutior redis.*
20. August. *Mor.* 34: *Novi multos esse sepulcrorum et picturarum adoratores. Novi multos esse qui cum luxuriosissime super mortuos bibant et epulas cadaveribus exhibentes super sepultos se ipsos sepeliant et voracitates ebrietatesque suas deputent religioni.* Also, on dangers of tombside drunkenness: Aug. *Confessions* 6.2.
21. August. *Ep.* 22.6: ... *super ipsas memorias non sint sumptuosae, atque omnibus petentibus sine typho, et cum alacritate praebeantur.*
22. CIL 6.26554: ... *amici et parentes habeatis deos propitios salvi huc ad alogiam veniatis hilares cum omnibus.*
23. CIL 6.2357 = ILS 8204: *Hospes, ad hunc tumulum / ne meias ossa precantur / tecta hominis, sed si gratus / homo es, misce bibe da mi.*
24. Sen. *Ep.* 12.8: *Pacuvius, qui Syriam usu suam fecit, cum vino et illis funebribus epulis sibi parentaverat, sic in cubiculum ferebatur a cena, ut inter plausus exoletorum hoc ad symphoniam caneretur:* βεβίωται, βεβίωται.
25. CIL 6.14672 = ILS 8156 = IG 14.1746 (trans. A. Foreman). μή μου παρέλθῃς τὸ ἐπίγραμμα, ὁδοιπόρε, / ἀλλὰ σταθεὶς ἄκουε καὶ μαθὼν ἄπι. / οὐκ ἔστι ἐν Ἅδου πλοῖον, οὐ πορθμεὺς Χάρων, / οὐκ Αἰακὸς κλειδοῦχος, οὐχὶ Κέρβερος κύων / ἡμεῖς δὲ πάντες οἱ κάτω τεθνηκότες / ὀστέα τέφρα <γ>εγόναμεν, ἄλλο δὲ οὐδὲ ἕν. / εἴρηκά σοι ὀρθῶς ὕπαγε, ὁδοιπόρε, / μὴ καὶ τεθνακὼς ἀδόλεσχός σοι φανῶ / Μὴ μύρα, μὴ στεφάνους λιθίναις στήλαισι χαρίζου· / μηδὲ τὸ πῦρ φλέξῃς ἐς κενὸν ἡ δαπάνη. / ζῶντί μοι, εἴ τι θέλεις, χάρισαι τέφρην δὲ μεθύσκων / πηλὸν ποιήσεις, κοὐχ ὁ θανὼν πίεται. / τοῦτο ἔσομαι γὰρ ἐγώ, σὺ δὲ τούτοις γῆν ἐπιχώσας / εἰπέ ὅτ<ι> οὐκ <ὢν> ἦν τοῦτο πάλιν γέγονα.
26. Lucian, *De Luctu* 19: τί δὲ ὁ ὑπὲρ τοῦ τάφου λίθος ἐστεφανωμένος; ἢ τί ὑμῖν δύναται τὸν ἄκρατον ἐπιχεῖν; ἢ νομίζετε καταστάξειν αὐτὸν πρὸς ἡμᾶς καὶ μέχρι

τοῦ Ἅιδου διίξεσθαι; τὰ μὲν γὰρ ἐπὶ τῶν καθαγισμῶν καὶ αὐτοὶ ὁρᾶτε, οἶμαι, ὡς τὸ μὲν νοστιμώτατον τῶν παρεσκευασμένων ὁ καπνὸς παραλαβὼν ἄνω εἰς τὸν οὐρανὸν οἴχεται μηδέν τι ἡμᾶς ὀνήσας τοὺς κάτω, τὸ δὲ καταλειπόμενον, ἡ κόνις, ἀχρεῖον, ἐκτὸς εἰ μὴ τὴν σποδὸν ἡμᾶς σιτεῖσθαι πεπιστεύκατε.

27. Artem. Oneir. 5.82: 'ὑπόδεχαι ἡμᾶς καὶ δείπνισον' ... ἔθος μὲν γὰρ τοῖς συμβιωταῖς καὶ εἰς τὰ τῶν ἀποθανόντων εἰσιέναι καὶ δειπνεῖν, ἡ δὲ ὑποδοχὴ λέγεται γενέσθαι ὑπὸ τοῦ ἀποθανόντος κατὰ τιμὴν τὴν ἐκ τῶν συμβιωτῶν εἰς τὸν ἀποθανόντα. Translation from MacMullen 1997, 62–63.
28. AE 1966, 404: *Hospes noli admirare / quod sic me in lecto vid(es) / recubante(m) dormient(em) / mortua sum.*
29. See also Wrede 1977; 1981.
30. On reading silently versus aloud, see Knox 1968; Saenger 1997.
31. *Anth. Lat.* 721: *Vivere post obitum vatem vis nosse, uiator? / Quod legis, ecce loquor: vox tua nempe mea est.* Cf. *CIL* 14.356, a fragmentary text from Ostia, which appears to contain nearly the same formula. On the phenomenon of speaking inscriptions, see Koortbojian 2006; Carroll 2007–2008.
32. *CLE* 1278, ll. 5–6 = *CIL* 13.2104: *quodque meam retinet vocem data littera saxo / vo[ce] tua vivet, quisque lege[s titu]los.*
33. *CIL* 14.480 = *CLE* 1255: *Hic ego qui sine voce loquor de marmore caeso ...*
34. Zanker 1995, 251–252.
35. Beard 1998; Hackworth Petersen 2003, 250–251 (*CIL* 6.1958b).
36. For example, Tomb E of Flavius' own necropolis underneath St. Peter's yielded an alabaster *oinochoe* (wine pitcher) and krater (punch bowl): Perna 2012, esp. 793–794.
37. Dunbabin 1986, 240–241, n. 208 (with prior bibliography).
38. Laderman 2005.
39. Pucci 1968/1969.

7 Flavius Agricola in Early Modern Rome

1. Barthes 1977, 148.
2. Benko 1980, 670–671.
3. Houghton 2015, 210–211.
4. Further on the fascists and the Roman past: Arthurs 2012; Kallis 2014; Sebastiani 2023.
5. Spivey 2019.
6. Early and important works related to object biographies: Kopytoff 1986; Gosden and Marshall 1999, 169–170.
7. Pucci 1968–1969.
8. Hibbard 1971, 155–188. On the *confessio*: Pergolizzi 1999.
9. *Liber Pontificalis* 2, 3.
10. Torrigio 1618, 53–54.
11. Drawing: McPhee 2008, figs. 2–3.
12. Liverani and Spinola 2010, 133–134.

13. D'Amelio 2005, 132. The key document is *Relazione di quanto è occorso nel cavare i fondamenti per le quattro colonne di bronzo*. For more, see D'Amelio 2005, 131–132 and n. 18.
14. D'Amelio (2005, 132–133) details the proceedings, with citations of original sources. Digging in the so-called Vatican Scavi in the mid twentieth century turned up a bronze box into which seventeenth-century officials had placed these bones. It was labeled with the following inscription: *Corpora Sanctorum prope sepulchrum sancti Petri inventa cum fundamenta effoderentur aereis columnis ab Urbano VIII super hac fornice erectis hic simul collecta et reposita die 28 iulii 1626*. Appollonj Ghetti et al. 1951, 69–70.
15. Ubaldi reprinted in Armellini 1887, 530–531.
16. Archivio Capitolare di San Pietro, cod. H 55, fol. 191 (letter dated August 26, 1626).
17. The document was found in the nineteenth century among the records of G. Manzi, a functionary in the Barberini library, and published in Melchiorri (1823). The document's author says he received a transcription of Flavius' epitaph from the only copier still living at the time of the pope's passing. The delay hinged on the inscription's content and the pope's threats against its publication.
18. Before reproducing the epitaph, the author writes, "I will give the aforementioned verses as they were passed on to me, but because they seem incorrect to me, perhaps because they were copied in subterranean darkness and with great fear, I will endeavor to emend them as I am best able."
19. Lumbroso 1875, 175–176. On Dal Pozzo, see Herklotz 1999.
20. For the relationship between the two men, see Rietbergen 2006, 388–390.
21. There is one small hint of a molding in the base's upper left portion, but the plinth is otherwise one of the least shaded parts of the drawing.
22. Pucci 1968–1969.
23. In March 2022, I was able to inspect the bottom side of the monument as it was being reinstalled at the Indianapolis Museum of Art. It consisted of a very clean and smooth surface.
24. Fabretti 1702, 420–421.
25. Volpi 1745, 668–669, no. 387.
26. Waddy 1990, 166. For a broader view of palaces and other residences across multiple registers of society, see Leone 2019.
27. Robertson 1867, 14 (a republication of several of Bargrave's essays).
28. Waddy 1976.
29. Waddy 1990, 173–180 (Sforza palace and arrangement), 204–212 (position and approach)
30. Tucci 2017, 68.
31. Scott 1991, esp. 125–197.
32. Intellectuals: Magnuson 1982, 238–239. Garden: MacDougall 1994, 23–36, 219–348. Music and theater: Hammond 1994. Poetry, patronage, and library: Rietbergen 2006. Architectural trappings: Waddy 2014.
33. Lavin 1975. For further discussion of Barberini programs involving ancient sculpture, see Faedo 2018.

34. Lurking next to the Republican temples in Rome's Largo Argentina is the Piazza dei Calcarari, while an 1191 papal record from Ostia mentions *sita in loco qui vocatur Calcaria*, on which see Lenzi 1998.
35. Key works for overviews of collecting practices: Haskell and Penny 1981; Christian 2010.
36. Vout 2018, 97–124.
37. Gensheimer 2018, esp. 21–27; Marvin 1983.
38. Plin. *NH* 36.33–34.
39. Beaven 2019, 391–394.
40. Seventeenth-century Barberini inventories: Lavin 1975.
41. Lavin 1975, 72–74 (May 22, 1626: III. inv. 26–31).
42. Santacroce: Christian 2010, 158–159 (sketch of Maarten van Heemskerck). Cesi: Bentz 2013, 138–140 (another sketch by van Heemskerck, painting of Hendrick van Cleve III). In these spots, according to Waddy (2014, 33), "a dignitary would take note of these signs of an owner's Roman-ness and his liberality in sharing these pleasures with the public."
43. Castagnoli 1942, 68.
44. The obelisk was intended to stand atop an elephant-shaped base designed by Bernini, and in 1678 a deep foundation was laid within the garden and in line with the *Ponte Ruinante*. Despite these and other plans, the obelisk sat in the palace's forecourt for nearly a century and a half. Elephant base: Golzio 1971, 40. Foundation and triumphal base: Waddy 1990, 261–262 (with archival sources).
45. *Documenti inediti per servire alla storia dei Musei d'Italia* 1878–1880, 4.45–46.
46. Joost-Gaugier 1985.
47. A similar sculptural overture, but of life-sized emperors rather than busts, greeted visitors who ascended the long square staircase to the grand *salone*: Lavin 1975, 691. Massimo: Beaven 2010, 33.
48. *Documenti inediti per servire alla storia dei Musei d'Italia* 1878–1880, 4.45–53.
49. Rossini 1693, 57. Followed largely by Rossi and Rossi 1697, 361.
50. Taddeo's investiture: Museo di Roma inv. 5700. Leone et al. 2002, 250–251. Saint Ignatius' canonization: Galleria Nazionale d'Arte Antica, Palazzo Barberini inv. 1445. Carnevale: Museo di Roma inv. 5698; Leone et al. 2002, 258–259.
51. For the sculpture, see Pizzorusso 1985. For the transaction, Goudriaan 2018, 280–282.
52. Ov. *Met.* 6.313–381.
53. Harper 2010, esp. 216–217. As a further index of the sculpture's importance, it was later positioned at the base of the monumental staircase leading to the grand *salone* hosting the palace's showcase events.
54. Boiteux 1977, 367: 60,000 *scudi* was the cost. Cardinal Guido Bentivoglio's 1634 pamphlet, *Festa Fatta in Roma, alli 25. di Febraio MDCXXXIV*, commemorated the events and included etchings illustrating different parts.
55. Individual banquets: Hammond 1999; Bacciolo 2015; Norman 2019. Culinary ceremony and diplomacy in general: Rietbergen 2006, ch. 4.
56. Waddy 1990, 5. The key text is Francesco Sestini's *Il Maestro di Camera*, first published in 1621 and republished many times thereafter. See also Girolamo Lunadoro's 1635 *Relatione della corte di Roma*, published in Padua, for another helpful text.

57. Waddy 1990, 5, drawing on an account generated by Cassiano Dal Pozzo (Barb. Lat. 5689, fol. 5).
58. Stenhouse 2005, quotation from 427.
59. Scott 1991, 193–197, and 216–219.
60. Waddy 1990, 251–263; cf. figs. 150–165.
61. Rossini 1715, vol. 2, 59–61. See also Mahon 1988, 16–17, on the Barberini painting collection in the early eighteenth century. For visitor accessibility in the late seventeenth century and thereafter, see Waddy 1990, 58–59.
62. *Lettera familiare* 1687, 14.
63. Maffei 1704.
64. Haskell and Penny 1981, 23–26.

8 Flavius in the Modern World

1. For the complicated history of the Barberini estate and its artworks, see Mahon 1988, esp. 13–21, on which the following relies heavily.
2. Mahon 1988, 18.
3. Guidebook: Barbier de Montault 1870, 429: "statue d'homme couché sur un lit funèbre," which is listed in the first room alongside several other pieces recognizable from the 1738 Barberini inventory, such as the colossal bust of Trajan. German inventory: Matz and von Duhn 1881–1882, vol. 2, n. 3415.
4. Matz and von Duhn 1881–1882, vol. 1, p. xi.
5. Marbles for sale: Barbier de Montault 1870, 430–432. Danish sales: Moltesen 2012, 162.
6. Mahon 1988, 18–19. *Dieci Quadri della Galleria Sciarra, fototipie a cura di Francesco Paolo Michetti con cenni storici e critici raccolti da Leone Vicchi*, Roma, Stabilimento Tipografico della 'Tribuna' 1889.
7. Hare 1893, 48–49.
8. Mahon 1988, 17–20; Mahon 1990, 6.
9. Mahon 1988, 19–20.
10. Moltesen 2003, 210–212. For the story of the bronze's acquisition, see Gjødesen 1970. (The Glyptothek in Munich had tried to make inroads into the Sciarra collection earlier in the nineteenth century: Wünsche 2007, 20.) For two other sculptures as well: Moltesen 2012, 168.
11. *Il Cracas*, April 8, 1923, "Cose Nuove: Note Cronistoriche, La Galleria Sciarra." Repeated July 8, 1893 (quotation from p. 256), "Cose vecchie e nuove: La Sentenza nella Causa della Galleria Sciarra incompleta, inefficace." "Honor and interests" elsewhere: April 8, 1894, "Note Cronistorische: La Sentenza nella Causa Sciarra e la sicura via per la rivendicazione dei quadri espatriati."
12. July 8, 1893, "Cose vecchie e nuove: La Sentenza nella Causa della Galleria Sciarra incompleta, inefficace."
13. April 1, 1894, "Note Cronistorische: La Sentenza nella Causa Sciarra e la sicura via per la rivendicazione dei quadri espatriati."
14. Fabréga-Dubert 2009.
15. *Il Cracas*, May 1892, "Tavole Necrologiche dell'arte moderna in Roma moderna."

Notes to pages 133–136

16. Arndt et al. 1893, vol. 17B, no. 5092. Poulsen and Glyptotek: vol. 17B, 32. Several of the artworks found homes in museums besides the Glyptotek, so it is clear that they were part of a broader pattern of marketing these pieces to collectors and institutions more broadly. For example, a head (no. 5059 [links]) is now in Munich after passing through the hands of a Rome-based dealer.
17. I have been able to access the Demotte archive at the Département des Sculptures at the Musée du Louvre, yet they consist largely of photographs of pieces that Demotte sold to the museum, and no written testimony. Additional financial information may be available at Les Archives Nationales in Paris, according to Christine Vivet-Peclet, whose assistance on this topic I acknowledge.
18. *Time*, December 17, 1923: "Demotte Fils."
19. *New York Times*, January 27, 1923: "Weary of Losses, Art Dealer to Give Treasures Away."
20. For full details of the episode, see Secrest 2004, 207–223, on which the following pages draw extensively.
21. *Le Matin*, May 22, 1923: "Un Miracle au Musée du Louvre: Les Statue Mortes qui Renaissent."
22. Secrest 2004, 215–218. Boutron's widow sought an enquiry; her husband had expressed his concern to a fellow sculptor that "they want to silence me," and, the day after the incident, Demotte pressed her not to ask questions. Her request was denied, and she maintained her silence until 1923 when Demotte's reputation was weakened in the press, and she pushed for the case to be revisited.
23. See Secrest 2004, 218, and notes for more spicy details. *New York Times*, June 19, 1923: "'Kidnapped' Statue Came to New York"; June 20, 1923: "Asserts Sculptor Faked Art Now Here"; June 23, 1923: "Demotte Defends Statues"; June 24, 1923: "Demotte Refuses Testimony on Statues"; July 15, 1923: "Will Not Re-Examine Gothic Ceramics Now"; July 19, 1923: "Impugns 3 Statues Sold to Americans."
24. In the world of Islamic Art, Demotte is infamous for his acquisition and then subsequent dismantling and sale of a fourteenth-century Persian manuscript, the Great Mongol *Shahnama*.
25. Brilliant 2000, 2–3, for two images.
26. Demotte's death, together with many details, were front-page news back in New York: *New York Times*, September 5, 1923: "Demotte Killed in Gun Accident." Secrest 2004, 222–223, for more details.
27. Romano (2018, 16) cites an April 10, 1935, document of guarantee for a statue; she is identified there as George Joseph Demotte's widow.
28. Brummer Gallery Records, Metropolitan Museum of Art, New York, www.metmuseum.org/art/libraries-and-research-centers/watson-digital-collections/cloisters-archives-collections/the-brummer-gallery-records.
29. Brummer Gallery Records, correspondence: E. Brummer to J. Brummer, October 20, 1936 (purchase); E. Brummer to J. Brummer, October 30, 1936 (shipping); list of objects and valuation: note with inventory from Rue de Berri and Depot, n.d.
30. Brummer Gallery Records: P13174_recto and P13174_verso (dates); correspondence: E. Brummer to J. Brummer, October 20, 1936 (warehouse).

31. Brummer Gallery Records, P141110_verso.
32. They concentrate especially in the Cloisters, the Met's outpost of medieval art in northernmost Manhattan, whose creation Rockefeller spearheaded. The partnership between museum and dealer earned Brummer election, in 1932, as honorary fellow for life by the Met's board of trustees.
33. The third auction appears to have grossed more than $100,000: The Brummer Gallery Records, price lists for sales May 12, 1947, through June 24, 1949.
34. The French and Company archives are held at the Getty Research Institute in Los Angeles. For a catalog of their holdings, see: http://archives2.getty.edu:8082/xtf/view?docId=ead/990051/990051.xml.
35. Houpt 2006, 27.
36. *New York Times*, November 30, 1959: "Mitchell Samuels Is Dead at 79; Art Dealer Headed French & Co."
37. The Brummer archive preserves prices quoted for two institutions before the sculpture was sold at auction: a price of $3,800 was quoted to the Royal Ontario Museum on May 5, 1937; $3,000 was quoted to the Rhode Island School of Design on April 2, 1938; and the piece went up for auction in 1949. Royal Ontario Museum: Brummer Gallery Records, Institutions-QR03_Nj_recto (May 5, 1937); Rhode Island School of Design: Brummer Gallery Records, Institutions-QR02_recto (April 2, 1938); Auction: Parke-Bernet Galleries 1949, 114.
38. Plut. *Luc*. 39: ἔστι δ' οὖν τοῦ Λουκούλλου βίου, καθάπερ ἀρχαίας κωμῳδίας, ἀναγνῶναι τὰ μὲν πρῶτα πολιτείας καὶ στρατηγίας, τὰ δ' ὕστερα πότους καὶ δεῖπνα καὶ μονονουχὶ κώμους καὶ λαμπάδας καὶ παιδιὰν ἅπασαν.
39. Other authors likewise finger Lucullus as a *piscinarius*, roughly "fish fancier": Cic. *Att*, I.19, I.20, II.9. Cf. Varro *RR* 3.2.17, 3.10, 17.9.
40. Plut. *Luc*. 40: οὐ μόνον στρωμναῖς ἁλουργέσι καὶ διαλίθοις ἐκπώμασι καὶ χοροῖς καὶ ἀκροάμασιν ἐπεισοδίοις, ἀλλ' ὄψων τε παντοδαπῶν καὶ πεμμάτων περιττῶς διαπεπονημένων παρασκευαῖς ζηλωτὸν ἀνελευθέροις ποιοῦντος ἑαυτόν. Not surprisingly, Lucullus' name was synonymous with a fancy lifestyle, to judge from a story in which a young and apparently flamboyant senator delivered a long and tiresome speech about frugality and temperance. Plutarch (*Lucullus* 41) reports that Cato interrupted his hypocrisy, "Stop there! You get wealth like Crassus, you live like Lucullus, but you talk like Cato."
41. Use of the adjective *Lucullan* in books in English, after a precipitous drop during World War I, steadily grew to peak in the years between 1940 and 1960, precisely when the French and Company ad was published. Many factors undoubtedly played a role in this frequency (I have chosen the adjective *Lucullan* instead of the proper name *Lucullus* to filter out scholarly treatments or references to the historical figure), such as disposable income, moral(-izing) sensibilities about displays of wealth, and the like. Whatever the reason, this notion of a Lucullan lifestyle was "in the air" when the ad was drafted. Google Books Ngram Viewer, "Lucullan" between 1900 and 2008.
42. French & Company records, 1910–1998, bulk 1950–1960, Getty Research Institute, Research Library, Accession no. 990051. "High priests": "Contemporary Gallery," p. 4. www.getty.edu/research/collections/collection/113YKV.
43. "Contemporary Gallery," p. 4: "It is regrettable to state that since 1929 French & Company has either completely missed, as in the case of Impressionists, or been late in anticipating commercial art trends" (underscore in original).

44. Quotation: Sawin 1959, 48. Overall: Temkin 2002, esp. 54–57.
45. French and Company Records, Getty Research Institute, "Preliminary Merchandising and Publicity Plans for the Opening of the French and Company Galleries, 1958," December 17, 1957, Publicity Consultants, Inc., p. 1. Another document, "Policy of New Galleries," reports that the new showroom space would be 35 percent of its predecessor.
46. French and Company Records, Getty Research Institute, "Preliminary Merchandising and Publicity Plans for the Opening of the French and Company Galleries, 1958," December 17, 1957, Publicity Consultants, Inc., p. 11. According to p. 3 of the same document, the advertisements stressed "the collection's scope and ma[de] it sound like a vast private assemblage to which the doors were being opened for the first time."
47. For the distinction, French and Company Records, Getty Research Institute, "To the directors: A general philosophy concerning policy at the new galleries and discussion of some problems, with suggested solutions," pp. 2–3.
48. French and Company Records, Getty Research Institute, "French & Company Advertising Campaign Story," Ray Josephs, July 31, 1957, p. 1.
49. "French & Company Advertising Campaign Story," Ray Josephs, July 31, 1957, p. 2. Page 5 summarizes as well: "In recent years, more and more Americans, as the Europeans before them, have developed a greater interest in all kind of luxury goods of which antiques and works of art are an unusually interesting example. As income levels rise, as taste heightens, as knowledge and understanding of the value of objects of beauty increases, more and more people will have to be reached by a new kind of advertising." A document two years prior, "Blueprint for French & Company, Inc.," dated January 3, 1955, notes several shifts in the art market, notably, "The change of the concentration of wealth in this country from a few multi-millionaires to many millionaires" (p. 2).
50. French and Company Records, Getty Research Institute, "French & Company Advertising Campaign Story," Ray Josephs, July 31, 1957, pp. 2–4.
51. "French & Co., Art House, Is Sold by City Investing," Sanka Knox, *New York Times*, January 30, 1969.
52. Hartman 1971. An exhibition organized in 1975 by Alan Hartman, entitled "Jade as Sculpture," traveled to Indianapolis after being shown in Minneapolis and the dealer's New York headquarters. It was open in New York simultaneously with the Joan Hartman-curated exhibition at China House Gallery, "Ancient Chinese Jades."
53. Value: Indianapolis Museum of Art, object file. Board of trustees: Hedy Hartman, in communication with the author.

Epilogue

1. Mart 2.29, 5.23; Hor. *Ep.* 4.15–16.
2. For a recent survey of the Meta Sudans, see Zeggio and Pardini 2007.
3. Provinces: Longfellow 2010.
4. Marlowe 2004; Zeggio and Pardini 2007, 8–9.

References

Adams, J. 1999. "The Poets of Bu Njem: Language, Culture and the Centurionate." *JRS* 89: 109–134.
Aldrete, G. 2007. *Floods of the Tiber in Ancient Rome*. Baltimore: The Johns Hopkins University Press.
Aldrete G., and D. Mattingly. 1999. "Feeding the City: The Organization, Operation and Scale of the Supply System for Rome." In *Life, Death, and Entertainment in the Roman Empire*, edited by D. Potter and D. Mattingly, 195–228. Ann Arbor: University of Michigan Press.
Allison, P. 2004. *Pompeian Households: An Analysis of the Material Culture*. Los Angeles: Cotsen Institute of Archaeology, UCLA.
Appollonj Ghetti, B., A. Ferrua, E. Josi, and E. Kirschbaum. 1951. *Esplorazioni sotto la confessione di San Pietro in Vaticano eseguite negli anni 1940–1949*. Vatican City: Tipografia Poliglotta Vaticana.
Armellini, M. 1887. *Le Chiese di Roma dalle loro origini sino al secolo XVI*. Rome: Tipografia Editrice Romana.
Arndt, P., W. Amelung, and G. Lippold. 1893. *Photographische Einzelaufnahmen antiker Sculpturen*. Munich: F. Bruckmann.
Arthurs, J. 2012. *Excavating Modernity: The Roman Past in Fascist Italy*. Ithaca: Cornell University Press.
Auguet, R. 1994. *Cruelty and Civilization: The Roman Games*. London: Routledge.
Bacciolo, A. 2015. "The Diplomacy of Taste: Maratti, Contini, Bellori, and a Banquet Hosted by Carlo Barberini for the Ambassador of King James II." *Storia dell'Arte* 142: 85–104.
Barbier de Montault, X. 1870. *Les Musées et galeries de Rome: Catalogue général de tous les objets d'art qui y sont exposés*. Rome: J. Spithover.
Barraco, M. 2020. *Larvae conviviales: Gli scheletri da banchetto nell'antica Roma*. Rome: Arbor Sapientiae.
Barrett, A. 2020. *Rome Is Burning: Nero and the Fire That Ended a Dynasty*. New Jersey: Princeton University Press.
Barthes, R. 1977. *Image, Music, Text*. New York: Hill and Wang.
Baslez, M. 2002. "Mobilité et ouverture de la communauté romaine de Délos: amitiés, mariages mixtes, adoptions." In *Les Italiens dans le monde grec: IIe*

References

siècle av. J.-C. — Ier siècle ap. J.-C.: circulation, activités, integration, edited by C. Hasenohr and C. Müller, 55–65. Athens: École Française d'Athènes.

Beard, M. 1998. "Vita inscripta." In *La biographie antique: huit exposés suivis de discussions*, edited by W. Ehlers, 83–114. Geneva: Fondation Hardt.

Beard, M., J. North, and S. Price. 1998. *Religions of Rome*. 2 vols. Cambridge: Cambridge University Press.

Beaven, L. 2010. *An Ardent Patron: Cardinal Camillo Massimo and His Antiquarian and Artistic Circle*. London: P. Holberton.

Beaven, L. 2019. "Elite Patronage and Collecting." In *A Companion to Early Modern Rome, 1492–1692*, edited by P. Jones, B. Wisch, and S. Ditchfield, 387–411. Leiden: Brill.

Beckmann, M. 2011. *The Column of Marcus Aurelius: The Genesis and Meaning of a Roman Imperial Monument*. Chapel Hill: University of North Carolina Press.

Bender, S. 2020. "Das Grabmonument des Flavius Agricola in Indianapolis (USA) und die Funktion der sogenannten Kasserollen." *ArchKorrBl* 50.2: 241–248.

Benko, S. 1980. "Virgil's Fourth *Eclogue* in Christian Interpretation." *ANRW* 31.1: 646–705.

Bentz, K. 2013. "The Afterlife of the Cesi Garden: Family Identity, Politics, and Memory in Early Modern Rome." *JSAH* 72.2: 134–165.

Birley, A. 1999. *Septimius Severus: The African Emperor*. London: Routledge.

Bohak, G. 2015. "Amulets." In *A Companion to the Archaeology of Religion in the Ancient World*, edited by R. Raja and J. Rüpke, 83–95. Chichester: John Wiley & Sons Inc.

Boiteux, M. 1977. "Carnaval annexé: essai de lecture fête romaine." *Annales (HSS)* 32.2: 356–380.

Borbonus, D. 2014. *Columbarium Tombs and Collective Identity in Augustan Rome*. Cambridge: Cambridge University Press.

Borbonus, D. 2021. "Countering Inequality through Organized Collective Burial in Imperial Rome." In *The Archaeology of Inequality: Tracing the Archaeological Record*, edited by O. Cerasuolo, 309–328. Buffalo: SUNY Press.

Borg, B. 2012. "The Face of the Social Climber: Roman Freedmen and Elite Ideology," In *Free at Last! The Impact of Freed Slaves on the Roman Empire*, edited by S. Bell and T. Ramsby, 25–49. London: Bloomsbury.

Borg, B. 2019. *Roman Tombs and the Art of Commemoration: Contextual Approaches to Funerary Customs in the Second Century CE*. Cambridge: Cambridge University Press.

Bradley, K. 1994. *Slavery and Society at Rome*. Cambridge: Cambridge University Press.

Brenk, F. 2022. "The Temple of Isis in the Campus Martius in Rome: Place, Space, and Identity in the Ancient Mediterranean World." In *Gods, Spirits, and Worship in the Greco-Roman World and Early Christianity*, edited by C. Evans and A. Wright, 1–22. London: Bloomsbury.

Bricault, L. 2019. *Isis Pelagia: Images, Names and Cults of a Goddess of the Seas*. Leiden: Brill.

Brilliant, R. 2000. *My Laocoön*. Berkeley: University of California Press.

Broekaert, W. 2012. "Welcome to the Family! Marriage as Business Strategy in the Roman Economy." *MBAH* 30: 1–18.

Bücheler, F. 1895–1897. *Carmina Latina Epigraphica*. Leipzig: B. G. Teubner.

Carroll, M. 2007–2008. "'Vox tua nempe mea est'. Dialogues with the Dead in Roman Funerary Commemoration." *ARP* 11: 37–80.

Castagnoli, F. 1942. "Due archi trionfali della via Flaminia presso Piazza Sciarra." *BullCom* 70: 57–75.

Castagnoli, F. 1992. *Il Vaticano nell'antichità classica*. Vatican City: Biblioteca apostolica vaticana.

Champlin, E. 1991. *Final Judgments: Duty and Emotion in Roman Wills, 200 BC–AD 250*. Berkeley: University of California Press.

Chris, F. 2018. *The Transformation of Greek Amulets in Roman Imperial Times*. Philadelphia: University of Pennsylvania Press.

Christian, K. 2010. *Empire without End: Antiquities Collections in Renaissance Rome, c. 1350–1527*. New Haven: Yale University Press.

Claridge, A., and E. Dodero. 2022. *Sarcophagi and Other Reliefs*. 4 vols. The Paper Museum of Cassiano dal Pozzo: Series A – Antiquities and Architecture, Part 3. London: Royal Collection Trust.

Clarke, J. 2003. *Art in the Lives of Ordinary Romans: Visual Representation and Non-elite Viewers in Italy, 100 B.C.–A.D. 315*. Berkeley: University of California Press.

Clausen, K. 2015. *The Flavian Isea in Beneventum and Rome: The Appropriation of Egyptian and Egyptianising Art in Imperial Beneventum and Rome*. Copenhagen: Det Humanistiske Fakultet, Københavns Universitet.

Closs, V. 2020. *While Rome Burned: Fire, Leadership, and Urban Disaster in the Roman Cultural Imagination*. Ann Arbor: University of Michigan Press.

Cohen, A. 1985. *Symbolic Construction of Community*. London: Routledge.

Cohen, S. 2011. "From Permission to Prohibition: Paul and the Early Church on Mixed Marriage." In *Paul's Jewish Matrix*, edited by T. Casey and J. Taylor, 259–291. Rome: Gregorian and Biblical Press.

Courrier, C. 2014. *La plèbe de Rome et sa culture*. Rome: Ecole Française de Rome.

Courtney, E. 1995. *Musa Lapidaria: A Selection of Latin Verse Inscriptions*. Atlanta: Scholars Press.

Cusmà Piccione, A. 2017. *Non licet tibi alienigenam accipere: Studio sulla disparitas cultus tra i coniugi nella riflessione cristiana e nella legislazione tardoantica*. Milan: Giuffrè Editore.

D'Ambra, E. 1988. "A Myth for a Smith: A Meleager Sarcophagus from a Tomb in Ostia." *AJA* 92.1: 85–99.

D'Ambra, E. 1998. *Roman Art*. Cambridge: Cambridge University Press.

D'Amelio, M. 2005. "Tra ossa, polveri e ceneri: Il 'fuoriasse' del baldacchino di San Pietro a Roma." *Annali di Architettura* 17: 127–136.

D'Arms, J. 2000. "Memory, Money, and Status at Misenum: Three New Inscriptions from the Collegium of the Augustales." *JRS* 90: 126–144.

Darwall-Smith, R. 1994. "Albanum and the Villas of Domitian." *Pallas* 40: 145–165.

Davies, G. 2007. "Idem ego sum discumbens, ut me videtis: Inscription and Image on Roman Ash Chests." In *Art and Inscriptions in the Ancient World*, edited by

References

Z. Newby and R. Leader-Newby, 38–59. Cambridge: Cambridge University Press.

Davies, G. 2018. *Gender and Body Language in Roman Art*. Cambridge: Cambridge University Press.

Dey, H. 2021. *The Making of Medieval Rome: A New Profile of the City, 400 – 1420*. Cambridge: Cambridge University Press.

Dixon, S. 1992. *The Roman Family*. Baltimore: Johns Hopkins University Press.

Dobbins, J. J. 1992. "The Altar in the Sanctuary of the Genius of Augustus in the Forum of Pompeii." *RM* 99: 251–261

Dolansky, F. 2011. "Honouring the Family Dead on the Parentalia: Ceremony, Spectacle, and Memory." *Phoenix* 65.1/2: 125–157.

Donahue, J. F. 2004. *The Roman Community at Table During the Principate*. Ann Arbor: University of Michigan Press.

Dunbabin, K. 1986. "Sic erimus cuncti ... The Skeleton in Graeco-Roman Art." *JDAI* 101: 185–255.

Dunbabin, K. 2003. *The Roman Banquet: Images of Conviviality*. Cambridge: Cambridge University Press.

Duncan-Jones, R. 1982. *The Economy of the Roman Empire: Quantitative Studies*. Cambridge: Cambridge University Press.

Duncan-Jones, R. 1996. "The impact of the Antonine plague." *JRA* 9: 108–136.

Duncan-Jones, R. 2008. "Payment of Dinner-Guests at Rome." *Latomus* 67.1: 138–148.

Duncan-Jones, R. 2018. "The Antonine Plague Revisited." *Arctos–Acta Philologica Fennica* 52: 41–72.

Durkheim, E. 1912. *Les formes élémentaires de la vie religieuse: le système totémique en Australie*. Paris: F. Alcan.

Ellis, S. 2004. "The Distribution of Bars at Pompeii: Archaeological, Spatial and Viewshed Analyses." *JRA* 17: 371–384.

Elsner, J. 2007. "Physiognomy: Art and Text." In *Seeing the Face, Seeing the Soul: Polemon's Physiognomy from Classical Antiquity to Medieval Islam*, edited by S. Swain, 203–224. Oxford: Oxford University Press.

Evans Grubbs, J. 2002. *Women and the Law in the Roman Empire*. London: Routledge.

Fabréga-Dubert, M. 2009. *La collection Borghèse au Musée Napoléon*. Paris: Musée du Louvre.

Fabretti, R. 1702. *Inscriptionum antiquarum quae in aedibus paternis asservantur explicatio et additamentum*. Rome.

Faedo, L. 2018. "Memory and Self-Presentation: Egyptian Antiquities Seen through the Eyes of Antiquarians and Aristocrats in 17th Century Rome." In *The Iseum Campense from the Roman Empire to the Modern Age*, edited by M. J. Versluys, K. B. Clausen, and G. C. Vittozzi, 317–331. Rome: Edizioni Quasar.

Fairweather, J. 1987. "Ovid's Autobiographical Poem, *Tristia* 4.10." *CQ* 37.1: 181–196.

Faraone, C. 2018. *The Transformation of Greek Amulets in Roman Imperial Times*. Philadelphia: University of Pennsylvania Press.

Fejfer, J. 2008. *Roman Portraits in Context*. Berlin: De Gruyter.

Foucault, M. 1986. "Of Other Spaces." *Diacritics* 16.1: 22–27.

Frier, B. 2000. "Demography." In *The Cambridge Ancient History*. Vol. 11: *The High Empire, AD 70–192*, 2nd ed., edited by A. Bowman, P. Garnsey, and D. Rathbone, 787–816. Cambridge: Cambridge University Press.

Garnsey, P. 1988. *Famine and Food Supply in the Graeco-Roman World: Responses to Risk and Crisis.* Cambridge: Cambridge University Press.

Gasparini, V. 2016. "'I Will Not Be Thirsty. My Lips Will Not Be Dry': Individual Strategies of Reconstructing the Afterlife in the Isiac Cults." In *Burial Rituals, Ideas of Afterlife, and the Individual in the Hellenistic World and the Roman Empire*, edited by K. Waldner, R. Gordon, and W. Spickermann, 125–150. Stuttgart: Steiner.

Gee, R. 2003. "The Vatican Necropolis: Ritual, Status and Social Identity in the Roman Chamber Tomb." Ph.D. diss., University of Texas.

Gee, R. 2008. "From Corpse to Ancestor: The Role of Tombside Dining in the Transformation of the Body in Ancient Rome." In *The Materiality of Death: Bodies, Burials, Beliefs*, edited by F. Fahlander and T. Oestigaard, 59–68. Oxford: Archeopress.

Gee, R. 2011–2012. "Cult and Circus 'IN VATICANUM'." *MAAR* 56/57: 63–83.

Gensheimer, M. 2018. *Decoration and Display in Rome's Imperial Thermae: Messages of Power and Their Popular Reception at the Baths of Caracalla.* New York: Oxford University Press.

George, M. 2005. "Family Imagery and Family Values in Roman Italy." In *The Roman Family in the Empire: Rome, Italy, and Beyond*, edited by M. George, 9–36. Oxford: Oxford University Press.

Giuliano, A., and M. Bertinetti, eds. 1981. *Museo Nazionale Romano. Le Sculture I*, 2. Rome: De Luca.

Gjødesen, M. 1970. "Fyrst Sciarras Bronze." *MedKøb* 27: 11–73.

Golzio, V. 1971. *Palazzi romani dalla rinascita al neoclassico*. Bologna: Cappelli.

Gosden, C., and Y. Marshall. 1999. "The Cultural Biography of Objects." *WorldArch* 31.2: 169–178.

Goudriaan, E. 2018. *Florentine Patricians and Their Networks: Structures Behind the Cultural Success and the Political Representation of the Medici Court (1600–1660).* Leiden: Brill.

Graf, F. 2017. "Sacred Meals in the Cults of Isis and Sarapis." In *Near Eastern and Graeco-Roman Traditions, Archaeology*. Vol. 3: *The Eucharist: Its Origins and Contexts*, edited by D. Sänger and D. Hellholm, 1747–1760. Tübingen: Mohr Siebeck.

Graham, E. 2005. "The Quick and the Dead in the Extra-Urban Landscape: The Roman Cemetery at Ostia/Portus as a Lived Environment." In *TRAC 2004: Proceedings of the Fourteenth Annual Theoretical Roman Archaeology Conference*, edited by J. Bruhn, B. Croxford, and D. Grigoropoulos, 133–143. Oxford: Oxbow.

Hackworth Petersen, L. 2003. "The Baker, His Tomb, His Wife, and Her Breadbasket: The Monument of Eurysaces in Rome." *ArtB* 85.2: 230–257.

Hackworth Petersen, L. 2006. *The Freedman in Roman Art and Art History*. New York: Cambridge University Press.

Hallett, C. H. 2005. *The Roman Nude: Heroic Portrait 200 B.C.–A.D. 300*. Oxford: Oxford University Press.

References

Hammond, F. 1994. *Music and Spectacle in Baroque Rome: Barberini Patronage under Urban VIII*. New Haven: Yale University Press.
Hammond, F. 1999. "The Creation of a Roman Festival: Barberini Celebrations for Christina of Sweden." In *Life and the Arts in Baroque Palaces of Rome: Ambiente Barocco*, edited by S. Walker and F. Hammond, 53–69. New Haven: Yale University Press.
Hare, A. 1893. *Walks in Rome*. 13th ed. London: George Allen.
Harlow, M., and R. Laurence. 2002. *Growing Up and Growing Old in Ancient Rome: A Life Course Approach*. London: Routledge.
Harper, J. 2010. "The Sun also Riseth: The Barberini Apollo Series as an Allegory of Rise, Fall, and Return." In *Tapestry in the Baroque: New Aspects of Production and Patronage*, edited by T. Campbell and E. Cleland, 204–231. New Haven: Yale University Press.
Hartman, J. 1971. *Three Dynasties of Jade*. Indianapolis: Indianapolis Museum of Art.
Hartnett, J. 2017a. *The Roman Street: Urban Life and Society in Pompeii, Herculaneum and Rome*. New York: Cambridge University Press.
Hartnett, J. 2017b. "Bars (Taberna, Popina, Caupona, Thermopolium)." In *Oxford Classical Dictionary*[4], edited by S. Goldberg.
Haskell, F., and N. Penny. 1981. *Taste and the Antique: The Lure of Classical Sculpture, 1500–1900*. New Haven: Yale University Press.
Heinemann, A. 2018. "Blessings of Empire: The Nile and Tiber River Statues from the Iseum Campense." In *The Iseum Campense from the Roman Empire to the Modern Age*, edited by M. Versluys, K. Bülow Clausen, and G. Capriotti Vittozzi, 161–178. Rome: Edizioni Quasar.
Herklotz, I. 1999. *Cassiano Dal Pozzo und die Archäologie des 17. Jahrhunderts*. Munich: Hirmer.
Heyob, S. 1975. *The Cult of Isis among Women in the Graeco-Roman World*. Leiden: Brill.
Hibbard, H. 1971. *Carlo Maderno and Roman Architecture, 1580–1630*. University Park: Pennsylvania State University Press.
Hopkins, K. 1978. "Economic Growth and Towns in Classical Antiquity." In *Towns in Societies: Essays in Economic History and Historical Sociology*, edited by P. Abrams and E. Wrigley, 35–77. Cambridge: Cambridge University Press.
Houghton, L. 2015. "Virgil's Fourth *Eclogue* and the Visual Arts." *PBSR* 83: 175–220.
Houpt, S. 2006. *Museum of the Missing: A History of Art Theft*. New York: Sterling.
Huemoeller, K. 2020. "Freedom in Marriage? Manumission for Marriage in the Roman World." *JRS* 110: 123–139.
Humphrey, J. 1986. *Roman Circuses: Arenas for Chariot Racing*. Berkeley: University of California Press.
James, P. 2020. *Food Provisions for Ancient Rome: A Supply Chain Approach*. Milton: Taylor & Francis Group.
Joost-Gaugier, C. 1985. "Poggio and Visual Tradition: 'Uomini Famosi' in Classical Literary Description." *Artibus et Historiae* 6.12: 57–74.
Joshel, S. R. 1992. *Work, Identity and Legal Status at Rome: A Study of the Occupational Inscriptions*. Norman: University of Oklahoma Press.
Kajanto, I. 1965. *The Latin Cognomina*. Helsinki: Societas Scientiarum Fennica.

Kallis, A. 2014. *The Third Rome, 1922–43: The Making of the Fascist Capital*. Basingstoke: Palgrave Macmillan.
King, C. 2020. *The Ancient Roman Afterlife: Di Manes, Belief, and the Cult of the Dead*. Austin: University of Texas Press.
Knox, B. 1968. "Silent Reading in Antiquity." *GRBS* 9.4: 421–435.
Koortbojian, M. 1996. "In commemorationem mortuorum: Text and Image along the 'Streets of Tombs'." In *Art and Text in Roman Culture*, edited by J. Elsner, 210–233. Cambridge: Cambridge University Press.
Koortbojian, M. 2006. "The Freedman's Voice: The Funerary Monument of Aurelius Hermia and Aurelia Philematio." In *The Art of Citizens, Soldiers and Freedmen in the Roman World*, edited by E. D'Ambra and G. Métraux, 91–99. Oxford: Archaeopress.
Kopytoff, I. 1986. "The Cultural Biography of Things: Commoditization as Process." In *The Social Life of Things: Commodities in Cultural Perspective*, edited by A. Appadurai, 64–92. Cambridge: Cambridge University Press.
Krause, J. 1994. *Witwen und Waisen im Römischen Reich. I, Verwitwung und Wiederverheiratung*. Stuttgart: F. Steiner.
Krautheimer, R. 1980. *Rome: Profile of a City*. Princeton: Princeton University Press.
Laderman, G. 2005. *Rest in Peace: A Cultural History of Death and the Funeral Home in Twentieth-Century America*. New York: Oxford University Press.
Laird, M. 2015. *Civic Monuments and the 'Augustales' in Roman Italy*. New York: Cambridge University Press.
Lanciani, R. 1883. "Notizie degli Scavi. XX. Roma and XIII. Roma (luglio)." *NSc* 207–212, 243–245.
Lavin, M. 1975. *Seventeenth-Century Barberini Documents and Inventories of Art*. New York: New York University Press.
Lelis, A., W. Percy, and B. Verstraete. 2003. *The Age of Marriage in Ancient Rome*. Lewiston: Edwin Mellen Press.
Lembke, K. 1994a. *Das Iseum Campense in Rom: Studie über den Isiskult unter Domitian*. Heidelberg: Verlag Archäologie und Geschichte.
Lembke, K. 1994b. "Ein Relief aus Ariccia und seine Geschichte." *MdI* 101: 97–102.
Lembke, K. 2018. "The Iseum Campense and Its Social, Religious, and Political Impact." In *The Iseum Campense from the Roman Empire to the Modern Age*, edited by M. Versluys, K. Bülow Clausen, and G. Capriotti Vittozzi, 29–40. Rome: Edizioni Quasar.
Lenzi, P. 1998. "'Sita in loco qui vocatur calcaria': Attività di spoliazione e forni da calca a Ostia." *Archeologia medievale* 25: 247–263.
Leone, R., F. Pirani, M. E. Tittoni, and S. Tozzi, eds. 2002. *Il Museo di Roma racconta la città*. Rome: Gangemi.
Leone, S. 2019. "Palace Architecture and Decoration in Early Modern Rome." In *A Companion to Early Modern Rome, 1492–1692*, edited by P. Jones, B. Wisch, and S. Ditchfield, 342–366. Leiden: Brill.
Lindsay, H. 2004. "The 'Laudatio Murdiae': Its Content and Significance." *Latomus* 63: 88–97.
Lindsay, H. 2009. *Adoption in the Roman World*. Cambridge: Cambridge University Press.

References

Liverani, P. 1999. *La Topografia Antica del Vaticano*. Vatican City: Tipografia Vaticana.

Liverani, P., and G. Spinola. 2010. *The Vatican Necropoles: Rome's City of the Dead*. Citta del Vaticano: Liberia Editrice Vaticani.

Longfellow, B. 2010. "Reflections of Imperialism: The Meta Sudans in Rome and the Provinces." *AB* 92.4: 275–292.

Lumbroso, G. 1875. *Notizie sulla vita di Cassiano dal Pozzo: Protettore delle belle arti, fautore della scienza dell'antichità nel secolo decimosettimo*. Turin: Paravia.

MacDougall, E. 1994. *Fountains, Statues, and Flowers: Studies in Italian Gardens of the Sixteenth and Seventeenth Centuries*. Washington: Dumbarton Oaks.

Mackey, J. 2022. *Belief and Cult: Rethinking Roman Religion*. Princeton: Princeton University Press.

MacMullen, R. 1997. *Christianity and Paganism in the Fourth to the Eighth Centuries*. New Haven: Yale University Press.

Maffei, P. 1704. *Raccolta di statue antiche e moderne*. Rome: D. de Rossi.

Magnuson, T. 1982. *Rome in the Age of Bernini*. Vol. 1. Stockholm: Almqvist & Wiksell International.

Mahon, D. 1988. "Fresh Light on Caravaggio's Earliest Period: His 'Cardsharps' Recovered." *Burlington Magazine* 130: 10–25.

Mahon, D. 1990. "The Singing 'Lute-Player' by Caravaggio from the Barberini Collection, Painted for Cardinal Del Monte." *Burlington Magazine* 132: 4–23.

Malaise, M., and R. Veymiers. 2018. "Les dévotes isiaques et les atours de leur déesse." In *Individuals and Materials in the Greco-Roman Cults of Isis*, edited by V. Gasparini and R. Veymiers, 470–508. Leiden: Brill.

Marlowe, E. 2004. "'The Mutability of All Things': The Rise, Fall and Rise of the Meta Sudans Fountain in Rome." In *Architecture as Experience: Radical Change in Spatial Practice*, edited by D. Arnold and A. Ballantyne, 36–56. London: Routledge.

Marvin, M. 1983. "Freestanding Sculptures from the Baths of Caracalla." *AJA* 87.3: 347–384.

Maschek, D. 2022. "Iconography and Style in Republican and Early Imperial Art (200 BCE to 14 CE)." In *Handbook of Roman Imagery and Iconography*, edited by L. Cline and N. Elkins, 169–199. Oxford: Oxford University Press.

Mathisen, R. 2009. "Provinciales, Gentiles, and Marriages between Romans and Barbarians in the Late Roman Empire." *JRS* 99: 140–155.

Matz, F., and F. von Duhn. 1881–1882. *Antike bildwerke in Rom*. 3 vols. Leipzig: Breitkopf & Härtel.

Mayer, E. 2012. *The Ancient Middle Classes: Urban Life and Aesthetics in the Roman Empire, 100 BCE–250 CE*. Cambridge: Harvard University Press.

Mazurek, L. 2022. *Isis in a Global Empire: Greek Identity through Egyptian Religion in Roman Greece*. Cambridge: Cambridge University Press.

McGinn, T. 1999. "Widows, Orphans, and Social History." *JRA* 12: 617–632.

McGinn, T. 2008. *Widows and Patriarchy: Ancient and Modern*. London: Bristol Classical Press.

McGuire, M. 2002. *Religion: The Social Context*. Belmont: Waveland Press.

McKitterick, R., J. Osborne, C. M. Richardson, and J. Story, eds. 2013. *Old Saint Peter's, Rome*. Cambridge: Cambridge University Press.

McPhee, S. 2008. "The Long Arm of the Fabbrica: Saint Peter's and the City of Rome." In *Sankt Peter in Rom 1506–2006*, edited by G. Satzinger and S. Schutze, 353–373. Munich: Hirmer.

Melchiorri, M. 1823. "Lettera del marchese G. Melchiorri socio ordinario dell'Accademia Romana di Archeologia, al ch. sig. cav. G. G. de Rossi socio ordinario della stessa Accademia sopra una antica Iscrizione metrica." *Effemeridi letterarie di Roma* 12: 163–167.

Miller, J. 1981–1982. "Propertius' Tirade against Isis (2.33a)." *CJ* 77.2: 104–111.

Miller, L. 2018. *Egyptian Imagery on Roman Walls: The Relationship between Roman and Egyptian Elements in the First-Century CE Roman Wall Painting* Isiac Ritual Worship *from Herculaneum*. MA thesis, University of Oregon.

Milnor, K. 2009. "Literacy in Roman Pompeii: The Case of Virgil's *Aeneid*." In *Ancient Literacies: The Culture of Reading in Greece and Rome*, edited by W. Johnson and H. Parker, 288–319. New York: Oxford University Press.

Milnor, K. 2014. *Graffiti and the Literary Landscape in Roman Pompeii*. Oxford: Oxford University Press.

Mol, E. 2018. "Present in Absence: The Imagination, Reconstruction, and Memory of Egypt and the Iseum Campense in Rome." In *Iseum Campense in Rome: Temple, Monument, Lieu de Mémoire*, edited by M. Versluys, K. Bülow Clausen, and G. Capriotti Vittozzi, 339–362. Rome: Edizioni Quasar.

Mol, E. 2020. "Roman Cyborgs! On Significant Otherness, Material Absence, and Virtual Presence in the Archaeology of Roman Religion." *EJA* 23: 64–81.

Mols, S. 1999. *Wooden Furniture in Herculaneum: Form, Technique and Function*. Amsterdam: J. C. Gieben.

Mols, S. 2007–2008. "Ancient Roman Household Furniture and Its Use: From Herculaneum to the Rhine." *AnMurcia* 23–24: 145–160.

Moltesen, M. 2003. "De-Restoring and Re-Restoring: Fifty Years of Restoration Work in the Ny Carlsberg Glyptotek." In *History of Restoration of Ancient Stone Sculptures*, edited by E. Grossman, J. Podagny, and M. True, 207–244. Los Angeles: J. Paul Getty Museum.

Moltesen, M. 2012. *Perfect Partners: The Collaboration between Carl Jacobsen and His Agent in Rome, Wolfgang Helbig, in the Formation of the Ny Carlsberg Glyptotek 1887–1914*. Copenhagen: Ny Carlsberg Glyptotek.

Morgan, T. 2007. *Popular Morality in the Early Roman Empire*. Cambridge: Cambridge University Press.

Mouritsen, H. 2011. *The Freedman in the Roman World*. Cambridge: Cambridge University Press.

Norman, J. 2019. "In Public and in Private: A Study of Festival in Seventeenth-Century Rome." In *Occasions of State: Early Modern European Festivals and the Negotiation of Power*, edited by J. Mulryne, K. De Jonge, R. Morris, and P. Martens, 229–246. New York: Routledge.

Nuno, A., J. Ezquerra, and C. Maza. 2021. "Total Sensory Experience in Isiac Cults: Mimesis, Alterity and Identity." In *Sensorivm: The Senses in Roman Polytheism*, edited by A. Nuño, G. Woolf, and J. Ezquerra, 389–426. Leiden: Brill.

References

Painter, K. 2001. *The Insula of the Menander at Pompeii*. Vol. 4: *The Silver Treasure*. Oxford: Oxford University Press.

Parke-Bernet Galleries. 1949. *Classical and Medieval Stone Sculptures, Part III of the Art Collection Belonging to the Estate of the Late Joseph Brummer*. New York: Parke-Bernet Galleries.

Pearson, S. 2021. *The Triumph and Trade of Egyptian Objects in Rome: Collecting Art in the Ancient Mediterranean*. Berlin: De Gruyter.

Pergolizzi, A., ed. 1999. *La confessione nella basilica di San Pietro*. Cinisello Balsamo: Silvana Editoriale.

Perna, S. 2012. "The Colours of Death: Roman Cinerary Urns in Coloured Stone." In *Interdisciplinary Studies on Ancient Stone*, edited by A. Guitierrez Garcia-M, P. Lapuente, and I. Roda, 787–800. Tarragona: Institut Català d'Arqueologia Clàssica.

Pfeiffer, S. 2018. "Domitian's Iseum Campense in Context." In *The Iseum Campense from the Roman Empire to the Modern Age: Temple – Monument – Lieu de Mémoire*, edited by M. Versluys, K. Clausen, and G. Vittozzi, 179–194. Rome: Edizioni Quasar.

Pizzorusso, C. 1985. "Domenico Pieratti: 'Primo suggetto nel suo mestiere in questa città'." *Paragone* 36: 21–42.

Pollini, J. 2012. *From Republic to Empire: Rhetoric, Religion, and Power in the Visual Culture of Ancient Rome*. Norman: University of Oklahoma Press.

Pomeroy, S. 1995. *Goddesses, Whores, Wives, and Slaves: Women in Classical Antiquity*. 2nd ed. New York: Schocken Books.

Pucci, G. 1968–1969. "L'epitaffio di Flavio Agricola e un disegno della collezione Dal Pozzo-Albani." *BullCom* 81: 173–177.

Riess, W. 2012. "Rari exempli femina: Female Virtues on Roman Funerary Inscriptions." In *A Companion to Women in the Ancient World*, edited by S. James and S. Dillon, 491–501. Malden: Wiley-Blackwell.

Rietbergen, P. 2006. *Power and Religion in Baroque Rome: Barberini Cultural Policies*. Leiden: Brill.

Robertson, J., ed. 1867. *Pope Alexander the Seventh and the College of Cardinals*. Westminster: Camden Society.

Roller, M. 2006. *Dining Posture in Ancient Rome: Bodies, Values, and Status*. Princeton: Princeton University Press.

Romano, I. 2018. "A Re-examination of the Glencairn Athena/Minerva and Its Relationship to the Sorgente Group Athena." In *Re-staging Greek Artworks in Roman Times*, edited by I. Romano and G. Adornato, 15–33. Milan: LED Edizioni Universitarie.

Rose, C. 2008. "Forging Identity in the Roman Republic: Trojan Ancestry and Veristic Portraiture." In *Role Models in the Roman World: Identity and Assimilation*, edited by S. Bell and I. Hansen, 97–131. Ann Arbor: University of Michigan Press.

Rossi, M., and P. Rossi. 1697. *Descrizione di Roma Moderna*. Rome.

Rossini, P. 1693. *Il Mercurio errante delle grandezze di Roma*. Rome.

Rossini, P. 1715. *Il Mercurio errante delle grandezze di Roma*. Rome: Pe'l Zenobj stampatore.

Rüpke, J., ed. 2007. *A Companion to Roman Religion*. Malden: Wiley-Blackwell.

Rüpke, J. 2016. *On Roman Religion: Lived Religion and the Individual in Ancient Rome*. Ithaca: Cornell University Press.

Rüpke, J. 2018. *Pantheon: A New History of Roman Religion*. Princeton: Princeton University Press.

Saenger, P. 1997. *Space between Words: The Origins of Silent Reading*. Stanford: Stanford University Press.

Sawin, M. 1959. "New York Letter." *Art International* 3.5–6: 48–50.

Scheidel, W. 2009. "Population and Demography." In *A Companion to Ancient History*, edited by A. Erskine, 134–145. Malden: Wiley-Blackwell.

Schmidt, M. 2014. "Carmina Latina Epigraphica." In *The Oxford Handbook of Roman Epigraphy*, edited by C. Bruun and J. Edmondson, 764–782. Oxford: Oxford University Press.

Scott, J. 1991. *Images of Nepotism: The Painted Ceilings of Palazzo Barberini*. Princeton: Princeton University Press.

Sebastiani, A. 2023. *Ancient Rome and the Modern Italian State: Ideological Placemaking, Archaeology, and Architecture, 1870–1945*. Cambridge: Cambridge University Press.

Secrest, M. 2004. *Duveen: A Life in Art*. New York: Knopf.

Shackleton Bailey, D. 1956. *Propertiana*. Cambridge: Cambridge University Press.

Solin, H. 2016. "Names, Personal, Roman." In *Oxford Classical Dictionary*, edited by T. Whitmarsh. Oxford University Press.

Sorek, S. 2010. *The Emperors' Needles: Egyptian Obelisks and Rome*. Bristol: Phoenix Press.

Speidel, M. 1992. "Roman Army Pay Scales." *JRS* 82: 87–106.

Spivey, N. 2019. *The Sarpedon Krater: The Life and Afterlife of a Greek Vase*. Chicago: University of Chicago Press.

Stenhouse, W. 2005. "Visitors, Display, and Reception in the Antiquity Collections of Late-Renaissance Rome." *Renaissance Quarterly* 58.2: 397–434.

Swetnam-Burland, M. 2015. *Egypt in Italy: Visions of Egypt in Roman Imperial Culture*. Cambridge: Cambridge University Press.

Swetnam-Burland, M. 2018. "Material Evidence and the Isiac Cults: Art and Experience in the Sanctuary." In *Individuals and Materials in the Greco-Roman Cults of Isis*, edited by V. Gasparini and R. Veymiers, 584–608. Leiden: Brill.

Takács, S. 1995. *Isis and Sarapis in the Roman World*. Leiden: Brill.

Tassinari, S. 1993. *Il vasellame bronzeo di Pompei*. 2 vols. Rome: L' Erma di Bretschneider.

Temkin, A. 2002. "Barnett Newman on Exhibition." In *Barnett Newman*, edited by A. Temkin, 18–75. Philadelphia: Philadelphia Museum of Art.

Thuno, E. 2015. "The Pantheon in the Middle Ages." In *The Pantheon: From Antiquity to the Present*, edited by T. Marder and M. Wilson Jones, 231–254. New York: Cambridge University Press.

Torrigio, F. 1618. *Le Sacre Grotte Vaticane*. Viterbo: Appresso i Discepoli.

Toynbee, J., and J. Ward-Perkins. 1956. *The Shrine of Saint Peter and the Vatican Excavations*. London: Longmans, Green and Co.

Treggiari, S. 1991. *Roman Marriage*. New York: Oxford University Press.

References

Tucci, P. 2017. *The Temple of Peace in Rome*. Cambridge: Cambridge University Press.
Vermeule, C. 1966. "The Dal Pozzo-Albani Drawings of Classical Antiquities in the Royal Library at Windsor Castle." *TAPS* 56.2: 1–170.
Veyne, P. 2000. "La 'plèbe moyenne' sous le Haut-Empire romain." *Annales (HSS)* 55.6: 1169–1199.
Vittozzi, G. 2006. "Una statua di Bes al Museo Gregoriano Egizio." *BMMP* 35: 53–78.
Volpi, G. 1745. *Vetus Latium profanum & sacrum*. Rome.
Von Hesberg, H. 2002. "Il profumo del marmo – cambiamenti nei riti de seppellimento e nei monumenti funerari nel 1. sec. D.C." In *Espacios y Usos Funerarios en el Occidente Romano*, edited by D. Vaquerizo, 33–49. Córdoba: Seminario de Arqueología, Universidad de Córdoba.
Vout, C. 2018. *Classical Art: A Life History from Antiquity to the Present*. Princeton: Princeton University Press.
Waddy, P. 1976. "The Design and Designers of Palazzo Barberini." *JSAH* 35.3: 151–185.
Waddy, P. 1990. *Seventeenth-Century Roman Palaces: Use and the Art of the Plan*. Cambridge: MIT Press.
Waddy, P. 2014. "Architecture for Display." In *Display of Art in the Roman Palace, 1550–1750*, edited by G. Feigenbaum, 31–40. Los Angeles: Getty Research Institute.
Wallace-Hadrill, A. 1994. *Houses and Society in Pompeii and Herculaneum*. Princeton: Princeton University Press.
Wallace-Hadrill, A. 2013. "Trying to Define and Identify the Roman 'Middle Classes'." *JRA* 26: 605–609.
Weaver, P. 1986. "The Status of Children in Mixed Marriages." In *The Family in Ancient Rome: New Perspectives*, edited by B. Rawson, 145–169. Ithaca: Cornell University Press.
Williams, C. 1999. *Roman Homosexuality: Ideologies of Masculinity in Classical Antiquity*. Oxford: Oxford University Press.
Witt, R. 1971. *Isis in the Graeco-Roman World*. London: Thames and Hudson.
Wrede, H. 1977. "Stadtrömische Monumente, Urnen und Sarkophage des Klinentypus in den beiden ersten Jahrhunderten n. Chr." *AA* 92: 395–431.
Wrede, H. 1981. *Consecratio in formam deorum: Vergöttlichte Privatpersonen in der römischen Kaiserzeit*. Mainz am Rhein: Von Zabern.
Wrede, H. 1990. "Der Sarkophagdeckel eines Mädchens in Malibu und die frühen Klinensarkophage Roms, Athens und Kleinasiens." In *Roman Funerary Monuments in the J. Paul Getty Museum*, vol. 1, edited by M. True and G. Koch, 15–46. Malibu: J. Paul Getty Museum.
Wünsche, R. 2007. *Glyptothek, Munich: Masterpieces of Greek and Roman Sculpture*. Munich: Beck.
Zanker, P. 1995. *The Mask of Socrates: The Image of the Intellectual in Antiquity*. Berkeley: University of California Press.
Zanker, P., and Ewald, B. 2012. *Living with Myths: The Imagery of Roman Sarcophagi*. Oxford: Oxford University Press.
Zeggio, S., and Pardini, G. 2007. "Roma-Meta Sudans. I monumenti. Lo scavo. La storia." *FOLD&R* 99: www.fastionline.org/docs/FOLDER-it-2007-99.pdf.

Index

Ariccia Relief, 70
Aelia Secundula, epitaph, 95–96
Alemanni, Nicolò, 113
ancient sculpture
   collecting/collections, 119–120, 128
   "informal" display in palazzi,
      120–121
   Italian sentiments in late
      nineteenth century, 131–132
   sale by once-grand families, 132
   treatment in Middle Ages, 119
Apuleius, *Metamorphoses*, 51, 55–56,
      57, 59, 63, 68
Augustine, 96
Aurelius Primitivus, 27, 31, 92, 104
   name, 47
   praise, 47
   relationship to Flavius Agricola, 47

Barberini Colonna di Sciarra, Maffeo
      (prince), 130–131, 132, 133
Barberini family
   See also Barberini, Francesco (cardinal); Barberini, Taddeo;
      Urban VIII (pope); Barberini
      Colonna di Sciarra, Maffeo
      (prince); Palazzo Barberini
   "casa grande," 116–117
   collection of antiquities, 121, 129
   exile from Rome and return,
      124
   history, 116–117, 123–124, 129
   public dinners and displays,
      125–127
Barberini, Francesco (cardinal), 115,
      117, 118, 124, 127, 138
Barberini, Maffeo (cardinal). *See*
      Urban VIII (pope)
Barberini, Taddeo, 117, 123
Barthes, Roland, 109, 110
Belvedere courtyard, Vatican, 119
Bernini, Gianlorenzo, 112, 113, 117, 145
   See also St. Peter's Basilica
   Ponte Ruinante, 121
Boscoreale
   silver cups, 80–81
Brummer Gallery, 137, 138, 147
   purchase of sculpture of Flavius
      Agricola, 136
Brummer, Joseph, 137

Campus Martius, 61–63, 66
Christina, Queen of Sweden, 124, 126,
      128, 145
Cicero, 37, 89
Column of Marcus Aurelius, 82
Constantine, 10, 20, 68, 109, 126, 138,
      145

Index

Dal Pozzo, Cassiano, 17, 114–115, 120
   See also funerary monument of Flavius Agricola: seventeenth-century drawing
Dea Pharia. See Isis
death
   See also funerary commemoration
   arena events, 83
   and dining, 85, 101–102
   disease, 81, 82
   diverse outlooks, 89
   and enjoyment of life, 83
   enjoyment of life, 102
   famine, 82
   imagery in dining contexts, 79–81
   memento mori motifs, 81, 83
   modern views, 103–104
   natural disasters, 82
   precariousness of life, 83
demography
   See also death
   age at marriage, 48
   infant mortality, 81
   widows, 48
Demotte, George Joseph, 134–136
   death, 135
Demotte, Inc., 138, 148
   leadership after death of George Joseph Demotte, 136
   New York gallery, 134
   Paris atelier, 135
   scandal about possible forgeries, 134–135
dining
   attendants, 36
   claims of status, 35–36
   clothing, 36
   communal, 34
   and death, 85
   and death imagery, 79–81
   and philosophy, 79
   posture, 35–36
   rarity, 34–35
   some social purposes, 34
   with the dead, 92–97, 101–102
   accommodations, 93–94
   birthday, 93
   Parentalia, 93, 97
   participation of deceased, 97, 98–100
   public festivals, 93
   raucous atmosphere, 97
   revelers' experience, 95–97
   skepticism toward participation of deceased, 97–98
   tombside stories, 96
Domitian, 61, 63, 64
Duveen, Sir Joseph, 134, 138

epitaph of Flavius Agricola, 15–18, 44–45, 55, 57, 58, 77, 92, 95, 104
   appearance of, 18
   correspondence with sculpture, 16, 43, 84, 100, 116
   dead speaking through epitaph, 99–100
   literary resonances, 32
   philosophical content, 100
   philosophy, 79
   poetic form, 30–33
   poetic quality, 32
   reference to disparate beliefs, 85–86
   removal, 16, 105, 115, 116, 129
   structure, 16
   treatment in eighteenth-century editions, 116
   treatments after separation from sculpture, 146–147
   use of different voices, 16, 31, 100
Euphronios krater, 110

Facist regime. See Mussolini, Benito
families
   See also marriage
   potential tensions, 104

families (cont.)
  various forms, 49, 102
Farnese family, 120
  collection of antiquities, 119
female virtues
  chastity, 53
  stock praise of, 47
  versus Greek attitudes, 46
Flavia Primitiva, 27, 44–60
  as *casta cultrix*, 52–55, 77
  described in formulaic terms, 46–47, 77
  life course, 45, 58–60
  marriage, 45–46
  as mother, 47
  name, 45
  personal meaning of Iseum Campense, 77
  potential remarriage, 48
Flavian Amphitheater, 3–4, 117
  coin issued by Titus, 4, 149, 150–151, 152–153, 154
Flavian dynasty, 26, 27
Flavius Agricola
  See also epitaph of Flavius Agricola; funerary monument of Flavius Agricola; sculpture of Flavius Agricola; tomb of Flavius Agricola
  corrective to generalizations, 102
  family background, 26, 28, 90, 102
  "literary literacy," 32–33
  marriage, 27, 46, 102
  name, 26, 47, 102
  presentation as diner, 37
  presentation as philosopher, 78–79
  relationship to Aurelius Primitivus, 47
  source of wealth, 30
  wealth, 27
  worldview, 78–89
  contrast with Flavia Primitiva, 85
  outlook on life and death, 84–85, 86
  potential alignment with Flavia Primitiva, 88
Forma Urbis Romae, 63–65
French and Company, 137–138
  See also Samuels, Mitchell
  advertisement featuring sculpture of Flavius Agricola, 138–143
  context and audience, 142
  change of business model, 142–144
  dissolution, 143–144
funerary commemoration
  See also dining: with the dead
  cena novendialis, 92
  dead speaking through epitaph, 98, 99–100
  labor, 34, 36
  leisure, 37, 90, 103
  mock rites, 97
  models, 33, 37, 90
  modern, 104
  offices, 33
  playfulness, 101
  rites, 38
  Silicernium, 92
  skeptical attitudes toward effectiveness, 97–98
  at tomb, 92–102
funerary monument of Flavius Agricola, 95
  See also epitaph of Flavius Agricola; sculpture of Flavius Agricola
  discovery and reaction, 112–116
  discovery of, 1
  potential cost, 27–28, 90
  removal of epitaph, 105, 110, 115, 116, 146

Index

reuniting of epitaph and sculpture, 105, 111, 115, 155
seventeenth-century drawing of, 17–18, 115, 133
toying with life-death dichotomy, 98–101

Giustiniani, Vincenzo, 120

Hadrian, 27, 32, 78, 89
Hartman, Alan, 144
Hartman, Joan, 144
Hartman Galleries, 138, 144
Herculaneum
frescoes showing rites for Egyptian deities, 71
Horace, 32, 53, 84, 88

Il Cracas, 131–132, 133
See also Maes, Costantino
Indianapolis Museum of Art, 1, 110, 144–145, 146
Iseum Campense, 53, 61–77
communal activities, 70–71, 75
as communal space, 71–73
decoration, 65–66
current locations, 67
diversity of worshippers, 76
Egyptian materials, 65
Egyptian style, 65
evolution, 75
as heterotopia, 66–67
importance, 63
layout, 63–65
location, 61–77
personal veneration within, 75
sources for layout and decoration, 63–65, 68
statue of baboon, 74–76
statues of Nile and Tiber, 65, 66
Isis, 49–60
See also Iseum Campense
aretologies, 56

encyclopedic powers and identities, 51
female roles in cult, 52–53
henotheism, 52
history of worship, 49
initiation, 69
moral outlook, 55–57
noninitiation activities, 69–76
potential effects, 72
Pharian goddess, 49
possibility of afterlife, 57–58, 85
practices of abstinence, 53–55, 71
promise of transformation, 59–60, 76
punishment of misdeeds, 56
reception in Rome, 49, 63
reputation of worshippers, 53
worship versus civic religion, 51, 52, 76
Isola Sacra, 94

Junia Procula, funerary altar, 48
Justice, 56–57

kline monuments, 17
C. Julius, 14, 99
in guise of Hercules, 41
Satorneinos, 41
young girl, 18, 99

La Tribuna, 130, 131
See also Barberini Colonna di Sciarra, Maffeo (prince)
Latin verse inscriptions, 31
See also epitaph of Flavius Agricola: poetic form
Laudatio Murdiae, 46
lectus, 98
Liber Pontificalis, 113
Licinius Lucullus, Lucius, 139–141
Lucullus. See Licinius Lucullus, L.
Lyaeus, 32, 42, 59, 88

Maes, Costantino, 131–132, 133
  See also Il Cracas
Marcus Orpheus, funerary altar, 35
marriage, 45–49
  "mixed marriages," 86–89
    Christian contexts, 86–87
    citizen-barbarian, 87
    different regions, 88
    legal status, 87
    patrician-plebeian, 87
  age at, 48
Meta Sudans, 152–153
Metropolitan Museum of Art, 135, 137–138
Misenum
  provisions for *Parentalia*, 93
Musée du Louvre, 134–135
Mussolini, Benito, 109–110, 153

New York Times, 135
  advertisement for French and Company, 138–140
  context and audience, 142
nudity, Roman attitudes toward, 39
Ny Carlsberg Glyptotek, 130, 133

object biography, 110
Ovid, 31, 32, 33, 53, 56, 93

Palazzo Barberini, 115
  architects, 117
  collection of antiquities, 119, 128
  cultural goods, 119, 129
  exterior, 117
    aesthetic of studied carelessness, 121
  garden, 116, 120–121
  guidebook for *salone*, 127
  images of Romanness, 117–118, 121, 123
  initial location of sculpture of Flavius Agricola, 120–121
  interior, 117–118, 121–123
  later location of sculpture of Flavius Agricola, 121–127
  location, 117
  Ponte Ruinante, 121
  rituals of reception, 127
  room B19, 123
  room B20, 122–124, 127
  room B29, 123
  visitors, 128
Palazzo dei Conservatori, 119
Palazzo Farnese, 119
Palazzo Sciarra, 130
Parke-Bernet Galleries, 137
Paul, First Epistle to the Corinthians, 86
Petronius, *Satyricon*, 30, 79
Pharian goddess. See Isis
philosophy
  celebration of life's joys, 81
  and dining, 79
  voiced by deceased, 85
Pieratti, Domenico
  Latona con i figli Apollo e Diana, 124, 126
Plutarch, 54, 79, 140–141
Pompeii
  altar from Temple of Genius Augusti, 49
  bronze vessels, 40
  food and drink establishments, 35
  literary graffiti, 31
  tomb of Naevoleia Tyche, 30
Propertius, 54, 86, 88
Raccolta di Statue Antiche e Moderne, 128

religion
  See also Isis
  civic, 50–51, 59, 89
  versus "mystery cults," 51
  differences in outlook between lovers or spouses, 86–87
  henotheism, 52, 89

Index

and morality, 55
power of ritual, 73
reciprocal behavior, 55
sociology of, 73
Rome. *See names of individual monuments and landmarks*
  cosmopolitan nature, 52, 76, 89
  "urban process," 68
Rothschild family, 131, 133
Rubrius Urbanus, C., funerary relief, 84

St. Peter's Basilica, 1–2, 10, 19, 20, 112, 117
  See also Vatican necropolis
  baldacchino, 1, 21, 112
    atmosphere surrounding erection, 113–114
  clergy, 113–114
  medieval statue of St. Peter, 75
  Old St. Peter's, 1, 21, 95
  reworking of *confessio*, 112–113
Samuels, Mitchell, 138, 143, 144
scavi Vaticani. *See* Vatican necropolis
Sciarra Amazon, 131, 134
Sciarra bronze, 131, 134
sculpture of Flavius Agricola, 12–15, 95
  in advertisement for gallery sale, 138–143
  auction and sale to French and Company, 137–138
  awkwardness, 14
  beard, 78
  body, 13, 37–39
    apparent disjuncture with face, 37–38, 39
    Greek precedents, 38–39
  circular cutting, 13, 101
  convivial sensibility in Palazzo Barberini, 125–127
  correspondence with epitaph, 16, 43, 84, 100, 116
  cup, 39–40
    nomenclature, 40
    shape, 40
  donation to Indianapolis Museum of Art, 144
  early twentieth-century photograph, 133–134
  exhibition in Indianapolis Museum of Art, 144–145
  face, 13, 26, 38, 42, 78
    apparent disjuncture with body, 37–38, 39
  formal analysis of, 14–15
  initial installation at Palazzo Barberini, 120–121
  later installation at Palazzo Barberini, 121–127
  lectus, 12, 35
  lifelike, 98–99, 102
  metal object inserted within, 13, 42
  mid-century American art world, 142–143
  monetary value in Baroque Rome, 122, 123
  movement to Palazzo Sciarra, 130
  movements in Manhattan, 138
  position within tomb, 22–23
  in possession of Demotte, Inc., 134–136
  possible movement in late nineteenth century, 131, 133–134
  potential cost, 27–28
  potential representation as divinity, 41–42
  potential urn, 13–14
  removal of lowest section, 116, 134
  "restoration" by Demotte, Inc., 135
  sale to Brummer Gallery, 136

sculpture of Flavius Agricola (cont.)
   scale, 29
   as stand-alone artwork, 111
   summary of viewers, travels, and projected meanings, 145–146
   symbolic value in Baroque Rome, 123
   use of marble, 28
slavery
   "social death," 45
social history, 3
   diversity of Romans, 104
   methodology, 3–5, 23, 25–26, 43, 58, 77, 103, 104–105, 146–148, 150–153
social mobility, 30

Temple of Isis and Serapis. *See* Iseum Campense
Temple of Vespasian, 117
Tertullian, 87, 96
Tibullus, 69
Tibur/Tivoli, 26–27, 32
tomb of Flavius Agricola, 19–23, 90, 114
   See also Vatican necropolis
   exterior, 21, 29
   hierarchy of deceased within, 24
   interior, 21–22, 29, 95
   libation holes, 22, 95
   neighboring tombs, 28–29
   position of sculpture within, 22–23
   potential cost, 27–28
   visitors' experience, 95–97
Totenmahl motif, 34, 101

Ubaldi, Ugo, 113–114
Urban VIII (pope), 112, 116, 121, 123, 124, 145
   and baldacchino project, 113–114
   election, 117
   reaction to discovery of funerary monument of Flavius Agricola, 114

Vatican necropolis, 9–10, 28–29, 68, 95
   history and development, 20
   location, 19
   Tomb A, 27
   Tomb F, 28, 95
   Tomb H, 28–29, 95, 98
   Tomb O, 95
   tomb of Peter (Field P), 20, 29, 112
   Tomb S. *See* tomb of Flavius Agricola
Venidius Ennychus, L., 25–26, 43
Vergil, 31, 89, 109
   reception, 109
Via Cornelia, 19, 61, 95